ERNS GRUNDLING

WALK IT OFF

QUEILLERIE

Queillerie,
an imprint of NB Publishers,
a division of Media24 Boeke (Pty) Ltd,
40 Heerengracht, Cape Town, South Africa 8000
www.queillerie.co.za

© 2019 Erns Grundling

Originally published in Afrikaans by Queillerie as *Elders* (2017)
Translated by Edwin Hees

Set in 11 on 14 pt Sabon by Susan Bloemhof
Cover design by Dian Wessels
Cover photography by jarcosa
Author pic by Timna Kirshenbaum

First edition, first impression 2019
ISBN 978-0-7958-0187-7
ISBN 978-0-7958-0188-4 (epub)
ISBN 978-0-7958-0189-1 (mobi)

For Catharien

"I particularly wanted to go alone, because one is so much more dependent and therefore so much more receptive if you go alone."

– Elsa Joubert, *Water en woestyn*

". . . I'm going to stay away for a long time so that I can become completely ordinary again . . ."

– Jeanne Goosen, *'n Uil vlieg weg*

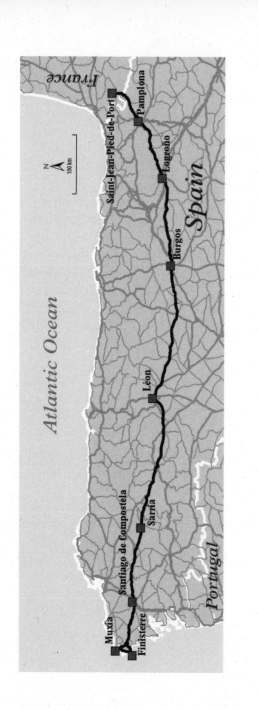

DEPARTURE

"If you are ready to leave father and mother, and brother and sister, and wife and child and friends, and never see them again; if you have paid your debts, and made your will, and settled all your affairs, and are a free man; then you are ready for a walk."

– Henry David Thoreau, *Walking*

WhatsApp to Sophia

Thanks for the lovely message. Wedding was wonderful but ja, afterwards I was bloody tired and got on the plane with Slagtersnek. I'm going to finish it between Doha and Paris, chuck my laptop into a bin and head for the Camino. I've had enough. It's not work's fault, or anyone there. I haven't been in such a bad space for a long time, but anyway, perhaps it's for the best for what lies ahead. Thanks again for your support, my goodness, yesterday especially. All I can hope now is this whole shitty business will make the Camino all the more meaningful. Ag, I'm going to stop moaning now – as Bun Booyens Snr said to Doc Craven after losing a game: "Grit the back teeth but smile with the front ones." This too shall pass.

* * *

My mother says we Grundlings are always rocking up with our ears flat, like rabbits, because everything is always such a bloody rush and a fuss. This morning I'm the rabbit with the flattest ears at the airport, tired and bewildered and bloody annoyed and struggling with my heavy red K-Way 35-litre rucksack, the monkey on my back for the next six weeks.

I'm sweating from the stress and last night's wine. I was

best man and incidental videographer at my friend Le Roux's wedding, on a farm on the Polkadraai road outside Stellenbosch. A wonderful, intimate Boland wedding, but I didn't get to sleep a wink afterwards. I actually had to sit and struggle with a *Go* travel magazine article I hadn't finished, on what was the eve of my Camino – a feature on the Slagtersnek Rebellion of 1815.

I shared a self-catering place with one of the wedding guests, who'd got a bit legless and had a rambling conversation on his cell phone in the middle of the night. "I'm feeling very randy now, honey." Then, he walked around the house repeating, like a mantra, "It's a fuckin' breakdown in communication."

At three thirty I realised what I had known for days: I wouldn't be filing the Slagtersnek article on time, before my brother arrives at seven to take me to the airport. The wedding guest was still awake, so we sat down together to watch the Floyd Mayweather–Manny Pacquiao fight on TV. Lauded as "The Fight of the Century", like so many things it was a massive anticlimax.

The Bag Wrap machine wraps my rucksack up in thick plastic, the two trekking poles poking out on either side like short kieries. It all seems completely absurd. As my friend Le Roux often says, "The lonely places we take ourselves."

* * *

"At Slagtersnek there is a triumphal arch that casts black shadows on the path taken by South Africa."
    – C.J. Langenhoven

Qatar Airways flight QR 1370 takes off. I take one last look at False Bay through the window, before the plane banks slowly northwards. If everything goes according to plan, I will see the Atlantic Ocean again in about five weeks' time, somewhere near Finisterre on the west coast of Spain. The carry-bag on my lap contains a handful of things: my wallet, sunglasses, notebook, a pen, cell phone, a range of wall plugs and a small Samsung N150 Plus laptop (actually a netbook). And J.C. van der Walt's book *Rebels of Slagtersnek 1815*. The iPhone and the laptop irritate me the most – they were not supposed to come with me. A voice makes announcements in Arabic and English. The seatbelt lights go off. My only thought is the desire to chuck the phone and laptop in a bin at Charles de Gaulle, then walk away all nonchalant as if I had thrown away an orange peel or a KitKat wrapper. But first, I have to finish the article. I am amazed at how my old patterns trip me up anew. Will these old patterns ever let us be?

* * *

The last thing I showed up on time for was my own birth. Actually, I was born much too early, at thirty-two weeks. My birth was a difficult one. My mother had kidney failure and very nearly died. When she told the doctor she wanted a little boy, all he said was, "Listen, let's just hope *you* get through this alive." The gynaecologist had a slightly different attitude: "This child is either going to be state president or a big crook." These days, it seems you can be both.

My grandmother Charlotte Rens, a dignified and deeply

religious woman, would tell me in later years that, while my mother was in theatre, she sat in the parking area and read the same verse from the book of James over and over again: "But let him ask in faith, nothing wavering. For he that wavereth is like a wave of the sea driven with the wind and tossed."

Now, thirty-five years later and twenty years after my grandmother's death, I'm leaving – an absolute sceptic – on a pilgrimage that will end in the cathedral at Santiago de Compostela, where this very apostle is said to be buried.

* * *

Douglas Adams wrote: "I love deadlines. I love the whooshing noise they make as they go by."

I know that whoosh all too well. I despise deadlines; they never go away. And I love testing and teasing them. There must be an arrogance underlying this, the kind of thing one's not eager to admit. Or total incompetence when it comes to time management. Or maybe a bit of both. I'm not sure exactly when this started. After all, the motto of my primary school, Laerskool Handhaaf in Uitenhage, was "Do it now". (This was years before Nike's Just Do It rallying cry . . .)

In my first year at what was then the University of Port Elizabeth, I realised my procrastination problem was getting out of control. I scratched around in the psychology section of the library and came across *Overcoming Procrastination* by Albert Ellis, a compact book with a purple cover. This I must read, I thought, and put it on my bookshelf at home.

Every morning I walked past the book, looked at it and thought: I'm reading *you* all right! Eventually, tail between my legs, I returned the book to the library, unread and two months late. And paid a hell of a fine.

* * *

Last Facebook post on 2 May before my departure

I'm going off the grid for a while. Into the mild. I'm flying to Europe the day after tomorrow to walk the Camino Francés, about nine hundred kilometres over forty days from Saint-Jean-Pied-de-Port in France to Santiago de Compostela, and then to the sea at Finisterre in north-western Spain. That's my plan, more or less. I'm leaving my phone in Cape Town, it's time for a digital detox and radical mindspace clean-up. Or as Toast Coetzer put it: "One man against himself." I will probably check in on Facebook again when I return later in June. Until then, adios! #intothemild

* * *

One man against himself. Toast, a good friend and confidant, and my neighbour in Go's open-plan office, knows me well.

For an incurable extrovert with a kind of teddy-bear persona, I can be extraordinarily hard on myself, especially in my quiet moments. But don't we all have all sorts of contradictions within ourselves? With masks that slip onto our faces so effortlessly, to the point where we struggle to distinguish between ourselves and our masks?

Walt Whitman wrote: "Do I contradict myself? / Very well then I contradict myself. / (I am large, I contain multitudes.)"

I often joke that I don't need anyone else to give me a hard time – I do it myself. All I need is a mirror to declare war against my greatest enemy.

* * *

Flickering across the plane's small TV screens are the first Batman movie, *The Big Bang Theory* episodes, unfathomable Bollywood hits, a golf game and the GPS map of our route; at the moment, we're still somewhere over the Great Karoo.

Time for a gin and tonic. I had my first high-altitude G&T in August 2001, when I went to cover the *Big Brother* eviction in Johannesburg for the Eastern Cape edition of *Die Burger*. Those were the early days of reality television – to this day it's a strange thought, to me, how the public and media made such a big thing of Ferdi and Brad's shenanigans in the garden. "S.A. peeps into the shower", said the headlines on the lampposts along William Moffett Avenue in Port Elizabeth.

It being the weekend of Govan Mbeki's funeral, the flight to Johannesburg was overbooked. In a surprise move, I was upgraded to business class. As is fit and proper for a student (I was still studying at the time and freelancing for *Die Burger*) with one foot still firmly in the trap of late adolescence, I got going on the gin and tonics, and had ordered my third before the plane had even flown over Cradock.

And so I started chatting to the passenger next to me, who had a *TopSport* tog bag with him. I assumed he was a TV sports presenter and launched with great conviction into a speech about just how pathetic the SABC's news coverage was. He mostly just listened; I didn't exactly let him get a word in edgeways.

A month later I saw him again at the Vodacom Journalist of the Year awards ceremony in Port Elizabeth. Turns out he was Phil Molefe, the awards' chief adjudicator, and head of news at the SABC . . .

* * *

The plane is not that full. I'm next to the window with two open seats next to me. There are two days of hard travelling ahead before I reach the starting point of my Camino, the little French village of Saint-Jean-Pied-de-Port at the foot of the Pyrenees:

- First I have to get the nine-hour flight to Doha in Qatar behind me.
- Then I'll spend the night in the new airport terminal at Qatar, before the seven-hour flight to Paris.
- In Paris, a train and taxi ride will get me to the Gare d'Austerlitz.
- From there I'll take an overnight train in a small compartment sleeping six people to Bayonne, near Biarritz in the south of France.
- In Bayonne, I catch a train that will stop an hour later in Saint-Jean-Pied-de-Port.

* * *

A scene from the film *500 Days of Summer* neatly sums up one of my life's great obstacles. The male lead pitches up at a party given by his ex-girlfriend, for whom he still has strong feelings. The screen then splits in two, with the same scene shown in both halves, but one with the title "Expectations" and the other "Reality". In the "Expectations" screen his ex-girlfriend greets him warmly, and they walk up the stairs to the deck, laughing and chatting. In the "Reality" screen she is still friendly, but keeps him at a distance; on the deck he hears, alas, that she is engaged to someone else. The background music to both the scenes is Regina Spektor's unsettling ballad "Hero". "I'm the hero of the story / Don't need to be saved."

Here on the plane, I am confronted with two such screens. In the "Expectations" screen I lean back peacefully in my seat, order another G&T, and do whatever I feel like: watch a movie, play a silly game, watch the other passengers, catch up on some sleep, or write a few serious and sensible thoughts in my Moleskine diary about the momentous journey ahead. Meditate, even.

In the "Reality" screen, though, I'm wound up, down a night's sleep, and can't stop hauling myself over the coals for not filing the Slagtersnek article before I left as I'd so solemnly promised. It's not the first time that something like this has happened, either.

Will these old patterns ever let us be?

* * *

"Our lived lives might become a protracted mourning for, or an endless tantrum about, the lives we were unable to live. But the exemptions we suffer, whether forced or chosen, make us who we are."

– Adam Phillips, psychoanalyst

* * *

My K-Way rucksack lies deep in the bowels of the Boeing, tightly bound in Bag Wrap plastic.

Years ago, former RSG presenter Fonnie du Plooy phoned me to arrange a radio interview. When I asked Fonnie what would happen if he ever lost his diary, his calm, super-polite voice answered, "Then, Erns, I am screwed."

If my rucksack goes missing between here and Paris, Fonnie, I too would be undeniably screwed.

* * *

I am already wearing the clothes I'm going to hike in: a K-Way fleece, a K-Way long-sleeve shirt, K-Way hiking pants (my only pair of pants: you can unzip the legs if you want to), a pair of black socks and a pair of brand-new Salomon trail running shoes. I bought them in a British size 10. I usually wear a size 9, but apparently one's feet swell on such a long hike.

The contents of my red K-Way rucksack:

- Two mismatched K-Way trekking poles. The grey one I used in September 2006 on Kilimanjaro and the orange one in July 2013 in the Fish River Canyon.
- A K-Way Chamonix 850 Eco sleeping bag, weighing only 850 grams. The "Recommended Sleep Zone" is between 3°C and 15°C. It's spring in Europe – I shouldn't get cold.
- A kind of sleeping sheet, folded up compactly and stashed in a Ziploc bag. Not as warm as a sleeping bag, but you can sleep inside it. I borrowed it from my friend Sarie, who has walked the Camino before.
- A pair of waterproof K-Way pants, bought – and probably last worn – back in 2006 for climbing Kilimanjaro.
- A light waterproof jacket, with the Solo cologne logo on it. No idea where I got it.

- Thermal underwear – long-sleeve vest and pants (possibly unnecessary, because it's not winter, but the weather can apparently change very quickly).
- A pair of grey K-Way shorts (to wear at night).
- A pair of gym/jogging pants.
- An extra pair of K-Way pants.
- A grey T-shirt with an *Ons Klyntji* logo (to wear at night).
- A compact, quick-drying K-Way towel.
- A hat.
- Two extra pairs of socks.
- A trump card, hopefully: three pairs of thin, ankle-length stockings to wear as a base layer when walking.
- Two extra pairs of underpants.
- Two handkerchiefs.
- Two pairs of Lycra tights – one pair is my flatmate Magriet's old cycling tights . . .
- One pair of pretty worn-in Reef slip-slops.
- A black bag, another disposable plastic bag I could use as a raincoat, and seven empty Ziploc bags of various sizes.
- In a large Ziploc bag, under my clothes: two Moleskine diaries for journalling, two pens (one an ordinary Bic, the other a fancier make with the Cricket SA logo, which my uncle gave me – who knows why anybody would want to travel with such a smart pen), the compact yellow Globetrotter's *Spanish in Your Pocket (Phrase Book and Two-Way Dictionary)*, John Brierley's *A Pilgrim's Guide to the Camino de Santiago* (the bible for thousands of pilgrims every year) and his *A Pilgrim's Guide to the Camino Finisterre*.
- A waterproof toiletry bag containing: a new Oral-B toothbrush in a holder, a small tube of Colgate tooth-

paste, my sunglasses in a case, two small bottles filled with Radox Shower Gel, 50 ml Nivea roll-on deodorant, 200 ml Nivea Sun suntan oil (factor 50), 50 ml Vaseline, 120 ml Proglyde Anti-Chafe Cream, a roll of Elastoplast plaster, Bactroban ointment, a strip of five Imodium tablets for diarrhoea, a strip of five Valoids for nausea, one bottle of Nexomist nasal spray for allergies. And twenty-two Provent plasters that I hope will help with the sleep apnoea.

- Another small bag: a red Victorinox pocket knife with the words "INTO THE MILD" engraved on it (a gift from friends), a cotton reel with six clean needles (if I have to deal with blisters), a small head torch, two carabiners to hang things on, four extra AAA batteries, a nail clipper and a blue spork (spoon-fork-knife combination).
- One last Ziploc bag: a small bottle of washing-up liquid, a small box of Omo washing powder, a plug (for washing clothes in a basin), eight clothes pegs.
- A coffee mug.
- A 100 g packet of raw almonds, 150 g of biltong, two packets of energy jellies.
- A one-litre Laken water bottle.
- 50 *Go* business cards.
- My Credencial del Peregrino, or Pilgrim Record, which I ordered in advance from the Confraternity of Saint James of South Africa.

The rucksack weighed 11,4 kg at Cape Town airport. That might not sound like much, but throw in about two litres of water and we're nearing 14 kg.

A strange prospect: for over 800 km and forty days, I'll be carrying the equivalent of a small child on my back.

I first heard about the Camino in 2004. One Sunday afternoon, I was sitting fairly anxiously (anxious because I was putting off the mountain of work I had to do) in the offices of the online journal LitNet above the Spur in Stellenbosch. Instead of working, I was aimlessly browsing the Brazilian writer Paulo Coelho's website.

I stumbled upon his publisher's contact details and wrote an impulsive email asking whether I could send Paulo a few questions. His novel *Eleven Minutes* had just been published and an Afrikaans translation of his international bestseller *The Alchemist* was also on South African shelves.

When you send emails like these – just another request for an interview from an obscure corner of the world – you don't usually hear back. But the very next morning, his publisher replied: "Paulo Coelho is currently on holiday on the French Riviera and would prefer to grant a telephone interview. He is available on Tuesday afternoon from 14:00 to 14:20. Here is his number . . ."

I nearly started hyperventilating. I spent a sleepless Monday night trying to come up with questions. I borrowed a speaker phone from a friend's parents so I could record the interview. Paulo was relaxed, friendly and extremely generous with his time – we ended up talking for over half an hour.

My last question was how he would like to be remembered, to which he replied: "As someone who died while he was alive. I'm going to be cremated and my ashes will be spread on the Santiago pilgrim's road. But if I had an epitaph or something written on a tombstone, it would be: 'He died while he was alive.' Because I see so many people who die before death arrives. They consider doing everything, they breathe, they eat, they make love . . . but they've lost their enthusiasm towards life. So I would like to be remembered as someone who died while he was alive."

* * *

The Santiago pilgrim's road . . . Paulo Coelho's last answer led to my discovering the Camino, the "pilgrim's way" that has led, since the ninth century, to the cathedral in the little town of Santiago de Compostela where it is believed the apostle St James lies buried.

It's believed that James, called a "brother of Christ" in the Bible (although they were not family), came to Galicia in Spain to do missionary work some years after the crucifixion (and ascension to heaven, depending on your faith).

John Brierley notes in his guidebook that there is no historical evidence of this, only anecdotal accounts.

But assuming that James did indeed come to Spain, he would have been one of the first of the apostles to carry out Jesus' injunction in Matthew 28:19: "Go ye therefore, and teach all nations, baptizing them in the name of the Father, and of the Son, and of the Holy Ghost: Teaching them to observe all things whatsoever I have commanded you."

At that time (about forty years after the birth of Christ), northwestern Spain was a hub of paganism – with Finisterre on the coast a kind of headquarters with stone altars, rituals and initiation ceremonies. The kind of place where Getafix the Druid from the *Asterix* comics would have felt entirely at home.

Finisterre (the Latin *finis terra* means literally the "end of the Earth") was likely one of the places where James tried his damnedest to convert the pagans to accept the message of the Man from Nazareth. But according to tradition – and its almost seamless fusion of fact, fiction and Catholic mysticism – James was no match for the pagans in Finisterre, so he headed for the little fishing village of Muxía, about thirty kilometres to the east. At Muxía he went to sit on a rock to lick his wounds, when out of the blue the Virgin Mary appeared before him in a small sailboat. She comforted him and encouraged him to return to Jerusalem without delay. Immediately after her appearance the sail of the little boat turned to rock, which is still there to this day.

James took Mary's advice and went straight back to Jerusalem, where he was promptly beheaded by King Herod in 44 AD. So, James became the first martyr in the name of Christ. Did Herod ever do anything but murder babies and chop people's heads off?

Despite his failed attempts to persuade the pagans of the error of their ways, James loved Spain, so a few of his followers brought his mortal remains back to the country by boat so that he could be buried at Finisterre. But the pagans didn't approve; James' followers fled to the interior and buried him somewhere there.

Almost eight centuries later, in the year 813 or 814, a shepherd named Pelayo or Pelagius had a vision of a bright star, which led him to the place where James had apparently been buried. This is the spot where the cathedral was later built and the little town of Santiago de Compostela established. The name of the town tells the story: Santo Iago (Saint James), Compos (field), Stella (stars). James is also the patron saint of Spain.

The first written record of a pilgrim walking the Camino dates from the year 940. In the subsequent centuries tens of thousands of people walked from every corner of Europe each year to pay homage at James' grave, and in the process be granted forgiveness for their sins. The Camino starts at your front door, the moment you put a foot over the threshold.

There were apparently also forced pilgrimages: instead of serving jail time, some of those convicted were made to walk the Camino. You could even "delegate" someone else to walk your Camino and to receive forgiveness on your behalf at Santiago de Compostela.

The Camino became so huge that it began to overshadow the other two famous and ancient Christian pilgrimages – those to Jerusalem and to Rome – in popularity.

Brierley mentions that this early growth must be seen against the background of the Catholic Church's attempts to consolidate its presence in Spain in the early Middle Ages, especially once the Moors had been expelled during the Crusades.

Here too the apostle James played a mythical – and controversial – role: He is known in Spain as Santiago Matamoros (Saint James the Moor-slayer). According to the legend, the apostle appeared on a white horse during the Battle of Clavijo and crushed a numerically vastly superior army of Moors with his sword.

From the Milky Way to the Moors . . . it remains a magical story that stirs the imagination of millions to this day.

* * *

9 March 1816: 5 rebels hanged . . . only Stephanus Cornelis Bothma's rope did not snap . . . prosecutor Jacob Glen Cuyler . . . . "It will perhaps be a satisfaction to His Excellency to hear the prisoners one and all died fully resigned to their fate . . ."

10 October 1815 . . . "ruffian" . . . Frederik Cornelis

*(Freek) Bezuidenhout (55) from the farm Baviaansrivier
... now Silverbrook (Johan Troskie) refuses to be arrested,
farm in Baviaansrivier ... shot at Pandoers ... shot and
killed, tried to hide in rock crevasse.*

My rough notes on the Slagtersnek Rebellion are becoming
unmanageable on my irritatingly small Samsung Netbook.

I can't stop thinking of the satisfaction I'll feel when I
chuck the laptop and phone away at Charles de Gaulle. It's
absurd: sitting up here in the sky on the way to the longest
holiday of my life, after all the flaming hoops I've jumped
through over the past few months, with an article that's still
not finished. It's enough to make you certifiably insane.

Bun Booyens, my first editor at *Go*, gave a talk at the
KKNK once in which he described how his journalists'
writing styles differ. Toast Coetzer's words flow like a
waterfall, and Bun imagines him writing with one hand,
while steering with his knees, holding a KFC Rounder in
his other hand. Dana Snyman has a different approach. He
is like a cat having kittens. Approach him cautiously, keep
your distance, and when you look again, there's a precious
new arrival.

And me? Erns sits in front of the laptop like a dog that's
swallowed poison ...

* * *

I yield to the temptation of the in-flight entertainment despite (or maybe because of) the pressure of work. The laptop's batteries are not going to last until Doha anyway;
I'll have to come up with another Slagtersnek plan at the
airport during the eight-hour stopover.

I scroll through the movies. My eye catches *Wild* (2014),

with Reese Witherspoon in the leading role, based on the bestseller with the same title by Cheryl Strayed.

Wild tells the story of Cheryl's epic solo hike along the Pacific Crest Trail in the USA. She covered almost 1 800 kilometres on her own in 94 days, with hardly any hiking experience and infinitely more baggage than she had in her rucksack.

Her hike began in the Mojave Desert in southern California. During the hike she has constant flashbacks to her childhood, the death of her mother, rough sex with strangers, and a heroin phase for good measure. Oh, and the collapse of her marriage, and an abortion. One is tempted to ask her, in the vein of a *New Yorker* cartoon: "Other than that, Mrs Kennedy, how was your trip to Dallas?"

The film is incredibly inspiring. I can't help making certain connections between Strayed's story and my own imminent hike.

Look, I don't foresee having to lick the dew off my tent when I run out of water, or covering the distances she covered without seeing a single soul. The Camino is far too popular for that. My guidebook tells me that in 2014 exactly 237 886 pilgrims arrived at Santiago de Compostela. Of these, 161 994 walked the Camino Francés, the route that I'm going to take.

But like Strayed, I also have a lot of baggage I'd like to get rid of. Physical and emotional. Baggage that has kept me very busy for a very long time, that I don't necessarily want to think about, but that is always lurking just below the surface. The cracks in the "room beneath the floor", as the psychoanalyst James Hollis refers to the unconscious. Let's face it, I don't think people decide, without reason(s), to take six weeks' leave to go and backpack around Spain alone without a cell phone, watch or camera.

I scribble a few quotes from the film in among my Slagtersnek notes, especially from the part where she reaches her destination at the Bridge of the Gods on the Oregon–Washington border after so many challenges, crises and adventures:

- "There is no way to know what makes one thing happen, and not another. What leads to what. What destroys what. What causes what to flourish, or die, or take another course? What if I forgive myself? What if I was sorry?"
- "We are never prepared for what we expect."
- "After I lost myself in the wilderness of my grief, I found my own way out of the woods. Thank you . . . for everything the trail had taught me and everything I couldn't yet know."
- "It was my life – like all lives, mysterious and irrevocable and sacred. So very close, so very present, so very belonging to me. How wild it was, to let it be."

* * *

What thoughts and sensations will I arrive at the cathedral in Santiago de Compostela with in about forty days' time? Or, firstly: will I make it there?

The obvious psychological challenges – in themselves a morass – aside, four physical aspects worry me constantly:

1. At 92 kilograms I am seriously overweight.
My body mass index (BMI) is a staggering 31,1 – so technically I am obese. A bit like the title of the Valiant Swart song: "Diknek en klein tandjies". So, getting over the Pyrenees on Day One won't be fun. I was full of good intentions and little schemes to take on the Camino considerably lighter and

leaner, but alas. It's a vicious cycle – I am an emotional eater, constantly stuffing my face to ward off the anxiety.

2.   I am unfit.
The story I keep trying to tell myself is one that travel author Dana Snyman once told in a *Go* article on club rugby in small towns. The one about the farmer who lives a little way out of town and won't travel back and forth into town on weekdays to train with the local team, because he "farms" himself fit. I hope I can "walk" myself fit on the Camino.

3.   I am injured.
I don't tackle anything with a measure of balance. It's always full-on or fuck-all – I've often thought this would be a good epitaph on my tombstone. On 2 January I hiked up Skeleton Gorge above Kirstenbosch, hung around for a bit at the reservoirs at the top, then bounded back down like a nimble mountain goat – only, I'm shaped more like a juvenile rhino. The next morning my right knee started hassling me, so much so that I couldn't bend it without a shooting pain. Several physiotherapy sessions and Pilates classes followed, as well as acupuncture needles from knee to hip. I even ended up at an orthopaedic surgeon, who took X-rays and diagnosed tendinopathy. That was ten days ago. The orthopaedic surgeon had good news and bad news. The bad news: I will definitely have ongoing knee pain, especially up steps or steep inclines. The good news: I'm not likely to mess it up more than it already is, especially if I start slowly and stretch regularly. He even claimed that my knee could start to heal with all this exercise.

This unsettles me deeply. In September 2006, I left for Tanzania to climb Kilimanjaro. I was also pretty unfit, and had the final stages of an upper respiratory tract infection. I boarded the plane with an irritating little cough, which only got worse. I don't know if the dreaded altitude sickness played a role, but it couldn't have helped. After four days I was so ill that I had to admit defeat, barely ninety minutes' walk from base camp, the start of the final climb. Being denied the sunrise from the roof of Africa was a huge disappointment.

4.   I have serious sleep apnoea.
In February I went for a sleep study at a clinic in Cape Town. My father had recently been diagnosed with sleep apnoea and now uses a CPAP device at night – an expensive affair at R20 000 with a mask that makes him look and sound a bit like Darth Vader from *Star Wars*.

My results were not good. Apparently I don't sleep deeply enough because of obstructive sleep apnoea – my throat muscles and tongue become so slack that I stop breathing, but I don't wake up. This may explain why I so often wake up dead tired. But sleep apnoea has all kinds of other scary and dangerous consequences: a higher risk of heart attacks, strokes, diabetes, obesity and accidents, because you could fall asleep while driving, for example.

My results showed an apnoea episode up to thirty times an hour; I sometimes did not breathe for as long as half a minute, during which time the organs need to work twice as hard. Sometimes you do wake up, gasping for breath, or choking, or from snoring loudly and irregularly, and with pounding heart palpitations – all symptoms I know well. Especially the snoring.

It's not really something I'm proud of, but I am a seasoned snorer. At university, a friend and I once went on a road trip from PE to Cape Town. One evening we pulled into a backpacker lodge in Knysna to overnight in its dormitory. Sometime in the middle of the night my own snoring woke me and I looked around. Only backpacks remained – everyone else had sneaked off to escape my thunderous snoring . . .

Weight also plays a big role in sleep apnoea – extra fatty tissue around your neck can add to the obstruction of the airway. After my tests the specialist immediately wanted to prescribe a CPAP device. But I resisted, especially when I heard about the new Provent plasters, which are practically invisible and much less of a drama than a machine. But the specialist insisted: I needed a CPAP device to help me get a good night's rest, to boost my metabolism and help me to lose weight, and also to prepare me for the Camino. In fact, in his view I did not stand much of a chance of completing the Camino without a CPAP device. He also recommended a special lightweight CPAP machine to make travelling easier. It all just felt too much like a one-sided push to sell me an expensive machine, so I went for a second opinion and decided to take my chances on the Camino with one packet of nice and expensive Provent plasters (R1 140 for thirty), which would hopefully bring some relief for my fellow hikers in the night if my snoring were to become unbearable.

* * *

The pilot announces that we are flying over Mecca and that those sitting on the right of the plane should be able to see it. I'm on the right. It's already pitch dark outside. Mecca's lights glimmer far in the distance, the holy place where millions of Muslims end their pilgrimage. From up here it looks like a massive power plant in the middle of nowhere.

Midnight at Hamad International Airport in Doha, Qatar. About 24 hours ago I was still at a Boland wedding, twirling a bridesmaid around on the dance floor with clumsy enthusiasm to Tina Turner's "Simply the Best".

It's a song that always brings back memories. At high school I was a sprinter, believe it or not. Our U-19 relay team at Uitenhage's Hoërskool Brandwag was pretty sharp. Our X factor was the guy who ran the home leg: Wylie Human, who played for almost every Super Rugby team in the country in later years.

Tina Turner's hit was our theme song. In the heats at the Volkswagen Prestige meeting on the tartan track at the University of Port Elizabeth, we were way ahead of all the other teams timewise. The final was going to be broadcast live on television.

I was to run the third leg of the race. But poor Gideon fell at the starting block and we literally bit the dust. Later that evening, watching the grown-up athletics, half-stunned, we heard "Simply the Best" blaring from the loudspeaker . . .

* * *

Doha's new airport is overwhelming. I feel like Dorothy's little dog Toto, in *The Wizard of Oz*, when she says, "Toto, I have a feeling we're not in Kansas any more . . ."

I reckon Qatar looks ready to host the Soccer World Cup in 2020 – but they're going to have to do something about the weather. It was uncomfortably hot and humid when we got off the plane – this, just before midnight.

I move with the mass of new arrivals in rows through

passport control and reach the shiny and hyper-modern arrivals hall with a TV screen as big as a tennis court. Images advertising the Al Khaliji banking group flash across the screen.

But the TV screen is nothing compared to the huge bloody bear in the middle of the arrivals hall. At first I thought the seven-metre-high yellow bear was a Lindt chocolate advert, but apparently it's a legendary work of art: *Untitled (Lamp/Bear)*. It was created ten years ago by Swedish neo-Dadaist Urs Fischer, and has been on display at Ludwig Mies van der Rohe's famous Seagram building in New York – the building, I might add, on which *Go's* home, Cape Town's Absa building, is modelled.

A member of Qatar's royal family bought the bear, which weighs about 20 tons, for $6,8 million at a Christie's auction. Impressive, but also a bit unsettling: a reading lamp sticks out behind the bear, as if someone has forced it into the teddy's back.

The reading lamp reminds me that Slagtersnek needs finishing. My flight leaves for Paris in under eight hours, just enough time to finish and email the article before Monday kicks off in Cape Town for my editor and colleagues. A sterile hotel room nearby would have been perfect; alas, I bought my ticket on special, so I don't qualify for accommodation.

* * *

I check in at the Oryx Lounge, a luxurious space that looks more like the domain of business class passengers, to bat out the night at the airport. My friend Le Roux often speaks of "the high premium on self-entertainment". Forty euros for eight hours in the Oryx Lounge is certainly a high premium, especially since what lies ahead for me can hardly be called entertainment.

But I really don't want to struggle with Slagtersnek in the arrivals hall, near the yellow bear, with the laptop on my lap.

The Oryx Lounge is clinical yet luxurious: a spacious room with laminate floors, hyper-modern standard lamps and rows of comfortable leather chairs. And no shortage of food: a buffet with dates, olives, dried fruit, rolls, cheeses, pastrami and a Nespresso machine. There is a family room, a games room with PlayStations and a computer area where the Macs' little white apples gleam.

I drink the first of many coffees and settle into a leather chair. Okay: time to wring this Slagtersnek article's neck. Starting the Camino without finishing this thing first would be career-limiting, to say the least. I might as well not bother going back to work when I get back to Cape Town in mid-June. The thought of walking for forty days with that sword hanging over my head makes me feel sick.

I've always found airports to be good spaces to work in. I've seen countless articles through their dying moments at airports, sometimes in transit between flights. I've even often wondered whether I should open an airport satellite office. I'm just more focused at airports, for some reason. Maybe it's just that, when an article is dangerously late, my tail feathers catch fire, so to speak, to such a degree that my grey matter really starts shifting gears.

The Man Who Wasn't There is a movie by the Coen brothers in which Billy Bob Thornton plays the lead. I also feel, sometimes, as if I'm not really present in the places I find myself. There's certainly a case to be made for the old AA saying "Wherever you go, there you are", but I don't always experience it like this. At least not psychically.

Around me tourists are lounging – people in transit, between airports, between past and future experiences, adventures, loves, disappointments, business transactions . . . Some are sleeping, others are trying to, squirming and fiddling. Most are absorbed in the small screens in their hands, earphones plugged in. It is quiet in here – no background music, just the soft clink of cutlery every now and then as people help themselves to something from the buffet. A long night lies ahead for all of us. A long night under bright neon lights that remind you of a university library.

The article is slowly taking shape. I'm listening to Micah P. Hinson, a troubled singer from Texas who, at the age of 33, has the gravelly, husky voice of an 80-year-old taking the last puff of a Lexington.

A deeply strange way of working, this. The man who wasn't there. How many times haven't I been in this position? Every time, I promise myself: this is the last time. But like an addict who buggers up the finest intentions and promises with a relapse, it's not long before I'm here again, in the discomfort zone I know so intimately.

The worst is when I embark on the next *Go* story before I've even completed the articles I'm still working on.

In a seedy two-star hotel in freezing Belfast (Mpumalanga's, not Ireland's) I once had to write an article about game ranger Christiaan Bakkes and his Jack Russell, Tiger, under extraordinary pressure – as all the town's characters reported to the bar, one by one.

In a guesthouse in Winburg I struggled half to death to finish an article about the Gifberg resort outside Vanrhynsdorp. In a rondawel in the old Transkei, with the sea as a soundtrack, I wrestled with the closing paragraphs of a piece about a road trip between Carolina and Barberton.

In Tsumeb I literally locked myself in a room at the Minen Hotel for a weekend to wrap up a story on the Knysna forest's characters (including two of the last true traditional foresters). A kind of boot camp for the psyche . . .

Here I am, freaking out at Hamad International Airport, building sloppy sentences in the vague hope of generating 2 500 readable words on Slagtersnek before the new day dawns at the start of the Cape Town week. The wi-fi is free: a good thing if you quickly need to check the details of a guesthouse in Cookhouse (near the Slagtersnek monument), but fatal for someone whose attention tends to drift.

I cannot wait to be without my phone for six weeks. To go completely under the radar and not feel constantly besieged by messages and marketing. To try to recall and relive what life was like before we all started walking around with smartphones.

But I'm already having some misgivings about turfing the iPhone and laptop. At the moment I'm just despondent, not visibly angered like before. I'm running out of time and options. Storing this stuff for forty days in a locker at Charles de Gaulle means an (unplanned) outlay of R4 000. I don't know anyone in Paris. When I got here I sent a quick WhatsApp to a former colleague who knows someone who lives in France, but I'm still waiting for a reply.

Hang on – last night at the wedding I sat next to someone who works in Paris frequently. Martine. We had a lovely chat and she gave me a few great tips on how to spend my last night in Paris on my way home. Before I left Cape Town this morning we said a quick hello on Facebook.

I send her a First World SOS:

Hi Martine, I'm at Doha airport. The only reason I'm still "digital" is that I've brought work with me that I have to finish before the Camino. I have a strange Paris request/ favour to ask: I'm finishing that work tonight here in Doha, and there's no way I'm taking the laptop and phone with me on the Camino. But the lockers at Charles de Gaulle seem expensive for 40 days' storage (about 320 euros) and I'm reluctant to mail/courier them to SA. You don't perhaps know of a person or a place in Paris where I can mail the parcel (I promise it's not contraband or something out of Breaking Bad) *from the airport and then pick it up on 15/16 June when I'm back there again? I'm waiting for an address from a colleague who knows somebody there, but it's dragging out a bit and I'm running out of time. I'll need to mail the parcel from the airport at about 3 p.m. tomorrow afternoon. Phew, this turned into quite a ramble. Maybe I should stick to organising bachelor parties. Looking forward to hearing from you!*

She answers quickly:

Just contacted a friend in Paris to find out whether you can mail the parcel to her – will let you know as soon as she replies. Enjoy the evening until then!

There you go – it's all working out nicely. The Nespresso is strong, the chair comfy, the wi-fi fast and, with a date from the buffet in my mouth, the word count is starting to rise.

* * *

With the address of a South African in Paris – Marcelle (also a journalist) – written in my Moleskine, and the Slagtersnek article now about three-quarters done, I board flight QR 039 for the Doha-to-Paris leg of my journey. It's just after eight on Monday 4 May. Six Nespressos through the night in the Oryx Lounge. And a gorgeous hot shower. But I haven't shut an eye for 48 hours. The lonely places we take ourselves . . .

This time I'm not alone in my row. There's a man on either side of me – on my left a Muslim gent with a long beard, in Islamic attire; on my right a young Indian guy who looks really nervous. Arjun has lived in New Delhi his whole life, and is flying abroad for the first time to go and work as a computer programmer in Paris. He is also scared of flying and heights.

Luckily, I don't have that problem. The worst turbulence I ever experienced was in a Boeing above Mossel Bay. People either screamed or started negotiating under their breath with their notion of divinity. A flight attendant went down on her knees, arms embracing the food trolley. Fortunately, the worst of the chaos was over within a minute.

Heights don't bother me: it's confined spaces that drive me to distraction. A few years ago I visited the Cango Caves to write a story for *Go*. I scraped through the Tunnel of Love, but by the Devil's Chimney my courage began to flag. Ahead of me, a young family were hauling themselves through the chimney. The father was egging on his chubby wife: "Are you in, Mouse? Are you in?" With barely half my body wedged into the chimney it felt like an All Black ruck had collapsed on me. I was out of there in a flash, and took the detour.

Just before take-off, the Boeing already powering up on the Doha runway, the pilot informs us in a heavy Arabic accent that there is a technical problem. We'll have to wait for technicians to investigate. Arjun is rubbing his hands together. There's not much we can do about it. When I'm sitting on the runway, I often get the feeling that a team of doctors is about to wheel me into the operating theatre. You are powerless, delivered unto others' mercy and expertise.

I read somewhere that the first ninety seconds of a plane's ascent are theoretically the most dangerous part of any flight. If something serious goes wrong during this critical period, your family will soon be wiping away the tears in a National Geographic *Air Crash Investigation* episode.

I have since developed a faintly obsessive habit. As the plane leaves Mother Earth, I diligently count up to ninety in my head and then relax into a false sense of security. "You realise it's not going to make any difference to your fate whether you count or not," a friend who likes to think logically has pointed out to me. Obviously she's right, but I do it anyway.

The technicians apparently on their way, Arjun and I start chatting about our fate in the air.

"Well, I guess if it's your time, it's your time, nothing you can do about it," he says stolidly.

"But what does it mean for us if it is the pilot's time?" I tease him.

Arjun laughs and shakes his head.

Again, a liminal place, a dormant no-man's-land. I was hoping to be in the air by now, laptop open, in the death throes of the article. Not here on the runway, where all our electronics have to stay switched off.

The minutes tick by.

* * *

-----*Original Message*-----
From: Erns Grundling
Sent: 04 May 2015 02:54 PM

To: Pierre Steyn
Subject: Here is Slagtersnek!
Importance: High

Hi Pierre

Attached find Slagtersnek. A bit long, but better now than never.

I'm now between Luxembourg and Paris. Altitude: 39 829 ft. Ground speed: 482 mph. Outside temperature -67 F. Still 525 miles to Paris, where a mad rush for trains awaits me. Tomorrow morning I'm mailing my laptop and cell phone from Bayonne to a journalist in Paris. I'm picking it up from her on the 16th.

Please give a quick heads-up that you've received the file. Because then my holiday's bloody close.

Au revoir!

Erns

The past few hours have been a manic blur. I notched up twenty dollars on my credit card to access the plane's wi-fi to check the last few facts and contact details for my Slagtersnek story. My laptop battery only just made it.

Not my best piece of writing, but for now the mantra "Don't get it right, get it written" is more important than producing a tour de force. I suspect, in any case, that the story of a small band of rebels who died under difficult – even unjust – circumstances two centuries ago is too depressing to make *Go*'s pages. It's not exactly a comfortable fit with the magazine's genial tone and its articles' uplifting escapism.

What an absurd little scene: desperately clicking "Send" somewhere between heaven and earth on the other side of Luxembourg so that a Word doc can announce itself with a bleep seconds later on my editor's computer in Cape Town, the old Muslim gent mumbling and bowing in prayer beside me, *Ice Age 3* paused on his screen, and Arjun, having abandoned the in-flight quiz shows, watching a Bollywood dance scene from *Slumdog Millionaire*.

Pierre lets me know all's good, and that I need spend only the first week of the Camino contemplating my deadline-related sins. Finally. I can shut the laptop for six weeks.

The last words I type are an Out-of-Office message:

I'm on holiday in Europe. Digital detox, into the mild. I'll be back at the office on Monday 22 June. Please email Esma Marnewick for any Weg/Go matters. Adios. Erns

* * *

Entry in Moleskine diary

Maybe it's like a train riding into rain, Gertjie. I'm somehow thinking of you now in the train between Charles de Gaulle and Saint-Michel–Notre-Dame. It's almost three years since my father and I were on a similar train not riding into rain but riding into the most autumnal autumn that I can remember and there are so few. Around me people are on their phones or reading books there are umbrellas and accents, I constantly feel I'm hearing Afrikaans but I'm mistaken the robot voice (woman's voice) of the train has just pronounced Parc des Expositions I just hear "Sex positions" my first impressions of Europeans are probably wrong but I detect a sophisticated indifference, almost as if ubuntu will never fly here – not that ubuntu flies in Africa anyway. At the airport Gert a quick young Frenchman started coming down on me in front of a whole lot of people in an ever-lengthening, stressful queue of Doha-Paris-bound passengers for deliberately brushing up against a woman, according to him, as if I wanted to dry-hump her in a split second like dolphins that have sex in a flash, but his outburst caught me off guard and I couldn't find the words "I didn't bump into her on purpose" and went into a whole long explanation of the trains I was chasing instead and said I was just in a rush and not looking where I was going and he just shook his head like the Head Boy of Life and said "Blablablabla" and spoke to the girl and her boyfriend in French and he almost became involved and people started staring and my only comeback was "You should come to Africa" but God knows why I defaulted to that maybe I just wanted to make a point about personal space in Africa or rather the lack of it and that he would have a lot to say in a queue at Home Affairs but there was no time to say everything but at that moment I became hyperaware of a type of pretentiousness and profoundly First World luxury and decorum. Anyway, Gert, God only knows why I'm not reading or doing crosswords rather I'm buggered Gert dead tired from sleep apnoea and fuck-all sleep. It's dismal in Paris. Hitting pause for a bit.

* * *

I feel a deep ambivalence towards the two Moleskine diaries I packed for the Camino.

I could easily have arranged in advance to write a freelance story or three to help cover expenses. And there's nothing stopping me from writing a column or a feature article for *Go* on my Camino experiences when I get back to Cape Town. I could even consider writing a book or a guide. But I just don't want to. Everything in me is fighting the thought. I'm just completely written out.

In "Famous Blue Raincoat" Leonard Cohen sings: "You're living for nothing now / I hope you're keeping some kind of record". I like the idea of "some kind of record", even if it's for me alone. And who knows? Maybe an idea or two finds me halfway along the Camino, in which case I'll definitely need pen and paper. Maybe I'll write a bit of poetry again. Or a song, for the first time in ten years. What happens to us when we detach ourselves from all the distractions, especially the cell phone screens that keep us so busy?

* * *

SMS to my father, Monday 4 May, 19:38 p.m.

Guess where I'm standing right now? At Notre Dame! Going to Bayonne just now, then mailing my laptop and cell phone to a journalist in Paris. I'll fetch them again on 15 June. Got all my work done, holiday starts NOW. Much love.

His reply:

Bon Voyage! Go well on the walk and so happy you are going to enjoy it to the full! Will miss you. Look after yourself! <3 Pa / Ma

Ja, Pa. Full-on or fuck-all.

Paris. The city of love. Hemingway's "moveable feast". "Paris is always a good idea," as Audrey Hepburn said. It was this city whose street life Jan Rabie described as "a history book of the whole world" in his diary. And the place about which André P. Brink wrote: "I was 'born' on a bench in the Luxembourg Gardens in Paris – when I was 23 years old."

After all the running around and battling with my luggage at Charles de Gaulle, I sit on a bench to catch my breath. There are heavily armed policemen everywhere, vigilant and intimidating and not missing a thing about their surroundings. The Charlie Hebdo attack was just four months ago. For the first time since leaving Cape Town, I feel truly alone. And I realise: I am completely dependent upon myself for the next forty days.

At the Saint-Michel station I totter up the stairs with my heavy rucksack to see the cathedral of Notre Dame de Paris (French for "Our Lady of Paris") looming ahead of me. I've always got excited about monuments, iconic buildings, even natural phenomena. I remember the first time I saw Table Mountain as a four-year-old through the car window in 1983. One of my uncles was an NP MP for Uitenhage and my parents and I stayed with him in Acacia Park. More than two decades later I stood in absolute amazement in front of the Taj Mahal in Agra and felt that childlike Table Mountain feeling again.

It felt the same to see Notre Dame, a cathedral I first got to know in a Disney movie about a gypsy, who was attractive even for an animated character, talking gargoyles and a kind-hearted hunchback.

This is my second visit to Paris. In September 2012 my father and I flew in to Charles de Gaulle and had less than four hours before catching a connecting flight to Verona in Italy. Rather than idling away a few empty hours somewhere in a restaurant at the airport, my father wanted to take a quick dash around Paris. The woman at the information counter strongly advised against taking the train into the city – she thought we wouldn't make it back in time for the connecting flight. We decided to take a train to Saint-Michel anyway. Near Notre Dame we enjoyed a glass of French champagne and some rabbit pâté.

The masses of tourists in front of Notre Dame on that beautiful autumn afternoon three years ago are not here tonight – there is just a cluster here and there, most with their backs to the cathedral taking selfies.

I stroll over the Pont des Arts, one of the city's famous bridges. Lovers attach so-called love locks to the bridge, often with their names written on them, then throw the key into the Seine. This tradition may only have started in 2008, but there are already hundreds – if not thousands – of locks of all sizes and colours all along the railings of the bridge. It's a tradition that has caused concern, as bridges have been damaged as a result. It's feared that the weight of all that love – or rather, the valiant declaration of it – could cause some of them to collapse.

I read some of the names on the locks: Jackie and Benn (17-05-12 Wedding), Eddy and Delia, Michael and Candice, one has only Rubí . . . Six months ago there was a name on my lips, too, one I would have liked to write on a lock next to my own and fasten it to this bridge.

* * *

I walk for about half an hour to the Gare d'Austerlitz, the station where the overnight train to Bayonne in the south-west of France awaits me.

Laurika Rauch sings about Austerlitz in her song "Hot Gates", a moving ballad listing historical battlefields and places of conflict. The station in Paris is named after a major battle fought on 2 December 1805 near the little town of Austerlitz in the Austrian Empire – one of Napoleon's most renowned victories.

The lack of sleep is beginning to catch up with me. At a busy intersection I look right as usual before crossing, and just don't see the motorbike coming from the left. We miss each other by what feels like centimetres . . . it happens too quickly for me to grasp how close it was. I freeze, then I realise how it happened: I crossed the street as if I were in South Africa. First look right, then left, then right again, as Daantjie Kat taught me on the record player way back in the early eighties – so I just didn't see the motorbike bearing down on me.

I suppose I could put it down to the shitstorm I've been through. Or to exhaustion. Or both. But even an hour later, having a pizza and a beer, I'm still rattled. I could have been killed, or at least seriously injured. My Camino could have ended in Paris before it had even begun. The difference between a sigh of relief and a hell of a drama was literally a fraction of a second. Why *did* nothing happen to me? Luck? Grace?

"There is no way to know what makes one thing happen, and not another."

* * *

At nine o'clock I step onto the overnight train. Bayonne is many hours away. My thinking was that I could just as easily sleep on the train as look up a cheap hotel in Bayonne.

Ahead of me in the queue there's a girl with a ponytail

and a green rucksack with something embroidered on it that looks like a flag or an emblem – a cluster of colourful blocks arranged diagonally. Could she be the first of my fellow walkers? I kind of hope we're in the same compartment.

The compartment is tiny, three bunks stacked on top of one another on each side. The woman with the rucksack is not in my compartment after all; Tom, a tanned young French surfer who lives near Bayonne, is. He's on his way home after a few months' surfing in Australia. While we're chatting, a middle-aged Frenchwoman and two Belgian girls also come in. The Belgians are on holiday in France; the Frenchwoman doesn't talk much. None of them is heading for the Camino. The Belgians are astounded to hear that I'm tackling it alone.

The train slowly pulls out of the Gare d'Austerlitz, creaking and groaning. It's so cramped that all we can do is lie like sardines in our bunks. The small talk stops. I go to brush my teeth. Standing in front of the mirror, I consider using the sleep apnoea plasters. No, I'll be too self-conscious – the others will just have to endure my snoring.

When I get back to the compartment, the lights are already off. I might as well have used the Provent plasters.

* * *

Train journeys always take me back to Uitenhage, where I grew up. I often say that Uitenhage is the most beautiful song Bruce Springsteen will never write. The Boss would feel at home there, especially near Volkswagen, the area's blue-collar mecca.

Sometimes, my father would take me to the nearby Willow Dam on Sundays, where we would ride three laps of the circular 300-metre track on a small steam engine, Little Bess.

My first trip on the Trans-Karoo, known these days as the Shosholoza Meyl, was in 2002 during my Honours year in journalism at Stellenbosch. Our annual class excursion that year was to Gauteng and we were able to persuade the lecturers to let us travel by train rather than by bus.

I was 22, full of plans and dreams and things. I remember the plastic bag with the five bottles that Gerjo, Borrie and I unpacked onto the little table in the compartment: Old Brown Sherry, Tassenberg, Smirnoff vodka, Bell's whisky and VO brandy. Sometime during the night, as the train rolled past Makwassie, a joint also did the rounds.

* * *

Despite having had so little sleep for two days, I keep waking up in my bunk. So much for the soothing sound of wheels on rails – instead, there's jangling and clattering. Sometimes it even feels like the coaches are being shaken from side to side.

At eight in the morning the train pulls into the station in Bayonne, almost 800 kilometres southwest of Paris. It feels good to get out of the stuffy compartment. I stumble out into the light drizzle and head for the station building. Once again I see the woman with the ponytail and rucksack with its flag.

"Hi, I guess you're also walking the Camino?" I try to start up a conversation.

"Uh-huh." (With a heavy American accent.)

"I'm Erns from South Africa."

"Oh wow, that's far from here! I'm Claire, from the US."

"Ah. You're also taking the train to Saint Jean?" I ask.

"Nah, I'm taking the bus."

"Oh, okay. I've got a train ticket. I guess I'd better go sort it out."

"Cool. Well . . . see you in Saint Jean."

There's already quite a crowd of walkers here – old and young, some in groups, an elderly couple here and there, and a few solitary souls with only their rucksacks and trekking poles.

According to the ticket I bought in advance on a French website, Capitaine Train, the train leaves for Saint-Jean-Pied-de-Port in less than two hours. I walk to the ticket office, where the man behind the counter – entirely predictably – seems prepared to help me in any language but English.

I have heard that you should just start speaking Afrikaans if this happens; it makes the French more sympathetic when they think you're not a Brit or an American. So, I wave my ticket and mumble something in Afrikaans. It works! The man's whole attitude changes. He explains in fluent English that the railway track to Saint Jean has been damaged in a storm and is currently being repaired, but that I can use my train ticket for the bus that leaves Bayonne at the same time.

But I need to find out something much more urgent from him: Where is the post office? I have to get rid of the laptop and cell phone right about now. Before boarding the bus to Saint Jean. I don't have much time. It's raining and I have no idea where to go.

After some vague directions and sympathetic hand gestures from the man in the ticket office, I head off down the street in search of the post office. The city is waking up. I walk past a few small shops and delis where old men sit reading the newspaper and sipping coffee. I could do with a coffee, but that will have to be my reward once the parcel is in the mail.

In the distance, on the other side of a bridge, a huge Gothic cathedral towers over the city. Half running, with my heavy red bag on my back, I spot a pharmacy and dash in to buy a few last-minute things: mosquito repellent, an ointment with a whole selection of insects on the box that looks as if it might protect me from bed bugs – one of the great potential evils of the Camino – and some cold and flu medicines that look like Grand-Pa headache powders. The pharmacist assures me, happily, that the post office is open today and only some hundred metres away.

Fortunately the woman behind the counter at the post office speaks good English. She looks slightly amused as I hastily unpack all my items on her counter: my laptop, the laptop's cable, my iPhone and charger, three different wall plugs (I had to make sure that my laptop would work in Doha and in France), the Croxley notebook, a thicker notebook, two pens and J.C. van der Walt's Slagtersnek book.

I find a five-kilogram box. For the last time, I see the glowing white apple with a bite out of it as I switch my phone off. I throw everything into the box. On it, I write the address of a person in Paris I do not know and have never had any contact with. I do not have Marcelle's email address or contact number, but I can get those at the end of the Camino. I pay seven euros; the box is sealed and thrown into a huge bag.

And suddenly I am free.

* * *

My digital detox has begun, but the feeling of emancipation is short-lived. Before I even get back to Bayonne station I'm experiencing the effects of going cold turkey. My left hand keeps reaching spasmodically for my pocket, like a reflex, for the iPhone that's no longer there.

The poor phone has been through so much it's a wonder it's still working. In October 2014 it fell into a toilet at the tourist bureau in Groot Marico. It had more than five hours of recordings of *Go* interviews on it that I hadn't backed up. If I lost them, I'd be screwed.

Luckily I remembered a trick involving rice that would help to rescue a phone with water damage – the rice absorbs the moisture. I charged off to a café; before the cash register had even stopped ringing I'd plunged the phone into a bag of Tastic. The Bangladeshi behind the counter was a bit surprised.

It worked, but I did not take into account the fact that grains of rice could find their way into the phone's sockets. Three grains of rice had a nice leisurely swell in the charging socket . . . This had me lying on my back on Egbert and Santa van Bart's stoep in Groot Marico on an inflatable mattress, wearing a head torch, trying to pick the rice grains out with a needle. Mercifully my efforts were successful, but hell . . . the lonely places we take ourselves.

For the next forty days, no one who knows me (or doesn't) will be able to phone or contact me. No one at work, not my parents or friends, not even the salespeople from those Unknown Numbers who phone you to try and sell you vehicle or funeral insurance or a cell phone contract you definitely don't need. No Facebook. No WhatsApp. No Google.

I thought this would be easier to deal with, but I should have known better. Isn't our dependence on – addiction to, even – the cell phone astounding? The longest I've ever been separated from my phone was five days in June 2014 when I went hiking in the Fish River Canyon.

Back at the station, and a bit unsteady on my feet – must be the lack of sleep – I go to a small café and order a baguette and coffee for four euros. There are many more walkers here now – you need to tread carefully between all the rucksacks and trekking poles and hats. I sit and look at the people. People watching remains my favourite spectator sport. I hear many languages: snatches of French, English, Spanish, German and something that sounds like Korean. A kind of United Nations of pilgrims. What brings all these people here? What brings *me* here . . . ? I have my reasons. But I hope to find even more reasons along the Camino itself.

Two large buses – France's answer to Greyhounds – stop in the parking lot. Time to leave for Saint-Jean-Pied-de-Port, where my Camino begins tomorrow. It looks like these buses will carry only walkers.

"You must be from South Africa?" somebody asks next to me, while I'm getting ready to load my rucksack into the belly of the bus. I've attached a piece of fabric with a few small South African flags to my rucksack.

I immediately recognise the accent. It sounds so familiar that I intuitively want to place it somewhere in the Eastern Cape. And would you believe it, Robert, the second pilgrim I meet, is from Port Elizabeth, where I was born! What are the chances?

Robert, a tall man in his early fifties, is really excited about meeting someone else from the Eastern Cape here in Bayonne. "I actually have no clue why I'm here, but here I am. I read about the Camino and thought why not, it's time for a new challenge," he says, laughing, and offers to help a young woman next to him with her big rucksack.

The bus driver is a lanky Frenchman with sunken cheeks who stood around grimly before our departure smoking Gauloises. A caricature. All he needs is a beret and a well-thumbed copy of Albert Camus's *The Outsider*. And a baguette under his arm. Local cartoonist Fred Mouton would have captured the likeness nicely.

I sit at the window and watch the scenes that flash by as the bus leaves Bayonne: a few suburban neighbourhoods with billboards, then the landscape turns into pure French countryside. It's spring in Europe and all the fields look cheerful and green. We travel through valleys, farmlands and forests, and approach the foothills of the Pyrenees; according to my guidebook, the Pied-de-Port in Saint-Jean-Pied-de-Port means "foot of the pass".

The bus is packed, but the seat next to me is open. The average age of the people on the bus is probably about 30. Almost everyone is busy on their phones or listening to music with earphones. I keep reaching towards my empty pocket.

Robert sits diagonally opposite me, Claire a few rows ahead of him. Between them is a young woman – probably in her twenties – with an alert sheepdog at her feet. The dog is clearly going to walk with her, and even has its own little rucksack with zips. A purple rucksack.

God, no. I could never lug a dog with me on a pilgrimage – the thought of the admin alone tires me out. Coping with my rucksack and two trekking poles is already enough of a challenge for me.

I can see, though, how a faithful dog could be a wonderful travelling companion. Jock meant a great deal to Percy FitzPatrick. And John Steinbeck's poodle Charley accompanied him on his road trip throughout the States.

Maybe it's because I've never really experienced the dog-as-man's-best-friend thing.

When I was about five, my first dog, a Jack Russell called Bobby, tore my orange blow-up octopus lilo to shreds. Things were never the same between us again.

My next dog, Guido, was the most asocial spaniel in the Eastern Cape in the eighties. In the garden, he would run around me in ever-diminishing circles and bark at all sorts of non-existent threats. Paranoia on four legs.

"So tell me, Erns," Robert says, turning to me, "what made you decide to do the Camino?"

The bus feels silent, as if I have an audience. Robert looks like a kindly soul who just wants to chat, but I am hesitant. "I'm hoping to find out along the way, Robert," I say and smile.

This is true, but it's only one of the reasons that made me decide to undertake this pilgrimage on my own.

* * *

I'm sitting on a small stone bench at La Porte Notre Dame, the gateway to the old part of the Basque town of Saint-Jean-Pied-de-Port. The old part of town lies along a steep and narrow cobbled street that stretches into the distance, the Rue de la Citadelle. On both sides of the street are white buildings with red-tiled roofs, some dating from the fifteenth century. It feels deeply Middle Ages here.

An information plaque on the wall states that dirt-poor pilgrims have been using this very bench for centuries, waiting for food and shelter.

Right next to me is a little church, the Church of our Lady at the End of the Bridge. In the Middle Ages there was a hospital here, too, that was linked to the church by an archway – in a way the hospital and the church were one and the same. Early tomorrow morning I'll walk through this archway again, in the general direction of the Pyrenees and Spain.

The Nive River, which has its source in the Pyrenees, flows close by. Some of the locals, and tourists, are strolling along the bank.

The Rue de la Citadelle is already part of the Camino. If I were to turn around and walk 1 000 kilometres north, I'd eventually end up back in Paris – where pilgrims have been starting from for centuries. You can start walking the Camino from many places all across Europe, such as Lisbon, Amsterdam or Geneva. In Spain alone there are six or so different Caminos that all end at Santiago de Compostela.

But Saint-Jean-Pied-de-Port is the most popular and practical starting point for modern-day pilgrims who want to walk the full 820 kilometres of the Camino Francés, or "The French Way", to Santiago de Compostela.

I feel a cold coming on, a scratchiness in my throat. Probably inevitable after all the flights, airports and train rides. All that breath. I've been wearing the same clothes for almost three days and last had a decent night's rest an impossibly long time ago. The French answer to Grand-Pa powders will have to work its magic. I mix the powder with water in my coffee mug and gulp it down. I don't know how I manage it, but the mug falls off the stone bench and cracks.

The clock tower shows it's half past one. I usually check the time on my cell phone, but from now on the churches and pilgrims along the route will be my time-keepers.

Our bus arrived in Saint Jean about ninety minutes ago and stopped about two kilometres from here, near the train station in the more modern (or less medieval) part of the town. It was a stiff walk up quite a steep hill to the Rue de la Citadelle. A warm-up for the mountain that lies ahead tomorrow, I reckoned.

I also realised, again, that I was by no means comfortable yet with the heavy rucksack and the two trekking poles that tick-tock-tick-tocked like a metronome on the cobbles. Well, sometime during the next forty days I'll hopefully find my rhythm.

Generally, you don't book accommodation in advance on the Camino. You walk every day at your own pace and decide which little town along the way you're going to find a hostel (or albergue) in. But for my first night, after the long journey from Cape Town to the south of France, I booked a place at an albergue: Beilari, a typical Basque house in the Rue de la Citadelle that sleeps eighteen.

According to the website, Beilari is the Basque word for "pilgrim", but the literal meaning is "one who awakes". The hostel only opens at two every afternoon, so when I arrived in Saint Jean I first went to the Pilgrim Office, which happened to be just across the street from Beilari.

* * *

I don't know how the Brits do it, but I detest queueing. My idea of hell (hang on, I have many ideas about this . . .) is to take the escalator into the bowels of the Absa building in Cape Town only to see a queue of twenty souls at the bank's Enquiries counter. Especially if all I need is some or other form or stamp.

I prefer the chaos of an Indian train station, where you vie in a desperate ruck for a chance to beg a man in a small glass booth for a train ticket.

Maybe it's an inborn irritability, or a fear of boredom, or an existential realisation of just how ridiculous and futile our attempts at control are . . . I don't know, queueing just gets to me. So much so that sometimes, I shamelessly squeeze in – or, let's be honest, push in – when my frustration gets the upper hand. And feel guilty about it for a long time. A vicious cycle, then.

An example: in December 2007, a group of friends and I arrived at the Noordoewer border post in Namibia for a four-day rafting expedition on the Orange River. It was about eight in the evening, and the snaking queue that met us reminded me of a voting station in the 1994 elections. It would take us at least four hours to get to customs. And we'd only get to the rafting camp long after midnight.

After half an hour I reached breaking point and began to worm my way into the queue fairly close to the front. I also managed to persuade – force, even – my mates to join me. They were, naturally, reluctant. Especially when a group of Americans right behind us began a loud protest.

It may have been the arrogance of my youth, which has hopefully been tempered a bit since then, but I didn't let the collateral damage bother me. I focused purely on the goal, which was only about two counters away.

But it's always possible to be too clever by half. I've found that selfishness or hubris of any kind catches up with you sooner or later, and not in a good way. Call it karma, or your just deserts, or life calibrating things in inexplicable ways . . . whatever you like.

It happened that very same night. There are many rafting camps along the Orange River. Over New Year, there are easily up to 2 000 rafters on the water. When you go on a guided rafting trip, you are generally divided into groups of twenty.

Lo and behold, when we arrived at the camp we found we'd been put in exactly the same group as the Americans. Things were really uncomfortable at first, but a day later we could at least make peace on the river over some beers – once I'd paid for my indiscretion.

* * *

Luckily there's not much of a queue at the Pilgrim Office in Saint Jean: four people, to be precise. The last thing I want to do is cause an international incident so soon after getting to the start of the Camino. The office is a tiny room. Three old guys are dutifully handing out and stamping booklets. There's a large map of the Day One route on the wall, from here over the Pyrenees to Roncesvalles.

Most walkers receive their Pilgrim Record or Credencial here, the most important document for the Camino. This booklet is your proof that you are a pilgrim. It gives you access to the albergues along the route, and discounts at restaurants – most eateries offer pilgrim menus so that you can enjoy dinner at a bargain price. You also need this passport if you want to get the official "Compostela" at the end of the Camino – the certificate showing that you have completed the pilgrimage.

You qualify for a Compostela if you have completed at least 100 kilometres on foot or on horseback up to Santiago de Compostela, or 200 kilometres on a bicycle. You also need to collect stamps (called "sellos") that you paste into your Camino passport from the albergues and restaurants you visit. If you start the Camino here in Saint Jean, for example, you need to collect one stamp per day and, if you walk only the last 100 kilometres, you need two stamps per day (for one restaurant and one hostel along the way, for example).

I had already received my Pilgrim Record from the Confraternity of Saint James of South Africa, so I needed only my first stamp in Saint Jean.

There is also a basket full of shells in the office. For a small donation (I put two euros in the little collection tin) you can choose a shell to take with you on your Camino. Most walkers tie the shell onto the back of their rucksacks with a piece of string. I pick a nice scallop shell – it looks a bit like the Shell logo. This shell, like the little yellow arrows indicating the route, is one of the symbols of the Camino.

There are several stories and legends about the symbolism of the shell. The lines on the shell apparently refer to the various routes that all converge at one place: Santiago de Compostela. In the Middle Ages the pilgrims used to tie the shells to their coats, hats or staffs. In fact, on my pilgrim's passport there is a sketch of a medieval pilgrim with two shells neatly tied to his coat, almost like lapels. It is also believed that in the old days the pilgrims used the shells as a small bowl for scooping water or soup. They obviously did not have the luxury of a range of outdoor products and stainless-steel mugs. And at that time, when the pilgrims reached Santiago de Compostela from wherever they'd started, they'd often walk another 100 kilometres to Finisterre. They'd collect scallop shells from the beach and take them back home as further evidence of the distance they'd travelled.

This is something we modern walkers easily forget: when the pilgrims of old had walked the 2 000 kilometres from Paris, or the 820 kilometres from Saint Jean, to Santiago de Compostela or Finisterre, they would walk all the way back home again. Unlike us, who get on a convenient bus or train or plane.

Legend has it that, at the very same Finisterre, the apostle James rescued a knight from the sea. Rising up from the waves, like a mythical sea creature, James was covered in shells. Before the arrival of Christianity, the shell was a pagan symbol of fertility and birth.

Outside the office, with my passport stamped and my scallop shell tied to my red rucksack, I run into Robert from Port Elizabeth again, who's standing in the queue. I have a sudden urge to let my father know I'm okay and ready to start the Camino. Robert takes a photo of me and texts it to my father with the words: "In Saint Jean and ready for the Camino! Lots of love, Erns."

I also see Claire again. She tells me she is heading for the Orisson hostel, about nine kilometres from here, already quite a way into the Pyrenees. I advise her to phone ahead and book a room: I had originally planned to spend the following night there, but it was already fully booked.

Maybe it's wishful thinking, maybe intuition, but I sense that my path and Claire's will cross again as she heads off towards the high green mountains on the horizon.

* * *

"Do you have wifey?" a man with a thick German accent and a wildish look in his eyes asks as we stand in the lobby of the Beilari albergue. For a moment I think the man is looking for a wife, or a female companion, maybe.

The host, Josele, answers firmly but with Zen-like calm. "Yes we do have wi-fi, but we don't switch it on for guests. The whole idea of the Camino is to be more present. If you really need wi-fi, there are coffee shops outside."

The German introduces himself as Karl-Heinz. He looks a bit unsettled to hear that there's no wi-fi. It doesn't bother me in the least; I don't even have a phone.

I try to remember the last thing I googled. It was most probably something about Slagtersnek. The last video I watched on my phone was a short clip leaked from the Kgosi Mampuru II jail showing Oscar Pistorius playing soccer with fellow inmate Radovan Krejčíř.

Josele is a neat middle-aged Frenchman, quiet and friendly. The pilgrims arrive one by one and introduce themselves. Reiner from Germany. Michelle from Ireland. Moss from the Netherlands. Chris and Ann, an elderly couple from Australia. George from Belgium. Bill from Canada, and Jim, an American who looks a bit like the old NP minister Piet Koornhof.

Karl-Heinz has calmed down a bit about the wi-fi. He mentions he's booked into the Orisson, so his first day won't be too bad at all. I feel a bit jealous that I left it too late to make a booking there.

The Beilari albergue is spacious, clean and tidy. Much cleaner than I imagined. I walk up the stairs to leave my bag in my room. There's an aerial photo of the lighthouse at Finisterre on the wall, with only the word *FINISTERRE* on it. End of the Earth. It looks a bit like Cape Point, but more beautiful.

When I arrive at Santiago de Compostela, the plan is to walk the additional 100 kilometres to Finisterre. To the point where you can literally walk no further. I like the symbolism, here at the very beginning of the Camino, of this glimpse of the final destination, about 920 kilometres away.

Next to the poster of Finisterre there is a quote by the Buddha (or rather le Buddha – it's in French: "Ne cherche

pas le chemin du bonheur, car le chemin c'est le bonheur."
My French is about as bad as my Spanish, so I write it
down and ask Josele to translate it. He smiles: "There is no
way to happiness. Happiness is the way."

I no longer need to pin my hopes on a Damascus moment or some or other revelation on the road. I'm glad I
came across le Buddha's words before starting the Camino.

* * *

In 1999, my first girlfriend gave me a small Buddha statue
as a gift. She apparently came across it in the caravan of
some old lady who was a freelance fortune teller. It was
a nice round, fat Buddha (is there any other kind?), with
long earlobes and the smile of someone experiencing en-
lightenment with a capital E in his every cell.

But what made this particular Buddha so distinctive was
the Afrikaans phrase on the statuette: *VIR GEWIGSVER-
LIES* (for weight loss). I was a bit surprised by the Afrikaans: the Buddha was still a bit of a cultural oddity for
the volk, especially in earlier years.

The poor Buddha has been no help at all for weight loss.
On the contrary, since the late nineties I've become something of a weight gainer, and I don't mean like a Bulgarian
Olympic muscleman with bulging veins. (I don't blame this
on the Buddha.)

In that same year, my girlfriend left me after just five
months. I didn't see that one coming. I was only nineteen
after all, young and naïve. My over-emotional response
was really not necessary: I stormed her bookcase like a
tarantula on tik to reclaim my books, ran sobbing to my
Volkswagen Chico, and only realised when I got there that
I'd left my keys on her bed.

It was also not necessary to sit her down on a seaside bench a week later and read long paragraphs from Viktor Frankl's *Man's Search for Meaning* out loud, to the soundtrack of screeching seagulls and the ice-cream cart's tinkling – my desperate attempt at using the insights of a Holocaust survivor to breathe life back into a feeling that had clearly died within her. Oh well. As Kevin Kline's character says in the movie *Life as a House*: "Hindsight. It's like foresight without a future."

When all my attempts had failed and I'd felt sorry enough for myself, my buddy Langes and I started experimenting with weed. "Experimenting" may sound a bit sinister, but it wasn't like that at all. I'd been Mr Exemplary at high school and hadn't so much as touched a cigarette, a beer can or a girl's hand. So the first ten times Langes and I smoked weed together, I didn't even know how to inhale. I puffed, at best, which naturally didn't get me high in the least. I don't know whether Bill Clinton was lying, but *I* can honestly say about my first attempts: "I didn't inhale."

I also acquired a small Zen garden, one that fitted easily into a flowerpot on my desk in my student flat in Summerstrand, Port Elizabeth.

A few months later, when I'd got over the worst of the break-up, I was sitting in the office of the festival newspaper *Krit* at the KKNK, typing a review with one hand, with a brandy and Coke in the other. Next to me actor Lochner de Kock, who had popped in, was speaking in his best Sarel Seemonster voice, much to everyone's delight.

My cell phone rang. It was my mother, who was phoning to tell me she was at my flat "to clean up a bit".

I got such a fright I sobered up instantly. My mother cleans well, for which I was deeply grateful as a lazy, spoiled student. But she's also inclined to scratch around. Forensically. And on top of my bookshelf was an FNB bankie full of weed.

I had hardly registered this when she asked, "Erns, when I dusted your bookshelf I found a little bank bag full of . . . seeds. Is it dagga?"

The lie just rolled off my tongue: "No man, Ma. They're seeds for the Zen garden on my desk."

"Oh, so how's it going at the KKNK?" she wanted to know next.

* * *

The afternoon at Beilari is quiet. I shower and wash my clothes. That's my fate for the next forty days – on the Camino you wash your own clothes. By hand, or you cough up a few euros to use a washing machine.

This is something I'm really looking forward to: the simplicity of washing my own clothes by hand, as often as possible. I never do it at home; my hands usually only work on the laptop.

I while away the rest of the afternoon sitting at the table with Josele and some of the other walkers. There's an eso-teric painting on the wall depicting a shell with a person standing in the middle of it. Two lines coil from the per-son's left leg and head, to create a kind of labyrinth and also to form the shell's inner lines.

It looks like something nice to try and draw. I may have no talent for this, but I do have some time on my hands. While everyone around me is chatting about logistics, or wondering about wi-fi and how bad tomorrow's walk across the Pyrenees will be, I try studiously to copy the painting into my diary. I'm not going to become an artist overnight, but I'm quite satisfied with the result.

* * *

Entry in Moleskine diary

It's just after five, and I'm sitting alone on the back terrace of a small French deli. I spent €6,50 on a workmanlike baguette with salami and an awesome artisanal beer – Bob's beer – a light-coloured beer, deeply workmanlike. A child is laughing in the background, there's French music on the speakers, a sort of Piaf Lite, and you know, life is good, as Liezel van Beek said after the Fish River hike: we live, and that's enough.

* * *

After my break at the French deli, I still have half an hour to stroll around Saint Jean before I have to be back at Beilari for our communal evening meal in the garden. I step into one of the souvenir shops and buy two pens and a new aluminium coffee mug.

The girl behind the counter speaks English and mentions how popular the Camino has become in recent years, even now in May. Just yesterday, 500 walkers started their Camino from Saint Jean alone.

I walk up along the Rue de la Citadelle to the gate of Saint James, through which walkers starting their Camino at three other points must also pass. At the gate, someone's graffiti: "Le voyage est la seule chose que tu payes et qui te rend plus riche." Travel is the only thing you pay for that also makes you richer.

This is deep rural France, pastoral scenes wherever you look. A short distance away a rugby team is training – must be the town team.

It reminds me of the local teams from my youth in the eighties: Old Collegians (OCs or Ousjas), Swifts and Despatch. My father was a teacher in those days and school psychologist at Daniel Pienaar Technical High School in Uitenhage. On weekends he was also a rugby referee, often for club matches.

I attended many of the local derbies at Uitenhage's Central Field, as it was known then. I'd sit among the spectators and watch my father in action. They'd complain about the ref and make all kinds of comments about him, not knowing his son was right among them.

It was only years later that I realised how privileged I had been to watch players like Danie Gerber and Frans "Domkrag" Erasmus playing club rugby.

Fists would often fly during these matches, especially when Despatch and OCs faced off. Inevitable, with hotheads like Adri Geldenhuys and Armand du Preez in a ruck.

But no one could touch Japan le Roux – at one stage captain of Uitenhage's first rugby team. Japan, a firebrand of an eighth man with a fine blond fringe, had a unique trick: he would go down with the scrum, but as soon as the men had locked he would drop to the ground, leopard crawl forward and punch the opposition's hooker in the face. The scrum would obviously collapse, but Japan would have had enough time to leopard crawl out of the scrum backwards. He'd then look up innocently from the back and ask the referee what had happened.

Japan got his comeuppance one evening years later when he knocked a referee unconscious during a match. I wonder where Japan is these days?

* * *

I walk up to the Citadel, a fort built in 1628. There's an information board here listing facts about the town and the origins of the Citadel. I catch myself jotting down *Go*-type notes:

- King of Pamplona, García Ximénez, founds the town in 716
- 12th century – San Juan del Piede Portus
- King of Navarre – King Sancho VII the Strong
- Pyrenees + Protectors – John Baptist
- 4 passes over Pyrenees: e.g. Lepolder (1 440 m)
- Stronghold, frontier town + commercial crossroads
- Wine and cider made here

It's going to be a challenge not to tackle the Camino as a *Go* article. I want to write as little as possible, actually.

To test my problem knee, I climb the 269 steps to the viewing site at the top of the Citadel. Here I can see the whole of the little town with its white buildings and terracotta roofs spread out before me, with the mighty and bloody intimidating Pyrenees on the horizon.

There's a quotation here from Aymeric Picaud, the twelfth-century monk and pilgrim who wrote the *Codex Calixtinus* on his own Camino pilgrimage. This is regarded as the first guidebook for pilgrims. Picaud writes about the Pyrenees: "It's eight thousand miles high and as much down." Look, he's exaggerating a lot, but I'm definitely going to have a hard time climbing up and then down that mountain on my first day. It's a full 25 kilometres from here to Roncesvalles in Spain.

I'm going to have to keep calm and walk myself fit – quickly.

I make a line drawing of the Pyrenees in my notebook,

really to stop myself from making more *Go*-type notes. All along the outline of the mountain I write: *So the plan is to climb this fucken high mountain tomorrow in one wild go because I am not a German who booked a room, for example, at the very cool hostel Orisson back in January. Now I and other walkers like the friendly Canadian Bill, for example, just have to put our heads down and get over the ± 27 km of bloody mountains down to Roncesvalles and get to the other side hopefully with our knees still in one piece and be okay.*

Another walker, a middle-aged woman, also comes to stand at the viewing spot. I really want a photograph of this moment, so I hand out the first of my *Go* business cards. My plan is to take no photos myself, but every now and again to ask a stranger to take one, hand them a business card, and then keep an eye on my inbox when I'm back in Cape Town.

* * *

During supper in the garden we play a kind of getting-to-know-you game – call it a Basque icebreaker. Not the weird icebreakers I remember from the CSA camps at Jeffreys Bay in the nineties, luckily, when we had to pass apples to one another with our chins. For our game, everyone at the table throws an imaginary ball to someone. If you "catch" the ball, you call out the name of your country and then throw the ball to someone else.

After that, everyone has to say why they are doing the Camino. Joe from the USA is almost 70 years old and is walking his third Camino. "I have to come back every year. It's the Camino," he says, his face a picture of peace and calm.

Chris and Ann from Australia do it to spend time in the outdoors and reflect on the past. The large and kindly Canadian Bill says confidently: "I know it sounds strange, but God wants me to be here. He has a plan for me."

Michelle, an Irish woman, has been caring for her mother, who had cancer. Her mother passed away two months ago; she is walking the Camino to process her death. "I will meet myself," is all that the wi-fi-less German Karl-Heinz says with great certainty.

My answer: "I hope to find out along the way why I'm doing it. I'm looking for new answers and new questions. And as a journalist I always travel with my camera and mobile phone. I've decided to leave it all behind and go for a digital detox."

Dinner is vegetarian and healthy: cabbage soup, carrot salad, green salad, brown rice and lentils. For dessert we have yoghurt, almost a kind of sorbet. And we drink red wine.

Josele is an inspiring host and calls us a "planetary family", from all over the world, of people who come together to walk.

He emphasises the importance of silence and a sense of "landing and grounding" that one should experience on the Camino. He points in the direction of the Pyrenees. "Don't be anxious. The mountain is ready for you. It's waiting for you."

Josele tells us about the Basque language – it's even older than Latin and developed entirely independently of other European languages. And he describes the Basque people's constant struggle for self-determination – the border between Spain and France cuts the Basque region in two.

He teaches us the word "ultreia", a word you can take

with you every step of the way on the Camino. It means "onwards, forwards".

Or on with the corpse, I think to myself.

Years ago I heard this little anecdote from a friend's mother. There was apparently an old man in a little village, let's call him Elias, who was exceptionally lazy. Uncle Elias was such a lazy good-for-nothing that the congregation decided it would be better to bury him alive. He was so lazy that he regarded this as a relief.

The day of the funeral arrived and, after the church service, the congregation headed for the cemetery. The pall-bearers solemnly bore Uncle Elias, lying very much alive in the coffin, towards the open grave. But one of the ladies from the congregation could not bear the thought of Uncle Elias being buried so prematurely. "Is there not even one little job that Uncle Elias wants to do around here?" she wanted to know. "Could he not chop a bit of wood, or . . ."

But before she could even finish the sentence Uncle Elias grumbled from the coffin: "On with the corpse! On with the corpse! What's this wood-chopping nonsense?"

* * *

By eight o'clock we're all in our rooms, getting ready for bed. Plastic bags and rucksacks rustle. No one talks; a time of quiet has descended. The sun is still bright outside.

I can sense the excitement, the light tension, in the room – the gnawing uncertainty. My plan is to get a good night's rest. I'm still exhausted after the three days of travelling and the chaos of Slagtersnek and everything I had to sort out in the week before I left.

"Would you mind if we walk up the mountain together?" Bill asks me, tentatively.

I immediately agree. Although I plan to walk mostly alone and can't see myself dealing with others' expectations or pressure, Bill seems like a good companion for the first leg. And, if I walk with someone, hopefully I won't push too hard on the first day.

* * *

No one complains about my snoring, so hopefully I didn't keep anybody awake last night.

We eat a quick, simple breakfast: croissants, biscuits, cheese and jam. Josele reminds us to visit a tree at the bottom of the garden. From it hangs a huge bag of small plastic balls. In each ball there is a slip of paper on which walkers have written what they wish to achieve on the Camino.

After breakfast I go and sit next to the tree in silence for a few minutes, take out a pen and write on one of the slips of paper: "To learn to love myself, be present, know my worth, walk the earth."

* * *

One Friday afternoon in November 2014 I was sitting head in hands in *Go*'s Skukuza conference room at my six-monthly performance appraisal with my editor, Pierre, and assistant editor, Esma.

I had just sketched out my difficult situation stemming from a personal crisis, not very elegantly or coherently. Maybe it was a desperate attempt to justify my inability to meet deadlines.

At that stage I was so messed up I no longer really cared. I had prepared myself for something like an official warning, or for someone in high heels from HR to stride up here to the fourth floor and set some process or other in motion.

I have always been bad with deadlines. My saving grace was that, when I did eventually submit something, it satisfied expectations and often even exceeded them. In fact, a previous editor gave me the nickname "Late but Great". Not something I'm proud of, necessarily, but at least I didn't lose my job.

But instead of taking disciplinary action or delivering a tirade (not that he is known for doing this anyway), Pierre said quite calmly: "Erns, I know now is not the time for platitudes, but this too shall pass."

This too shall pass. It's a common saying, and yes, sometimes even a platitude, but Pierre's words nevertheless resonated somewhere deep within me.

On my way back to my desk after this meeting, a quote from Dana Snyman on the wall caught my eye: "By travelling we not only discover this beautiful, awe-inspiring earth; we also discover our own humanity and that of other people. That is why I shall always be a traveller."

I remembered that as a young child – I was probably seven or eight – I found a book in my father's study called *Light From Many Lamps*.

It was one of those books with inspiring anecdotes from all over the world. The only one I remember very well was a story about a ruler in the Far East who had many worries and concerns. One day he presented his wise advisers with a challenge: come up with a universal phrase that will apply to all times and situations, good and bad. And, make the phrase short enough to be engraved on a ring.

The advisers puzzled over this for a long time and eventually came back to the king with the following words: "This, too, shall pass away."

I googled "This too shall pass" when I was back at my desk. Several photos of people who had these words as tattoos came up. And further down the following:

This too shall pass.
Until then,
Fetch wood,
Carry water,
Walk the Earth.

Fetch wood. Carry water. Walk the Earth. I instantly appreciated the simplicity of this. And as far as "Walk the Earth" was concerned, only one word came to mind: Camino.

FIRST STEPS

"People usually consider walking on water or in thin air a miracle. But I think the real miracle is not to walk either on water or in thin air, but to walk on earth."

– Thich Nhat Hanh

Day One, Wednesday 6 May
From Saint-Jean-Pied-de-Port to Roncesvalles
(25 kilometres)

At seven thirty in the morning, in the Rue de la Citadelle, I take my first official step on the Camino.

A new journey begins.

My red rucksack feels damn heavy and uncomfortable. Joe and Bill are standing praying outside Beilari, then Bill joins me. Tick-tock, tick-tock, tick-tock, our trekking poles on the cobbled street. Other walkers emerge from other hostels with huge rucksacks on their backs.

It's a windless, cloudless day. We are really lucky – last week it rained every day and was windy.

Just outside Saint Jean, the road forks. We can either take the route directly over the Pyrenees, or we can take the Valcarlos route, an alternative that my guidebook recommends in case of bad weather. Bill and I do not hesitate for a moment. Ultreia! We are going to tackle the difficult fair-weather route over the mountain. Anything between six and ten hours of walking lie ahead of us.

But we need to proceed carefully; the Route de Napoléon has claimed many lives, and not only when Napoleon and his troops crossed the mountain here. And as in most high mountains, the weather can change very quickly.

The first of the graffiti, painted on the tarred road, speaks directly to the message I left in the plastic ball in Josele's garden: a large heart with the words "Help yourself" and "Love yourself" and, underneath it, "Ultreia!"

* * *

Careful yet focused, Bill and I take on the Pyrenees. I suspect that neither of us is remotely fit enough for the uphills and exertions that lie ahead. But it helps that we walk at the same pace.

It looks like most of the walkers who left Saint Jean this morning have also decided to walk the Route de Napoléon. I can see why: The weather is perfect. If up to 500 people do indeed start their walk here on some mornings, we're lucky they're not all here now.

I stop every now and again to look back at Saint Jean, which gets ever smaller the higher up along the narrow tarred road we walk. At Go, we steer clear of anything that sounds like a cliché. But this morning, Saint Jean in the distance, with its narrow streets and red roofs and church and fort, looks just like a postcard of a medieval village in the French countryside.

Bill and I don't talk non-stop, but we do chat comfortably. He mentions almost shyly that he is a minister in London, Ontario, a preacher of the gospel. He is 53 years old and serves with a ministry called Promise Keepers Canada, which focuses mainly on men. It sounds like a kind of Mighty Men in Canada, without the potato-farmer pastor, of course. The ministry's motto is "Leave no man behind".

A year ago Bill saw the film *The Way*, a Hollywood box-office hit with Martin Sheen and Emilio Estevez. He tells me a bit about the storyline, which is about a father who comes to walk the Camino when his son dies in a snowstorm in these very mountains. When Bill walked out the cinema, he heard the call of the Camino. And now he's here. In the evenings he wants to write a blog about his experiences and perceptions for the people back home.

There's an entire prayer group there praying for him.

We are walking, now, through some of *The Way*'s opening scenes. Bill is quite surprised that I haven't seen the film. But I deliberately did not want to see too much of the Camino before I got here. The only video I watched was a short preview of the documentary film *Six Ways to Santiago*.

Bill is a pleasant, friendly guy, not a zealot in the least. He tells me how he used to go walking early in the mornings before work, and how hard this was during Canada's freezing winter months.

We also walk comfortably in silence for fifteen minutes at a time. When a faster walker passes us, or we pass other walkers, the greeting is always "Buen Camino!" – "good walk" or "good road", a centuries-old blessing that pilgrims use to acknowledge one another's presence and wish one another well.

My thoughts drift back to South Africa. My parents. We have a close bond and get on well, despite our differences. My father is a full-time teddy bear, a psychologist who prefers on the whole to see the good in others. He can be extraordinarily brave. My mother can be a bit more cynical, but her razor-sharp sense of humour, and ability to observe and describe things in ways that I sometimes envy, tempers this.

They supported my plan to walk the Camino from the very beginning. My mother was a bit concerned when she heard that I planned not to take my cell phone. "But what if I die while you are walking?" she wanted to know. "As sad as that would be, you'd be dead, so you wouldn't have to worry," I replied.

It does take root in my mind from Day One, though: never before have I had no contact with my parents for a full forty days. There have been *Go* stories, such as a 4×4 tour of almost two weeks deep in Kaokoland, where I was cut off from everyone and everything for quite a while, but forty days is a very different matter.

My parents are both 62 and in good health, but you never know. If something should happen to either of them in the next six weeks, there would be no way to get hold of me.

It's Wednesday morning. In Cape Town, most of my colleagues will be sitting in the Absa building's open-plan office. And here I am, walking, tick-tock, tick-tock, with a Canadian in the Pyrenees.

We're climbing ever higher up the mountain – still on a narrow tarred road, but the walkers are beginning to spread out. A woman who looks to be in her seventies walks determinedly past us. "Buen Camino, how many have you done?" she asks. I gesture that this is my first. "Ah, then you're a chicken!" she says and walks away, cackling to herself. Bill and I just look at each other, smile and push on.

The rucksack is feeling even heavier. My slip-slops and fleece and towel hang out of it, swinging around. I'm sweating like an ox. The morning sun beats down on us and sharp pains shoot through my right knee . . . on with the corpse!

Eight kilometres later we walk past Orisson. It's festive, with people sitting on the deck drinking coffee and eating croissants and baguettes. The albergue itself looks like an old barn. I'm glad now that it was fully booked and that we're pressing on to reach Roncesvalles in one day. My body is protesting, but I want nothing but to carry on walking. There's not much else to do, anyway.

In his book *What I Talk About When I Talk About*

Running, the Japanese novelist Haruki Murakami writes about his two great loves: writing and running marathons. He talks about the mantras that he and other marathon runners sometimes chant out loud to themselves while they are running, in those moments when the body and the spirit no longer want to cooperate. He talks about the marathon runner who always said to himself: "Pain is inevitable, suffering is optional."

Time for our first real break. We sit in the grass next to the road and take off our shoes and socks to air our feet a bit. Bill says he plans to do this every few hours, and also to rub Vaseline on his feet before he starts walking again. This sounds like good advice to me. If there's a thing I want to avoid at all costs, it's blisters; my Salomon trail-running shoes are still brand new.

I almost took on the Camino in my Hi-Tec hiking boots that I bought a year ago for the Fish River Canyon. A few weeks before the Camino, luckily, I attended a valuable information session arranged by the South African Confraternity of Saint James in Milnerton. During this session, the aunties recommended staying away from hiking boots. A few gruesome PowerPoint photos of bloodied ankles and blisters quickly convinced me.

I lie back in the grass using my rucksack as a pillow. The green mountains roll into the distance as far as the horizon, the highest peaks still covered in snow. I grew up with no snow whatsoever, the NG Kerk services in the eighties being the closest I ever got to a white Christmas.

This is pure bliss, exactly what I had hoped for on the Camino: to lie dog-tired but carefree in the grass, fully in the moment, nothing urgent hassling me. In the background I hear the varied rhythms of other walkers' footfalls. A cheerful "Buen Camino!" rises, then there's silence, or a passing conversation in one of a profusion of languages. A young couple bustles past, hand in hand. There are many ways to walk the Camino – but what do you do if you start arguing with your partner somewhere along the 800-kilometre way?

Hardly a hundred metres away from us three griffon vultures rise up into the sky. This reminds me of standing on the edge of the Drakensberg escarpment after a helicopter flight, once, watching a bearded vulture gliding on the thermals.

In "Nijmegen deur my trane", Gert Vlok Nel sings about a bearded vulture sweeping across the skies: "Dalk daar bo in die lug waar die lammergeier sweef, dalk daar . . ." And about the buck that live in constant fear as a result.

Bill and I walk on. We hear the clanging of the cowbells even before we see the cows. A few ponies graze the green slopes lazily. I'm not sure how these things work, but the road is not nearly as busy now as it was earlier this morning. Probably because people all walk at a different pace. It's difficult to know whether we are ahead of or behind most of the walkers.

Ultreia! Spain is only a few kilometres away.

We eat a late-ish lunch at a lookout point with a statue of the Virgin Mary. For four euros, we bought a large baguette and an omelette each from Josele to eat along the way. Bill asks me to take a photo of him.

The weather is turning. Mist rolls in and it's much cooler than it was this morning. When we get up, I put my fleece on.

We continue along the narrow tarred road, inching ever higher into the Pyrenees. We're together, but don't talk much. I prefer it this way, a kind of silent meditation on the move. Or rather, that's what I *try* to do.

Meditation is actually very simple, which is what makes it so difficult, of course. My friend J.P. from Grahamstown always said meditation is about two things: It must be something almost menial, and you must be able to repeat it. Like sitting still and focusing on your breathing. Or sitting and staring at a campfire for a long time. Or walking, step by step, and remaining aware of what is happening in your immediate environment: first your breathing, then each step you take, twigs snapping beneath your feet, perhaps, bird sounds.

But this is much easier said than done. Even here in the Pyrenees. My thoughts constantly want the upper hand, swirling and eddying and racing off like wildfires.

A few weeks before I left, I read an essay on walking by Henry David Thoreau on Brainpickings.org. He firmly believed that a daily stroll was essential, and regularly went walking for up to four hours in the afternoon.

He writes about how difficult this is. "I cannot easily shake off the village. The thought of some work will run in my head and I am not where my body is; I am out of my senses. In my walks I would fain return to my senses. What business have I in the woods, if I am thinking of something out of the woods?"

Another mantra: "What business have I in the woods, if I am thinking of something out of the woods?" How often aren't we actively busy with something, but our thoughts and attention are elsewhere, or trying in vain to focus on more than one thing?

Two taxis pass us from the direction of Spain, both full of people in hiking clothes and with rucksacks. They could be injured walkers heading back to Saint Jean, but more likely they are just people driving from Spain to Saint Jean to start the Camino Francés.

I can hardly believe my eyes when I see a little food stall under a gazebo. It must have taken the two entrepreneurs a great deal of effort to set up here, so high up the mountain. I hope it's profitable. I buy coffee for me and Bill at €1,50. "This your last French stop," the guy behind the counter says with a smile. He says we still have eight kilometres or so to walk before we get to Roncesvalles, of which the last five are a steep downhill.

Just past the stall we leave the tarred road and follow a route marker with a yellow arrow to a footpath. The route gets even steeper. We just have to press on to Roncesvalles. The only shelter here, high in the mountain, is a small, primitive shepherd's hut built of stone. There's a little pile of ash in it; somebody must have made a fire recently.

I see snow right next to the path. It must have snowed here a day or so ago! Bill finds my excitement pretty amusing: where he comes from, snow is as common as sunshine in South Africa. For the first time in my life I touch snow. It feels like I have pressed my hand into a giant Slush Puppy.

We walk past a cement route marker that reads *Saint-Jacques de Compostelle 765 km*. Shouldn't that be 790 kilometres? I read somewhere that the kilometre figures on the route markers can sometimes be misleading. But who am I going to split hairs with about exact distances, so close to the Spanish border, anyway? The bottom line is this: I still have a hell of a long way to walk.

I try to put it into perspective: I'd cover about 765 kilometres in my Suzuki Jimny each year, during the December holidays, between my flat in Green Point and my parents' home in Uitenhage. That trip takes about eight hours, depending on how long I get stuck at the Wimpy in Riversdale. I have more or less the same distance ahead of me now, and I want to cover it on foot in just over a month with a heavy rucksack and aches and pains everywhere. Crazy.

At the Fontaine de Roland we can fill up our water bottles and catch our breath.

Bill and I are finished, and we still have at least two hours of walking ahead of us. I start seeing myself stumbling into Roncesvalles like the 80-year-old Wally Hayward at the end of his last Comrades. The images of this old legend vomiting blood after the murderous ultramarathon were pretty much the most disturbing thing I have ever seen on TV. The worst was the misunderstanding between Allan Donald and Lance Klusener at Edgbaston in 1999 . . .

No one will ever know exactly when Hansie Cronjé started his match-fixing, but I always thought that something in him finally broke that day at Edgbaston. Four years later, with Hansie already dead, I watched the Proteas' World Cup venture in Durban come to an end in the rain, apparently because they got the Duckworth-Lewis calculation wrong.

The cameramen, probably just sick of showing the shattered Proteas, focused on a large frog sitting in the rain next to the boundary rope. Seconds later my phone rang. It was my mother: "Erns! Did you see the frog? It's Hansie!"

How my thoughts are roving. I could probably tell Bill the frog story, but I doubt the kindly Canadian would see the point; by the same token, I wouldn't understand the context of some ice-hockey goalkeeper's scandal.

We cross unannounced into Spain. No border post, customs office or Welcome to Spain sign. Just a cement route marker with the word *Navarra*, the name of the province in which I now find myself.

At 1 450 metres, Col de Lepoeder is the highest point of today's route. We've climbed one and a half Table Mountains today, and now face a steep 500-metre downhill. According to my guidebook, we should have a great view from Col de Lepoeder and should even be able to see the roof of the Roncesvalles monastery way down below us, but the mist is too thick.

There is a slightly longer but less steep route to Roncesvalles from here, but we stick to the shortest route through the beechwood forest. I'm not amused: dog-tired, dripping with sweat, and feeling all sorts of aches in my feet, ankles, calves, hips and back – pains that keep me so busy that I almost forget about my right knee, which is sore enough as it is.

What I do realise fully is that I must not rush through these woods. I need to keep a clear head – any further damage and I might as well quit my Camino before Pamplona. So I take things extremely slowly and carefully, one step at a time. Bill quickly gets 50 and later even 100 metres ahead of me. He has quite an unorthodox technique for this downhill: He tries walking backwards, almost falling a couple of times. I'm not even going to attempt it. It looks as if most of the other pilgrims decided (wisely, probably) to take the less challenging roundabout route.

Walking gently and cautiously with my trekking poles, and becoming increasingly aware that my other knee is also starting to give trouble, I hear a sudden "HOLA!" and the hum of bicycle wheels. Three cyclists almost knock me over. I didn't see them coming at all. I'm angry at first, but then I welcome the adrenalin.

A girl with long curly hair and a red rucksack walks past me, carrying a large Nikon camera. I mumble a tired, half-hearted "Buen Camino". She turns around. Wow – she is gorgeous, with high cheekbones and big blue eyes.

"Cómo?" she asks. Ah, she speaks Spanish. My fine intentions to learn Spanish before the Camino came to nothing.

This is how I meet Rubí, from the city of Aguascalientes (which means "warm waters") in Mexico. This is Rubí's second Camino. She walked over 300 kilometres from León (in Spain, not France) to Santiago in 2013. Now she's back, but only for three weeks. She is walking the Camino Francés up to Pamplona, then travelling north to San Sebastian to take on a section of the more remote Camino Norte (the Northern Way) along the coast. She is 28 and already owns a travel agency, which she recently took over from her mother. Before the Camino, she was with a tour group in Turkey.

We walk the last few kilometres to Roncesvalles together, with Bill still some 100 metres ahead of us. She stops regularly to take photos of the forest. I give her one of my business cards and step off the path for a photo. I hope she emails it to me later, so I'll have a record, at least, of my first day on the Camino. But I don't look where I'm going and my Salomons sink into almost ankle-deep mud.

Rubí giggles at my dirty shoes. She has braces on her teeth (at school we used to call them train tracks), but even they look sexy.

Relax, Erns. Keep it together. I didn't come all the way here to fall in love with the first girl I've said more than "Buen Camino" to. Before even reaching my first albergue in Spain . . .

"We're here!" Bill calls out in front of us. At last I see the spire of the Real Colegiata de Santa María – a Gothic cathedral dating from the thirteenth century – sticking out above the treetops.

Bill says it's already past five. We've walked for more than nine hours today, but it's not time to rest yet. First I must make sure I have a bed at the albergue.

Roncesvalles dates back to 1127, when a hospital-hostel for pilgrims was set up here. It still looks medieval. The albergue has hundreds of beds, thank goodness. But even though it's still early May and not peak season (June to August), many people, especially Spaniards, start their Camino here. So, accommodation is not always guaranteed. I certainly don't want to spend the night in an expensive guesthouse or hotel that would set me back 40 euros or more.

If you are smart about your spending, 30 euros a day is more than enough for food and accommodation, plus a beer.

Fortunately, Bill, Rubí and I are in time to get a bed in the albergue for eight euros each. Mine is on the ground floor in a room with twelve other basic bunk beds. It's a stuffy room, with clothes, rucksacks and trekking poles scattered all over the place. Rubí also sets her bag down on a bed in this room, but I don't know where Bill settles down for the night.

Three young Italian women stand chatting in the room. It's an intense discussion – in English for some reason, although one of them sometimes switches to Italian – about what time they should get up tomorrow morning, how far they should walk . . . One of them feels that they should get going as early as six, another wants to walk beyond Zubiri to the next town, Larrasoaña.

I unfold my sleeping sheet and listen to their chattering. It seems they're under pressure to be in Burgos by a certain day and return from there to Italy. Of course, it is very easy and relatively cheap for Europeans to travel to Spain and walk sections of the Camino. Not everyone has the "luxury" of taking six weeks' leave to walk the whole Camino in one go.

But I am so relieved that, unlike the three Italians, I am here alone. I can decide what time I want to get up (although one usually has to be out of an albergue by eight), how far I'm going to walk on any given day, and which town I'm going to overnight in.

I've booked no accommodation for the next forty nights, except for the last night in Santiago at the Hospedería San Martín Pinario, because I need to get a taxi to the airport the following morning for my flight to Paris.

Top priority: a shower. Outside our dormitory there are showers in huge containers that look a bit like temporary classrooms, but they are all jam packed at the moment. A middle-aged man beckons me to come closer. At first I'm a bit suspicious, but he explains that I should try two floors up, as there are modern showers there, and not many people. A spot of ubuntu on the Camino. I take the Samaritan's advice and find a neat, upgraded bathroom where I can shower in peace. I may have climbed up and down a mountain today, but I'm still chunky.

My "evening wear" for the next forty days: grey shorts, my *Ons Klyntji* T-shirt, black slip-slops and a blue fleece top. I really don't feel like doing my washing by hand this evening. It won't dry by tomorrow morning, anyway. There is a laundry service here. I happily pay the four euros to have my long-sleeve shirt, trousers, socks and ski pants washed and dried. I rinse my hat and hang it on a large drying rack outside, along with hordes of other people's clothes.

The girl with the dog I saw on the bus yesterday comes stumbling out of the woods. She and her dog look as if they've had a wild Wednesday in the Pyrenees.

I have supper at the La Posada restaurant near the cathedral. I wanted to sit with Rubí or keep a place for her, but I am shown to a table where two middle-aged Frenchwomen are already seated. They are so utterly French that I do not even catch their names. We look at each other uncomfortably, but I reckon all three of us are too tired to talk anyway, even if we could understand one another.

Bill sits down next to me – he happened to be next in the restaurant queue. He tries bravely to strike up a conversation with the two Frenchwomen, but quickly gives up. The atmosphere around the table is the opposite of the previous evening's. Bill also looks like he misses the congenial table at Josele's albergue.

We order from the pilgrim menu. For nine euros we get a bottle of wine between the four of us, spaghetti bolognaise as starter, a whole fish (I have no idea what kind of fish), and a small unflavoured yoghurt for dessert. One of the Frenchwomen does not want wine, so I help myself to a second glass.

Bill says he wants to get going early tomorrow morning, just after six. "I need to go at it alone tomorrow," he says. We greet warmly; Bill was a good companion on the first day of my Camino.

I have no idea whether I will see Bill again. But isn't this true of every goodbye? Like me, he plans to arrive in Santiago in about thirty-five days. Who knows, maybe our paths will cross again.

The restaurant is full now, and some of the other tables are much more festive than ours. At a table in the corner Rubí and the three Italians and a few other young people are clearly having a good time. The extrovert in me gets the upper hand and I go to sit down with them, taking my half-glass of wine. One of the Italians introduces herself as Nora, an anaesthetist from Milan.

I have mixed feelings. My whole body hurts like crazy

and I'm nearly falling asleep from exhaustion, but this is such an interesting situation, just to sit back and hear the Italian, Spanish and English rolling off the tongues of those around the table.

A very loud and boisterous elderly American woman comes marching into the restaurant, still in her hiking clothes and boots. She immediately strikes me as a character.

"Oh my Gawd . . . I think I'm going to die. I'm sleeping in the igloo tonight!"

The whole table starts clapping and Rubí jumps up to give her a hug. The "igloo" refers to the containers outside the albergue, the very last available accommodation option for pilgrims.

I remember walking past this woman earlier. There was a young woman with her, in my blind spot. It must have been Rubí.

Angie is 70 years old and is from New York. Day One nearly broke her. Rubí tries to comfort her and says she wants to start walking with her tomorrow. I also want to walk with Rubí. This idea irritates me slightly; I must guard against being a bloody pilot fish on the Camino, swimming in the wake of other fish. I need to do my own thing – or rather, *learn* to do my own thing. And I suspect I can only start learning this on my own.

Nora says she is keen to attend mass in the cathedral. But the clock strikes nine and we realise it's already over. On the Camino, mass in the village churches usually starts at eight in the evening.

We stroll to the cathedral anyway. I test the limits of small talk with the very charming anaesthetist and tell her that her counterparts have been concerned about me on the operating table in the past.

Nora finds this amusing and stops in her tracks. "Let me have a look. Say ah . . ." She gives the universal consulting room instruction. But we're not in a consulting room; we're standing next to a cathedral in Spain.

Still, the doctor has spoken, and so I "Ah . . .".

"I can see why you gave the anaesthetists grey hairs," she says and smiles.

The cathedral looks quite ordinary from the outside, but inside it's overwhelming. Gigantic lead-glass windows, pillars and a large statue of Mary at the altar.

There are eight other people sitting on the church pews. I sit on my own a little way from Nora. You don't have to be a Catholic or even a Christian to appreciate the silence in this centuries-old cathedral after a long day's walk. There is something to be said for the mystical after all. I focus on my breathing. In . . . and out . . . in . . . and out . . . Scenes from the day flash through my mind: Saint Jean, the mountain, the snow, Bill, Rubí . . . but I always return purposefully to my breathing.

Back at our sleeping quarters Nora and her two Italian walking companions are once again in council. Their plan is to set off at seven. "No breaks, no breaks," one of them says strictly.

No thanks. My plan is to make the next forty days one long, extended break.

* * *

A self-conscious moment in the container bathroom at Roncesvalles

It's a few minutes before ten, when the hospitaleros lock the main door. If I don't get a move on there'll be drama, or I'll have to sleep outside in the cold. I wait until everyone is out of the container bathroom: I want to use my sleep apnoea plasters tonight. These poor people are all exhausted and I don't want to be the reason why none of them gets any sleep. I have had three glasses of red wine, which usually turns up the volume. I must choose between two embarrassments: being the guy who snores, or being the guy who sleeps with two ludicrous plasters on his face. I choose the latter.

A quiet, lonely moment in front of the mirror. I open the Ziploc bag on which Sophia wrote *SNORE ZZZZZ* with a koki pen, carefully open the Provent packet and stick two plasters across my nose. It's a strange business: you can inhale freely through your nose, but there is tremendous resistance when you breathe out. This makes you exhale mainly through your mouth.

I left my head torch in my rucksack, so I stumble from the bathroom in the dark, negotiating bags and sleeping pilgrims, back to my bed. Almost everybody is already asleep, with only a faint glow from a cell phone here and there. At least I feel less self-conscious about the plasters. I climb into my sleeping sheet and use my little inflatable cushion, wrapped in my fleece for additional padding.

And then I hear it: one after the other, from every corner of the albergue, the loud snoring of walkers who could also do with some plasters. A cacophony of snoring and gasping.

Day Two, Thursday 7 May
From Roncesvalles to Viscarret
(20 kilometres)

"Wake up, little Susie, wake up! Wake up, little Susie, wake up!"

I wake up completely disorientated. Where on earth am I and what are all these beds and people around me and why is somebody playing the guitar? Relax, I tell myself. You're at the albergue in Roncesvalles. It's your first morning in Spain.

I don't know if it was yesterday's 25-kilometre trek over the Pyrenees, or the intervention of the Provent plaster, but I was in a deep sleep. A Rip van Winkle-type deep sleep.

The hospitaleros at the albergue – they all wear red T-shirts for some reason – are strolling through all the rooms playing the guitar and singing to the walkers. It must still be very early.

Rubí is sitting cross-legged on the bed and smiling in a symphony of dimples and braces. She claps in time with the music and sings along. I realise it again: I'm slightly in love with this blue-eyed Mexican.

But I must tread carefully. I need to respect my own pilgrimage as well as that of the other walkers. This will just complicate things. But it's also not easy to control or suppress emotions like these. Maybe this is one of my first lessons of the odyssey to Santiago.

The hospitaleros sing "Morning Has Broken" before moving on. What a great way to wake up! I wouldn't mind dragging my tired body out of bed like this every morning.

* * *

During his 2008 world tour Leonard Cohen performed with the beautiful Webb Sisters, Hattie and Charley Webb. While singing "Tower of Song" he turned to them between verses and said: "Don't stop. Please don't stop. Sing me to sleep, and sing me through the bitter morning."

* * *

There's nothing bitter about this morning, but my calves, hamstrings and hips hurt like hell. As do my back, shoulders and neck. Is this how a retired Springbok rugby player in his forties crawls out of bed every morning?

It's all systems go for the three Italians, who are packed and ready. It's all just zipping up bags and a few final instructions in passionate Italian.

I'm a lot less bothered. I have lots of time and nothing to prove to anyone. No one waiting for me, and no one to wait for. No waiting, no expectations.

I have always assumed that Koos du Plessis's "Skielik is jy vry" ("Suddenly you are free") alludes to death, but perhaps during the Camino I'll experience something of the peace he writes about:

Dis tog so eenvoudig:	It's so very simple:
dis jy, alleenlik jy;	It's you and you alone;
en die groter sorge	and the bigger troubles
gaan vanself verby.	disperse on their own.
Niks om te verhaal nie,	None to tell or tally,
net die vrede bly.	peace alone remains.
Niks om te betaal nie –	No payments to be made –
en skielik is jy vry.	and suddenly you're free.

* * *

Runners and hikers – especially overweight ones – will know: chafing between your legs is one of the evils of Creation. It's an evil I'm very familiar with.

I'm trying to prevent it at all costs on the Camino.

This is why one of my morning rituals right from the start is to apply Proglyde Anti-Chafe Cream generously before I head off for the day.

The worst chafing I've ever experienced was during the Fish River Canyon hike in June 2014. I waddled wide-legged up to the 50-kilometre mark, my seven hiking buddies as my audience. Like John Wayne on the set of a Western.

* * *

I brush my teeth, fetch my basket of clean laundry, get dressed, pack my bag and walk wearily up the stairs to reception. There I find a coffee machine in a room full of walkers staring at their phones and tablets.

Welcome to the "Wi-fi Room".

I look around to see if Karl-Heinz from Beilari is there, but then remember he spent the night at Orisson and will only get here tonight. He will be quite taken with this room.

It has been two days since I mailed my phone to Paris. Yesterday I kept patting my pocket to check something on my (non-existent) phone, but today I don't miss it at all.

It's a bit absurd, really, all these walkers so focused on their phone and tablet screens, paging through Facebook news feeds, frantically updating blogs . . . I empathise with people with loved ones at home who may be concerned about them, or with whom they want to share this experience. But it looks so unnatural: all these people in hiking gear, in a centuries-old site, drinking deeply of the wi-fi.

Rubí walks out of the wi-fi room. I'm keen to walk some of the way with her and chat a bit more.

The hospitaleros with the guitars are now standing in the lobby and launch into the well-known Mexican song, "Cielito Lindo":

Ay, ay, ay, ay,
Canta y no llores,
Porque cantando se alegran,
cielito lindo, los corazones.

I ask Rubí what the lyrics mean. "It means sing, don't cry," she explains. "Because when singing you are happy in your heart, then you don't cry."

* * *

I wait for Rubí outside the albergue while she tries to find the 70-year-old Angie.

An elderly man walks past and sings softly in a British accent, barely audible: "The future's not ours to see, what will be, will be."

For a moment I wonder if he's not a well-disguised John Cleese. Even if he was, I wouldn't have wanted to stop him, despite being such a Monty Python fan. Besides, I don't have a phone to take a selfie.

"What will be, will be."

I remember singing this in the eighties in singing class at Laerskool Handhaaf in Uitenhage. I sat cross-legged in the front row on a wooden floor. I wore a green safari suit. The teacher sat behind the piano. First we sang from the red *Jeugsangbundel*. Song Number 37 – about speaking in angels' tongues – then "Dis 'n land", about a country "that will never pawn its most precious possessions, the many peoples who are its lifeblood" ("Daar's 'n land wat nooit verpand sy kosbaarste besittings / vele mense volke wat sy lewensaar sal bly"). While a military Casspir patrolled outside our school and people were dying in the townships.

And at the end of every lesson we sang "Whatever Will Be, Will Be". "Que sera, sera, whatever will be, will be . . ."

As with the song about "our country", we had no clue what we were singing about. This morning, almost three decades later, I still wonder about the words "what will be, will be".

I struggle with that kind of acceptance, frequently pushing back against the reality of the way things are.

* * *

We're a bit of a motley crew, Rubí and Angie and me. We were among the last to leave Roncesvalles this morning and amble along the tree-lined road next to the N135 highway. We really are ambling; Rubí is in front, I'm dawdling along in the middle and Angie is bringing up the rear.

A road sign tells us: *Santiago de Compostela 790.* That's the distance by road if you take the highways.

I've chosen to take it easy after yesterday's Pyrenees expedition. I've read that many pilgrims overdo it in the first few days and have to throw in the towel at Pamplona, or rest for days to recover from tendinitis and other injuries.

Again, I experience walking as meditation. It's simple, really: (1) Breathe. (2) One foot in front of the other. (3) Repeat (1) and (2).

At Burguete, a village three kilometres outside Roncesvalles, we stop at the Café Frontón. I get a chance to try the very basic Spanish I have managed more or less to master.

"Hola señorita." ("Hallo madam.") "Uno café con leche por favor." ("One coffee with milk, please.") "Gracias." ("Thank you.")

I eat a chocolate croissant with my coffee. Rubí buys a long baguette that she ties to her rucksack. I buy packets of salami and cheese for a euro each. No need to haemorrhage euros on the Camino.

Very much like little platteland towns in South Africa, Burguete is dominated by a view of the church, in this case the Iglesia de San Nicolás de Bari, a saint who took pity on medieval pilgrims. I read in Brierley's book on the Camino, however, that not everyone was protected here: in the sixteenth century, five women were burned on the square in front of the church for alleged witchcraft.

The village is quiet and deserted. Large white houses with red roofs are packed close to one another on both sides of the road.

My guidebook also tells me that Ernest Hemingway stayed here in the 1920s and wrote about Burguete in his novel *The Sun Also Rises*. He apparently also signed the piano in the Hotel Burguete and scratched the date 25/07/1923 on it. I have read only *The Old Man and the Sea* and am in no way a Hemingway groupie, but I'm curious and would like to see the piano.

I knock at the door of the Hotel Burguete. A woman opens, looking troubled from the outset. She doesn't understand a word of English, or pretends not to.

I say "Hemingway" a few times and wave my fingers pianistically in the air, but she just shakes her head. If I were writing a *Go* story I would have persisted, but I leave her in peace and walk on. I'm not here to write articles.

* * *

People tend to think that my work at *Go* is one long, lazy, extended holiday. I clearly thought this would be the case too before I started working at the magazine. As a teenager I would page through *Getaway* (long before *Go* arrived on the scene) and read the articles by Don Pinnock and Justin Fox. It looked like fun.

I am very passionate about my work. Seven years in, it is still a privilege for me to take to the road and find stories for our readers. But everything in life comes with a price. It's no glamorous, five-star life. You're buggered after weeks on the road. And relationships get very challenging.

As my mother always hears in the Spar: "I see that boy of yours is on holiday again, and getting paid for it."

* * *

I lie on my back in a field of small white and yellow flowers next to a farm road. Rubí takes photos and puts a little white flower behind her ear. I roll around, pull faces and lie with open arms, staring at the blue sky.

It's exactly what I had hoped for: to stroll around carefree in rural Spain, and sit or lie wherever and whenever I felt like it. To live in the moment for a while again, to play and laugh and enjoy the simplicity of it all. The stress of preparing for the Camino and the manic packing session, the struggle with Slagtersnek and the long journey to Saint Jean now feel very far away.

One of my favourite books is Dr Seuss's *Oh, the Places You'll Go!* It's not just a children's book – I often buy it as a birthday gift for my adult friends.

In the book the character sets out on a journey, effectively the journey of life:

It's opener there
in the wide open air.
Out there things can happen
and frequently do
to people as brainy
and footsy as you.
And when things start to happen,
don't worry. Don't stew.
Just go right along.
You'll start happening too.

* * *

The main street in Espinal looks like an abandoned film set. It's too early for a siesta, but this little town looks fast asleep. Or like nobody lives here permanently. All the doors and windows are tightly shut, except for one café, where I down my first Spanish cerveza (beer).

Rubí is self-conscious about her braces, which are only coming off in six months. "I guess it sounds vain, but in Spanish we say 'Le belle cuesta'. It means beauty comes with a price," she jokes.

What precious little knowledge I have about Mexico is strewn with stereotypes. I know Speedy Gonzales, I know it's the holy ground of tequila, Maradona scored his "Hand of God" goal in the 1986 Soccer World Cup, and there were some truly terrifying villains from Mexico in the HBO series *Breaking Bad*.

Rubí wants to recite a Spanish poem about walking, but can remember only the first line: "Caminante, no hay Camino."

I instinctively reach for my phone in my pocket. I would usually do a quick Google search for something like this.

After all, Google has become the Encyclopaedia of Life. But then I remember that my phone is somewhere in a five-kilogram box, hopefully on its way to Paris. I was so judgemental about the people in the wi-fi room this morning. Now I miss my iPhone.

* * *

"And sometimes you will go on the most valuable journey of all, the one between one person and another, intimate and quiet and seldom lasting, but always precious." These words of André P. Brink, who passed away a few months ago, keep running through my mind as we walk through a beautiful forest.

My Standard 1 teacher was really intense. She was like Heidi's Fräulein Rottenmeier, only stricter. We had to do exactly what she told us to do. Once we had to write an essay about custard. The teacher wrote the first sentence of the essay on the board: "Creamy, dreamy, thick yellow custard." This was her first sentence, so it had to be everyone's first sentence.

Something in me rebelled. My essay rejected her first sentence and opted for a more biographical approach. I wrote about the time I accidentally knocked a pot of custard off the stove and my mother chased me around the house with a wooden spoon.

The teacher was not impressed at all. She crumpled it up in front of the class and said: "Don't you bring your André P. Brink manners to my class."

I was upset. It put me off writing for a long time, especially essays. But later I realised she had actually paid me an unintended compliment.

* * *

In his short story "Soos eers" ("As before"), P.G. du Plessis writes about the phenomenon of the "bieg-gesig" – "confession face". I like this word of his a lot. It has nothing to do with your physical appearance. If you have a "confession face", though, you'll know all about it: people will keep coming to you with all kinds of stories and secrets.

I suspect I have a bit of a confession face. Maybe I just like listening to people's stories, and don't keep interrupting them.

It's not long before Rubí starts to "confess" a bit. She describes a relationship of seven years that ended last November. She really wanted to marry this guy, but he wasn't sure. When the relationship ended, though, he was desperate to get her back.

They now communicate regularly, even during her Camino. She's really confused. "It's a little bit complicated," she says, on more than one occasion. But she hopes to find the answers during the Camino.

I am inclined to want to intervene: jump in immediately, be the "good guy" and try to "rescue" her from this predicament. And although this kind of thing never ends well, I find it difficult to unlearn. Another of my lessons on the Camino: not to relapse into old ways of thinking and doing. And to be more conscious, to stand back a bit and not try to impress or change anyone.

What will be, will be.

* * *

I find it interesting that Rubí's disappointment in love occurred in November 2014. Mine happened at the same time. So I decide to tell her my story, too.

I had been in a serious relationship with a girl in Onrus for thirteen months. Her background seemed very exotic to me: born in Suriname, her parents were French and Dutch, and she grew up in places like Togo, the island of São Tomé, and Botswana. Her ancestors were gypsies and the gypsy blood flowed strongly in her.

We met one Sunday evening in Vermont when my friend Toast's band, The Buckfever Underground, played a house concert there. I hadn't even planned to go, but was in the area and wanted to deliver a belated birthday present, Homer's *Odyssey*, personally before Toast left with the band on a countrywide tour.

A different, unforeseen, odyssey began that night.

She had a three-year-old daughter from a previous relationship. The daughter's biological father was an absent parent and I very quickly began to take on that role. It was an all-or-nothing arrangement. I loved her as if she were my own child. I was soon talking about my "instant family" and we started planning a future together.

But then one Friday afternoon in November 2014, my phone rang. I was packing a bag for the weekend at Onrus. My girlfriend ended the relationship over the phone. I have my blind spots, and didn't expect this at all. I never saw her or the little girl ever again.

Veronica Shoffstall writes in a poem that "futures have a way of falling down in mid-flight", an appropriate metaphor for the shock I felt after that phone call.

I confess all this to my new Mexican friend while we follow the yellow arrows in the general direction of Zubiri.

Disappointments in love happen. But I'm heartbroken and disillusioned.

It's all just part of the universal story. Cheryl Strayed from *Wild* says there are really only three narratives that have been repeated since the beginning of all things:

"It's about sorrow, it's about redemption, it's about journey."

* * *

I worry about Angie. I'm scared she's going to have a heart attack or collapse from exhaustion. She moves slowly, like a chameleon, falls far behind, and then Rubí and I have to wait a long time for her to catch up.

"You two go ahead!" she calls out. "I don't want to hold you back!"

Sometimes she just stops and leans forward over her trekking poles. The mountain path up Alto de Erro is a narrow, stony footpath, up and down, up and down. We are far from villages or the main road; phoning a taxi, and getting to one, would be an expensive and time-consuming business.

Angie complains of blisters. She is also starting to get shin splints. It's a dismal picture: a New York pensioner dripping with sweat and on her last legs in a forest in Spain. Her water is also finished. I give her some of mine. I'm not feeling too fresh myself; it's stiflingly hot and we still have at least eight kilometres to Zubiri.

The sun is still high, but I doubt we are going to be in time for a bed at one of the albergues. According to my guidebook, there are only 112 beds in Zubiri. The next refuge for the night is six kilometres further at Larrasoaña, and I know for a fact that none of us is going to make it all the way there today.

I can think of only one solution. "Rubí, I know we're both tired, but we've got to help Angie and carry her backpack."

Rubí does not hesitate for a second. "Yayaya, let's do it. At least it's not the Pyrenees."

Angie resists at first, as she can see that we are also exhausted. But I insist. Rubí and I each grab a strap of Angie's big, heavy, light-blue rucksack. It swings between us as we struggle up the hills. Angie is about 100 metres behind us. As we get to the top of a hill, we stop for a break. Over and over again we decide to press on just as Angie is about to catch up with us. Ultreia!

We see no one else, and I begin to wonder whether we are the last three walkers between Roncesvalles and Zubiri.

Rubí plays music on her cell phone. First we listen to a reggae/ska band, Bedouin Soundclash, which I don't know at all. I usually can't stand it when people go walking in nature – like up Table Mountain – with music blaring from their cell phones. But here, battling with Angie's rucksack, which is a bit ridiculous anyway, I'm not going to protest about a soundtrack. Another surprise along the way.

So this is how we tackle the last few hills: me and Rubí staggering with the huge rucksack between us, and Angie weak and wobbly just behind us. And Tom Odell's pulsing "Another Love": "And I wanna kiss you, make you feel alright / I'm just so tired to share my nights / I wanna cry and I wanna love / But all my tears have been used up / On another love, another love."

* * *

We're on tarred road again. Zubiri is still four kilometres away. Here, in the middle of nowhere, there's a food truck: Bar Alto Erro, with red tables and chairs.

We buy coffee and fruit and plonk ourselves down. The owner, Fernan, is very chatty, but only in Spanish. Fortunately Rubí and Angie understand everything. I wish I had gone to more trouble with that Spanish course I bought last Christmas.

There's a crate full of underwear in front of Fernan's truck. A notice reads: *Leave what you don't need. Take what you need.* And another: *Looking for husband? Leave your underwear here. Looking for wife? Magic happens!!!*

Fernan apparently originally set the crate down there to get underwear to donate to charity. But then a young woman who had donated something met her future husband further along the Camino, and this inspired Fernan to adapt the notice.

I packed only three pairs of underpants, but scratch around in my bag and throw one into the crate. You never know. Rubí does the same.

There are some pamphlets on the red table. One has a poem in Spanish by Antonio Machado, with an English translation next to it. A line catches my eye: "Caminante, no hay camino." Rubí and I are both dumbfounded. This is exactly the poem she couldn't recall earlier:

Walker, your treads are
the path and nothing more.
Walker, there is no path,
the path is made by walking.
When walking the path is made
and when looking back
you see the path that never
has to be walked again.

Fernan, Rubí and Angie start a lively conversation – maybe it's the Spanish dialect, but everything sounds like it's being said with great enthusiasm. The news that Angie translates for me is not good: Fernan says we are hopelessly late to find a bed in Zubiri, and even the more expensive guest-houses will be full by now.

It is already seven o'clock. Although the sun is still shining, we just don't have it in us to walk another ten kilometres today. Luckily Fernan is a man with a plan. He makes a phone call; again, the conversation is passionate. He arranges accommodation for us in Viscarret, a small village we passed through earlier in the day. It will cost us ten euros each. Even better: The owner will come and fetch us here in half an hour and will return us to the same spot tomorrow morning to continue our walk. The Camino provides.

While we wait for the people from the guesthouse, a man comes walking up from the direction of Roncesvalles. I can't believe someone else is only getting here now.

Luiz is from Brazil. He is built like an athlete or a soccer player. When he hears that I am from South Africa, he says that the only other T-shirt he has brought on the Camino is an Orlando Pirates shirt he received as a gift from a South African doctor years ago.

Luiz is not in the least bit concerned about where he will sleep tonight. He has already walked over thirty kilometres today. Yesterday he started too late from Saint Jean and had to shelter in one of the mountain huts in the Pyrenees. It was apparently freezing cold in the night; there was wood close to the hut, but he had nothing to start a fire with.

"Were you afraid that you could die?" Angie wants to know.

Luiz smiles. "How can you be afraid of something you are so sure will happen?" he replies. "You just don't know when."

* * *

You just don't know when. Alain de Botton writes in his excellent book *How Proust Can Change Your Life* about the writer Marcel Proust, who once responded to a question in a newspaper. The question was more or less: Imagine you have one hour left to live before a meteorite hits the earth and wipes out all life. What would you do?

There were many different answers. One person said that half of humankind would rush to church, while the other half would jump into bed.

But Proust had an interesting idea: Why do we need such a question in the first place? Why do we need such an urgent deadline to make us decide to do all the things we keep putting off, right now? Because the point is, as he puts it so simply and strikingly: "Death may come this evening."

* * *

Two friendly Spanish women, the guesthouse owner Ruthie and her sister, arrive in a purple Kombi to pick us up at Fernan's food truck. I didn't expect a Kombi ride just two days into the Camino, especially not one headed away from Santiago. It seems I'll just have to make peace with the fact that most of my expectations of the Camino will be turned upside down.

The house we stop at is a genuine villa, double-storey with en suite bedrooms and a spacious balcony looking out over the village, a green hill and the Pyrenees in the distance. We can hardly believe our luck. To save money, we decide to share the room with three beds. No one else is sleeping here tonight, so we have the entire top floor to ourselves.

Ruthie has also recently renovated a flat in Burlada, a suburb on the outskirts of Pamplona, which she wants to rent out to walkers. She offers it to the three of us for tomorrow night. We'll be her first guests.

The three of us immediately agree. Rubí wants to take a bus from Pamplona to San Sebastian anyway, Angie wants to stay in Pamplona for at least two days, and I'm simply going to carry on walking from Pamplona. This motley crew is going to spend another day on the Camino together.

Ruthie must go to prepare the flat in Pamplona tomorrow and they offer to take our rucksacks with them, so tomorrow we won't be as weighed down.

Ruthie's husband, Miguel, owns a restaurant in the village and they invite us for supper there, where we are each handed a free beer (charmingly called 'San Miguel'). When Miguel hears that Rubí is from Mexico he immediately fetches a sombrero from the bar and wears it for the rest of the evening.

We eat like royalty: mutton soup for starters, and then chicken and chips. The red wine flows and we talk and laugh like friends who have known each other for years.

The weather forecast indicates an approaching heatwave. The temperature tomorrow could reach 37 degrees.

Miguel asks if any of us can play the guitar. This is something I have neglected badly over the years, but I offer to play something – Koos Kombuis's "Lisa se klavier", one of the first songs I learnt back in the mid-nineties. It turns into a fun experiment: I sing a line in Afrikaans and then translate it into English for Rubí and Angie. Rubí then translates it into Spanish for Miguel, Ruthie and the waiters.

Later that evening I'm lying in my bed. Rubí and Angie are already asleep. I'm not sure if I'm a little bit drunk or just in a very good mood. In just two days on the Camino, so many of my preconceived ideas and expectations have been demolished. I think this is part of the Camino's enchantment: every day along this journey brings the possibility of fresh surprises.

Day Three, Friday 8 May
From Viscarret to Burlada
(29 kilometres)

When I was a child I would sometimes lie on my bed, shut my eyes and try to think of eternity. Eternal Life. Try to imagine what is beyond comprehension on so many levels – perhaps even capture it, just for one moment.

Sometimes these thoughts would completely overwhelm me and I would feel a kind of brain freeze, like when you eat ice cream too quickly. I would jump off the bed light-headed, as if I had been woken up with a fright from a deep sleep.

This morning I had a similar feeling when I realised that a whole 38 days of walking still lay ahead of me. That's almost as long as the six-week vacation of my school days.

Outside, the clock strikes eight. Being without a watch has made me more aware of the church bells ringing.

We wanted to be on the road by now. But Ruthie said we could let them know anytime this morning when they should take us back to the food truck. Angie is also awake and I make coffee for the three of us. There's also yoghurt, biscuits and small croissants for breakfast. I take Rubí coffee in bed.

"Hola princesa, here's some coffee." She appreciates this little gesture immensely. I don't ask, but I suspect she doesn't get coffee in bed regularly, if ever.

Rubí and I sit on the balcony and look out over the mountains. The Camino passes right in front of the guesthouse. There's a steady stream of walkers. The road coming down from the hill makes an S-bend. In the distance we can see a shepherd drive a large flock of sheep towards the village. A peaceful, rural scene. The flock comes closer and then runs into the S-bend. We sit amazed, watching several hundred sheep fill up the whole turn. I hear the bleating, the desperate pattering on the gravel road and a shepherd calling.

Rubí wants to run and fetch her cell phone to take a picture, but it's already all over. I would probably have wanted to do the same if I had a camera with me. Ultimately, photos – a video, even – would have been unnecessary. This would never have been the same on YouTube. The sheep on the S-bend were dreamlike, something from an art film.

* * *

Karl-Heinz, the German I met at Beilari in Saint Jean, lies stretched out on the grass next to Fernan's food truck. I don't disturb him; he looks utterly relaxed. He doesn't seem to be missing the "wifey".

* * *

I feel a bit guilty that I'm not carrying my rucksack today. It's only the Discovery running pack on my back. It's much easier walking through the forest with so little to carry.

We reach Zubiri, where we'd initially planned to overnight. The name of the fine medieval bridge across the Río Arga is Puente de la Rabia. The "rabia" in the bridge's name refers to the legend that you can cure a rabid animal by leading it across the bridge three times. I am neither a dog nor rabid, but I would not have minded walking over the bridge three times for muscles that hurt less.

We buy chorizo and cheese at Embutidos Arrieta in Zubiri. Though the accommodation stamps in your Credencial are the most important, you can also get stamps at eateries and cafés (generally called "bars"). The stamp from this place is really quirky – a graphic depiction of six little pigs' hindquarters.

I drink coffee and order my first tortilla de patatas, an omelette with potato. It looks more like a quiche cut into slices but is without doubt going to be my first choice for breakfast from now on.

* * *

Rubí and I chat about the Mexican Day of the Dead festival. She says it takes place over three days and is a colourful celebration of friends and family who have died. Many people build altars to commemorate those in the afterlife and even invite them to come for a visit. Food and other tokens are often placed at the altars. During the festival you eat a special kind of sweet bread, the pan de muerto. Bread of the dead. La Catrina, a female skeleton wearing an elegant hat, is one of the festival's iconic symbols.

I would love to attend this festival one day. I find the Mexican view of life and death, the fluid relationship between these two "worlds", very appealing.

Rubí teaches me my first Spanish sentence: "Los Mexicanos nos reímos hasta de la muerte." ("We Mexicans laugh to the other side of death.")

I see two guys walking towards us at quite a pace, no rucksacks or trekking poles. What are they doing on the Camino? I feel the hair on the back of my neck rise. I'm walking a little way ahead of Rubí and Angie, but can't see them.

The Camino is very safe, but I have read about thieves – although mostly just pickpockets – near the big cities. We happen to be on the way to Pamplona. I keep an eye on them and begin walking back to the women. Just in case. My instinctive reaction is usually flight, not fight – not something I'm necessarily proud of – but no one must start any trouble with Rubí or Angie.

Luckily I see them walking towards me. They were also suspicious of the guys, but it was a false alarm.

* * *

We've probably got about eight more kilometres to walk before we get to Pamplona. Since first starting to read about the Camino, I've had these images of yellow wheat fields in my mind. It's spring, though, and the fields are still green.

Rubí and I reach a wheat field amid villages and decide to play a trick on Angie, who's blissfully bringing up the rear. We hide in the wheat field. As she passes by, we jump out, shouting like hell.

She freezes, gasps, then works out what's happening. "You fucks! You fucks!" she shouts in her deepest New York accent. We all burst out laughing. She sounds like a female Joe Pesci in a mafia movie set in the Bronx.

When we look back from the top of a hill, we see the wind create the illusion of waves rolling across the wheat fields. The wheat surges, wave upon wave. Like the sheep on the S-bend this morning, a photograph would only diminish this moment.

It's getting late. Rubí points out that it's after eight. At our current pace, we will only reach the flat in Burlada at nine thirty. We started walking hopelessly too late this morning. Rubí's phone rings.

It's Ruthie, wanting to know where we are. As luck would have it, she has just finished up at the flat in Burlada. She's less than 500 metres away with her purple Kombi.

We are very happy to get into back the Kombi. It does mean there will be a few kilometres of the Camino that we haven't walked. But who's making these rules? There are many ways to get to Santiago and I think they are all valid.

Day Four, Saturday 9 May
Pamplona

I wake up in the self-catering apartment in Burlada, on the outskirts of Pamplona. It sounds like Rubí and Angie are still sleeping in the other room. We hit the sack quickly last night, after I'd bought us take-away chicken and chips.

I look out the window and see the buildings of Pamplona, the capital of Navarre, just four kilometres away.

My calves and ankles are sore this morning. In fact, my entire body is in shock after these three days of walking about 75 kilometres. It's just as well I didn't need to carry my rucksack yesterday, or my back and shoulders would have been feeling even worse.

I want to explore Pamplona a bit and then move on, perhaps even as far as Puente la Reina. And this morning

I have to say goodbye to Rubí and Angie, with a heavy heart. We've become close during our short time together, something I could never have foreseen.

But the Camino called each one of us separately, for reasons we still have to discover. We have coffee and Rubí and I write letters to each other in our diaries. I suggest writing to her in Afrikaans, and that she writes to me in Spanish. Then, we read the letters to each other.

Letter written in Rubí's journal

Rubí, I am so happy that the Camino brought us together for a short while. Thank you for all the wonderful moments. I hope you find all the answers you are seeking along the Camino. I'm sure you will, because everything you need to know is already within you. You have the answers. You are beautiful, inside and outside, don't ever forget that. I can see that you are a free spirit with a big heart. Life is short. Don't settle for just anybody, be with someone who can see and appreciate the light within you. Please remember to send me a few photographs, and you're always welcome in Cape Town, the mountains and the forests are waiting for you. Whatever lies ahead, remember, it's not the Pyrenees, and may your road ahead be full of yellow and white flowers and sheep on S-bends and winds rolling across wheat fields like waves. If our paths cross again, I want to be able to speak better Spanish and look like a stick man. Remember your Afrikaans sentence: Die Meksikane lag tot anderkant die dood – Mexicans laugh to the other side of death. Until then, buen Camino. Erns xxx

* * *

Angie can hardly walk this morning, poor thing. Perhaps she shouldn't have tried to keep up with us from Ronces-valles, and rather walked at her own pace. She's spending another night in the flat, though, and is just going to rest today.

There's a bus stop right next to the flat. Angie wants to take the bus to Pamplona. Rubí and I decide to ride with her, have a quick bite in the city and then go our separate ways.

Pamplona is famous for the San Fermín festival (the running of the bulls), which takes place every year in July. Hemingway was especially fond of Pamplona and visited the city many times. He writes about San Fermín in his first novel, *The Sun Also Rises*. There's a street near the bullfighting arena – the third largest on earth – named after him. We walk past the arena. I immediately feel attracted to Pamplona. It's a city bursting with life, a colourful assault on the senses.

The Plaza del Castillo looks geared towards partying. It's not even lunchtime yet and the square's already buzz-ing: so many restaurants and cafeterias, and crowds of people wearing pink hats raising glasses of champagne.

The next minute, Rubí is in a pink hat too, and shoves glasses of champagne into our hands. I have no idea where she got them.

We stroll to the Albergue de Jesús y Maria, the main municipal hostel in the old part of Pamplona. Rubí stored some of her things here before her trip to Saint Jean, and wants to collect them before boarding the bus to San Se-bastian.

I'm still considering my options: I can explore Pamplo-na and stay in this albergue overnight, or even spend the night in the flat in Burlada. Or I can start walking now and look for an albergue in the village of Cizur Menor five kilometres away. If Cizur Menor is full, well, I'll just keep walking until I find a place to sleep somewhere else. The Camino will provide.

Rubí discovers that the next bus only leaves later tonight. The narrow streets and the restaurants of the old part of Pamplona beckon: rows of eateries on top of each other that all sell pinchos (Navarre's answer to tapas). We order beer and pinchos before making any further decisions.

Then, the afternoon builds a momentum of its own. A group of friendly Spaniards, all young professionals from Pamplona, start to chat to us. Soon we're socialising like old friends: I meet a teacher, a doctor and an accountant. The beer flows and the pinchos are constantly replenished. Rubí goes to the bathroom and returns in a blue dress, evidently her party outfit.

A young glamour boy – whom I silently dub the Poor Man's Rafa Nadal (he looks very much like the tennis star) – starts flirting with her shamelessly, but I'm not bothered.

"Look, I got some pot!" Angie calls out, and laughs a belly laugh. She's managed to get her hands on a joint in a single conversation.

Our new Spanish friends take us to their stomping ground, not far from the cathedral, where the locals apparently go. I don't see any other pilgrims here. There's a viewing point overlooking the Arga River and the city. I play the guitar again. The Spaniards all know about Rodriguez and his South African connection thanks to the Oscar-winning film *Searching for Sugarman*.

I could never have guessed that one day I'd be sitting on a lawn in Pamplona playing "Sugarman" on an out-of-tune guitar for a group of Spanish lovers of life.

Day Five, Sunday 10 May
From Pamplona to Muruzábal
(21 kilometres)

I wake early with a hell of a hangover, but it's time to walk.

We got into it properly in Pamplona last night. After partying with the Spaniards, Rubí, Angie and I wandered around the Plaza del Castillo eating ice cream. It was past nine, which is actually when the Spanish only start to get going. There was such a family atmosphere: parents drinking wine, eating pinchos and talking loudly, while children laughed and chased one another around the square. I'm liking the Spaniards and their lifestyle more and more.

I say a final farewell to Rubí and Angie at the bus stop outside the flat in Burlada.

For the first time, I walk entirely on my own. It feels good, as if a new chapter of this surprising journey is now starting. I'm glad I didn't take the bus into Pamplona, because now I can walk over the medieval Puente de la Magdalena XII bridge back into Pamplona's old city. The network of narrow cobbled streets holds an almost magical attraction. There's a half-marathon on this morning, so some of the streets have been closed.

It's Mother's Day. Like me, my mother is not sentimental about things like Mother's Day. But I miss her today. She would really enjoy Spain.

I'm eager to visit the Catedral de Santa María and get my Credencial stamped. It's too early, though – the cathedral is not open yet.

I recognise the red rucksack and the pink hat immediately. It's Rubí. She's also come to see if the cathedral is open before boarding the bus to San Sebastian. We hug and laugh about the coincidence, as if the Camino just won't allow us to go our own ways. What are the chances that we would bump into each other again today?

* * *

It's just after nine. Rubí and I sit in a café in Pamplona. We order our last coffee together; within an hour she'll be on the bus to San Sebastian to walk the Camino del Norte, and I'll continue the Camino Francés.

We're sitting at the bar and my eye catches a bottle of gin: Voortrekker. Can it be? Apparently it's a Dutch gin. But alas it's too early for that, especially on a Sunday.

A brass band is playing outside the café. Inside, a Whitney Houston CD is playing: "Don't walk away from me, no. Don't walk away from me. Don't you walk away from me."

Jeez! It's absurd. Why would this song be playing just at *this* moment?

We both try to postpone the inevitable as long as possible. As if, after coffee, we're both just going to pick up our rucksacks and hit the road again, together. I wrestle with a wild idea: What if I buy a bus ticket too, and go with her to San Sebastian?

* * *

My friend J.P. is my mentor. We met late one afternoon in 1998 at Van's Tuck Shop on the campus of what was then UPE (these days NMMU). I was a first-year student. He was sitting there having a smoke, and I was paging through a newspaper. We started chatting about the newspaper. The headline story was that P.W. Botha had refused to appear before the TRC.

J.P. had a degree in psychology and was an intern in the

psychology department. We got up, said goodbye and then realised we were walking in the same direction, and to the same place: a writing course that Marlene van Niekerk had come to present at UPE. This was the uncomplicated start of a close friendship.

J.P. introduced me to psychology, philosophy and Zen. I believe his favourite philosopher is Arthur Schopenhauer, who once said: "Life swings like a pendulum between pain and boredom." But J.P. is not exclusively cynical.

These days, J.P. is a psychologist in Grahamstown. In his free time he started a tree-planting project at the hospital where he works. He has already planted over a thousand trees on the grounds. When I visit him, we usually go to the hospital first to water the trees. "The trees can't wait for water," he always says.

J.P. doesn't believe in giving advice. At the age of 22, with my studies behind me, I had to make a decision: accept a job as a reporter at *Die Burger Oos-Kaap* in Port Elizabeth, or sign up for a postgraduate course in journalism at Stellenbosch. I was torn.

J.P. lit a cigarette and said: "Whichever one you choose, you'll regret it."

* * *

What do I want to regret more?

I will regret impulsively getting on the bus to go to San Sebastian with Rubí. And I will regret saying goodbye here in Pamplona and probably never seeing her again. But – and I think this is what J.P. was implying – both these decisions could also have benefits I cannot even begin to foresee.

I am more serious, these days, about boundaries and

about giving myself and others more space. Before the Camino my therapist, Peter – another mentor who has played a significant role in my life – quoted the Vietnamese poet and Zen monk Thich Nhat Hanh: "Dear one, do you have enough space in your heart and all around you?"

I decide to stick to my plan to walk the Camino Francés. Rubí and I have our own questions and answers to tease out along the way. For that, we need space.

Rubí is looking at something on Facebook. I tell her about the Facebook group Berlin Artparasites. Over the past few months, I've got a lot inspiration from this group's posts. She reads the post quoted this morning by a young Filipino poet, Sade Andria Zabala: "I understood myself only after I destroyed myself. And only in the process of fixing myself, did I know who I really was."

Exactly. It's time to carry on with the repair work.

One of my favourite movies is Sofia Coppola's *Lost in Translation*, with Bill Murray and Scarlett Johansson. They play two people who meet coincidentally in a hotel in Tokyo and spend a few days together. The chemistry between them is palpable, but they are never physically intimate. Towards the end of the film they whisper something to each other that the viewer cannot hear.

It's like that at our parting on that Sunday morning in Pamplona, in a narrow street near the cathedral. We hold hands for a few seconds. Neither of us wants to be the first to let go. Each heading in a different direction, to another life. We met on the Camino, and we part, too, on this centuries-old pilgrim route.

I walk away, and turn back after fifty metres or so. But she's gone, already out of sight. A Tom Petty line comes into my head. "You can look back babe, but it's best not to stare."

* * *

I follow the silver scallop shells etched into the pavements until I reach the outskirts of Pamplona. Tick-tock, tick-tock . . . I wonder if I'll bump into Angie before she reaches Cizur Menor.

Lo and behold, about half an hour later I see her in the distance ahead of me. Her little waddle and light-blue rucksack make her immediately recognisable. I walk quickly to catch up to her. We don't talk much. The sadness is palpable, the realisation that our paths are truly going to diverge, probably for the last time.

Strange, isn't it? How an interaction can be so short yet so intense. And how you know intuitively that an experience is going to stay with you for a long time. Angie is going to overnight in Cizur Menor. Just five kilometres for her today – her body is still very sore.

In Cizur Menor I buy a banana and a big green apple at the supermarket. I eat them in a little park for a bit of energy, and fill my water bottle. According to my guidebook, I am near the place where Charlemagne and his Christian forces defeated the Muslim army of a certain Aigolando in the eighth century. I find it difficult to imagine bloody scenes of war in this tranquil environment.

The kilometres roll by. For a long time, I see no other walkers. Occasionally, I pass someone, greet them with a "Buen Camino" and march on.

The questions keep milling around in my head: Is Rubí already on the bus? Should I have gone with her to the Camino del Norte? But what about my own journey – isn't that why I'm here, after all?

There goes my heart, again. But no, it's better this way; the experience was good and beautiful and quiet and intense. What am I afraid of, though, and why is everything of value so vulnerable, as Lucebert said?

There was speculation about my Camino among some of my colleagues – that afterwards, I'd elope, bag and baggage, with a woman I'd meet along the way . . .

But there's something I do already know: You can travel halfway around the world, mail your phone and camera somewhere, walk for forty days with only eleven kilograms' worth of possessions, and try to avoid every possible distraction. But wherever you go, you travel with yourself.

It sounds so simple it's almost laughable, but that's how it is. You cannot escape from yourself and your issues and blind spots and the stuff that keeps you awake at night. It follows you everywhere, like your shadow.

When you walk, especially without the excuse of digital distractions, you begin to confront things about yourself that make you uncomfortable. As the psychoanalyst James Hollis puts it: "Those parts of myself that when brought to consciousness I find troubling . . . and yet they're there. And they show up."

I once watched a wildlife documentary about Komodo dragons hunting a water buffalo. One dragon risks getting close enough to the buffalo to bite it. Just one bite, on the leg. It then falls back, and waits. About eight other Komodos join it.

For days they walk patiently with the buffalo, which weakens increasingly from the toxins from that single bite. I know it's nature, and it's not necessarily cruel, but it's a macabre procession to watch: eight Komodo dragons awaiting their opportunity, not leaving the buffalo alone for a second.

When the buffalo eventually collapses, they attack. Within three hours there's nothing left of the buffalo.

My dragons are walking with me to Santiago, I think. I must make sure they don't get the chance to bite.

* * *

I'm taking a breather under one of the few shade trees on today's route. Soon a few other out-of-breath walkers arrive and plonk down their bags. A young Korean man sits down right next to me. He is wearing earphones and the music is so loud that I can hear it's electric guitars making the racket. It sounds like Jimi Hendrix and a bit of Iron Maiden. No "Gangnam Style" here between Pamplona and Puente la Reina.

At first he just nods his head to the rhythm. Then he picks up of one his trekking poles and starts playing air guitar. Not for attention, it seems – he just likes it. He is not concerned with the rest of us. With happy abandon, he's playing an air guitar solo with his trekking pole in Spain.

Who am I to judge?

* * *

Nirvana's Kurt Cobain committed suicide in 1994, but I first heard of him a year later reading an article in *Time* in my dentist's waiting room in Port Elizabeth.

I was 16 years old, in puberty's injury time. My hormones were all over the place and I was recovering slowly from a sports injury that became a hip operation. And then I went and fell hopelessly in love with an unattainable matric girl who was also the leader of my CSA group.

In a shaky hand I wrote the lyrics of Bon Jovi's tear-jerker ballad "Always" in a Valentine's card for the unsuspecting lass. And then installed it anonymously, with a little lion soft toy, for her attention on the matrics' veranda.

This was me making an early acquaintance with the cul-de-sac of unrequited love. But also my first skirmish with the Black Dog, as Winston Churchill used to refer to depression.

I don't have to look too far back into my lineage to find the Black Dog. My maternal grandfather was a farmer near Kruisrivier outside Uitenhage. He'd apparently sit down at the kitchen table with his morning coffee, take the first sip, sigh deeply and say: "Ai, it's bitter to be human."

As a teenager I shared my grandfather's sentiments, and in Nirvana's music I found an appropriate soundtrack for the cataclysmic shitstorm that was my disposition. That was another era, before cell phones and email. You couldn't just google or download a song or album. Even CDs were still a novelty. Nirvana's *Unplugged in New York* was one of the first CDs I bought with my pocket money. I got hold of some of the other Nirvana albums on TDK tapes.

Kurt Cobain also inspired me to start guitar lessons. I think my parents were only too happy that I wanted to do something besides lying around all day with the door closed listening to Nirvana. I paid a fortune to order the sheet music of the *Unplugged* album from the USA. I sat in my room hammering out the chords from "Jesus Doesn't Want Me For a Sunbeam" and "All Apologies" to my heart's content.

What really worried my parents was my fanatical devotion to a person who screamed mostly morbid thoughts in a hoarse voice, then blew himself away with a double-barrelled shotgun.

Then I attended a CSA camp at Jeffreys Bay. One of

those camps where emotions – and, with hindsight, guilt – build and build, until the Saturday night's soothing gospel music performance in the hall. Then the dominee asks all those who want to give their hearts to Jesus anew to please to stand up.

I stood up. And I'd also fallen head-over-heels in love, this time with another girl who was also at the camp. One weekend, two conversions.

I needed to make a decision about Nirvana. And I don't do anything half-heartedly.

In a box somewhere in my parents' home there is a photograph of me taken shortly after this camp: I'm sitting on the bed and wearing my school's white honours blazer. Around me lie the torn and tattered remains of my Nirvana collection.

I'm smiling broadly. Looking directly at the camera. And clasping a Bible.

* * *

This hill is bloody steep. My legs have had it. They're heavy, as if I'm wearing batting pads for cricket. Not since Day One on the Pyrenees have I struggled this much on the Camino. And I'm really missing Rubí and Angie.

The heatwave will just not let up either. I drink more water. My thoughts are circling again, back to the chants from the stands at interhouse athletics: "Go, legs, go. Go, legs, go."

If I were fitter and more sure-footed, I would turn around, appreciate the view of Pamplona in the distance, and look back proudly over the long road I've walked so far. But I don't care about views right now, I just want to get to the top.

Close to the summit I walk past a dry fountain with an interesting legend. A medieval pilgrim apparently stopped here once, exhausted and dehydrated. The devil appeared to him and offered him some water, but only if he rejected God. Old Beelzebub was disguised as a pilgrim, as is often the case in Camino legends.

The pilgrim refused the devil's request, and a miracle occurred: the apostle James himself appeared, led him to a fountain and gave him water to drink from one of the Camino's scallop shells.

I wonder whether I'll bump into the devil somewhere between here and Santiago. Or will my struggle be largely with demons of my own?

* * *

Either I have an overactive imagination, or I was just a very sensitive child. Both, maybe. But when I was very young, I was petrified of pictures – or even talk – of the devil.

I wasn't even particularly comfortable with pictures of Our Lord Jesus. Except for the Jesus in *Ons eie Kleuterbybel* (*Our Own Children's Bible*). He was okay. With his dark, wavy hair, he looked like he'd just stepped out of a Timotei advert, not like he was roving around with a bunch of fishermen and preaching. (Although, years later I did find it distressing that the Jesus in *Ons eie Kleuterbybel* had the same skin colour as the dreaded "flesh-coloured" Colleen pencil crayon).

I remember visiting one of my friends once. His mother pulled out a photo that someone in a Boeing had taken. The photo seemed to show Jesus up in the clouds. I flatly refused to look at it, and buried my face in a cushion instead.

Any monstrosity with red eyes also sent my anxiety levels through the roof. My mother experienced this at first hand when we went to a children's theatre production in Port Elizabeth. The director thought it a good idea to give the lion character little red lights for eyes; my mother had to flee the theatre with her shrieking child.

But the worst was when I visited another friend and his mother told us about the Antichrist. This same mother had burnt her son's He-Man figurines because poor He-Man, Man-at-Arms and Skeletor were apparently "devilish". She told us about the Antichrist who would arise in the East at the end of days. And that the end time was close at hand.

I understood very little about these things, but I did know one thing: my bedroom window faced east, because the sunlight streamed in there every morning. If the Antichrist were to decide to arise, he would look into my window straight away.

In my imagination the Antichrist looked something like a cross between an Egyptian pharaoh and the Ayatollah Khomeini. He *was* going to rise up and come to fetch me. It was just a question of time. For a whole week, I went to bed anxious about waking up.

So, if the devil is going to look me up on the Camino, he'd better be very well disguised. For everyone's sake.

* * *

The hill is called Alto del Perdón, the Hill of Forgiveness. It is one of the iconic points along the Camino, a place where pilgrims once received forgiveness. A foretaste, perhaps, of what ultimately awaited them in Santiago.

The thirty or so wind turbines placed along the ridge are a more modern development, however.

I catch my breath, take off my shoes and socks, and sit for a while. I'm still following Bill's advice to air my feet at every break and treat them with a bit of Vaseline before putting my shoes back on. My feet are sore, but I haven't had any blisters yet, luckily.

There's a wrought-iron monument here by the sculptor Vincent Galbete depicting pilgrims through the ages. Some are walking, others are on horseback, in medieval dress or carrying bags on their backs. These words appear on one of the figures: "Donde se cruza el camino del viento con el de las estrellas." ("Where the path of the wind crosses that of the stars.") This is a reference to the legend that led to the founding of the Camino, when the shepherd followed the course of the stars all the way to Santiago.

The view from up here, of all sides, is spectacular. It was worth the sweat. Now for a steep descent; the road past the villages of Uterga, Muruzábal and Obanos is a thin white line all the way to the horizon.

I still have no idea how far I'm going to walk today or where I'm going to sleep tonight. It doesn't worry me in the least. There will be a bed for me somewhere. The Camino provides.

Ultreia!

* * *

Santa María de Eunate is a little church dating back to 1170. Its octagonal shape and cupola remind one of the Holy Sepulchre in Jerusalem. According to legend, this little church was built by the Knights Templar.

I don't know much about the Knights Templar, except that they were secretive and have links to the Ark of the Covenant and the Turin Shroud. They protected travellers and pilgrims along the Camino against highwaymen and other rogues.

The church is two kilometres from Muruzábal, the village where I have now arranged accommodation for tonight. I rode here on a bicycle I borrowed from the albergue.

It's been years since I rode a bike. The bike itself is basic – no gears, and you don't need special shoes for the pedals. I wear my "evening wear" and slip-slops. The landscape – green hills, dirt roads and lots of white and yellow flowers – reminds me very much of the Overberg, the area around Bredasdorp and Napier.

On a hill the wind turbines are turning like crazy. The sky is filled with white stripes – the vapour trails of aeroplanes. I'm still trying to get used to them – it's not something you see often in South Africa.

I'm glad I read about this church in my guidebook. It's a mysterious place. A place of silence.

I stub my toe at the entrance and break the sacred silence with an "Ouch, fuck". But at least there's no one else here.

Compared to the church in Roncesvalles, the interior of this one is modest. There's a statue of the Virgin Mary with the infant Jesus on her lap behind the altar. For a donation of €0,20, you can light an electronic candle.

I'm not big on this kind of ritual, but I like the symbolism of lighting a candle for someone – in this case, Rubí and Angie. Even if it's an electronic one.

The clock strikes six. I have to head back to the albergue.

* * *

The Camino has been described as a "500-mile journey to yourself".

In Cape Town I'd say to my friends, tongue firmly in

cheek, that I hoped to meet up with myself somewhere along the route. Little did I know that this would happen, literally, before I'd even walked 100 kilometres.

I'm at a table with four Germans at the Albergue El Jardín de Muruzábal. I've just finished off a substantial pasta with broccoli. This is a new albergue, which opened just fifteen days ago. The family that owns it moved from Pamplona to the sticks, bought the house and converted it into a hostel.

There are fourteen bunk beds and I was glad to hear of one still available for ten euros. These private albergues also often have en suite double rooms, but you pay a premium for privacy – such a room for two guests can easily cost 40 euros per night.

On the Camino you soon get used to the question "Where are you from?", especially since you are often at the table with other walkers. The Germans sound faintly interested when they hear I'm from Cape Town, but quickly begin speaking German among themselves again.

Then another person comes to sit down. At first I think he's German too, but Robert tells me he is from Graz in Austria. He rolls his eyes about the Germans and mutters under his breath that they deliberately don't want to speak English.

Robert is 26 and works for a software company. He used to be a photographer in conflict zones like Israel and Jordan. He has a brand-new Sony camera that he can control with his smartphone, as he carefully shows me. A bit of a tech geek, then.

He walked his feet raw during the first few days to Pamplona, so he spent two days nursing his blisters in a hotel.

Robert is considering resigning and becoming a student again. And he's licking his wounds from a relationship that didn't work out – apparently one of the reasons he came to walk the Camino.

We get on well straight away, and have the same sense of humour. But the strangest thing is how closely we resemble each other. I have walked right into my European doppel-gänger.

Day Six, Monday 11 May
From Muruzábal to Estella
(27 kilometres)

Robert and I set off together. He is carrying the biggest ruck-sack I have seen on the Camino. It looks like he's packed for an Arctic expedition. It must weigh at least twenty kilo-grams, but he insists it doesn't bother him one bit.

After two kilometres we reach Obanos, a small village with an interesting story. Towards the end of July of every second year, the Mystery of Obanos festival is held on the village square. Up to 600 people, more or less the entire village, take part in a theatre piece depicting the story of San Guillén and Santa Felicia.

San Guillén, the Duke of Aquitaine in France, walked the Camino with his sister sometime in the Middle Ages. When they arrived at Obanos, Felicia wanted to stay and provide comfort and assistance to the pilgrims. San Guillén would have none of this. In a fit of rage, he murdered her. He then felt so guilty that he walked to Santiago to ask for forgiveness, and on the way back he settled near Obanos. For the rest of his life he did exactly what his sister had wanted to do: provide comfort and assistance to pilgrims and the poor.

San Guillén's skull, encased in silver, is preserved in the

church of San Juan Bautista. During the festival in Obanos the skull forms part of a parade and the priest pours wine through the skull as a blessing.

I didn't realise the Catholics have so many intense myths, legends and rituals. It all feels light years away from the NG Kerk of my childhood.

* * *

Outside the town of Puente la Reina, a life-size statue of a medieval pilgrim stands guard. Two of the Camino routes, the Camino Francés and the Camino Aragonés, converge here. The Camino Aragonés is 160 kilometres long and starts at Somport on the border between Spain and France.

Charlemagne apparently spent a night here in Puente la Reina after triumphing over the Moors. All the towns so far have had a medieval feeling, but Puente la Reina trumps them all. The large Romanesque bridge with its six arches over the Arga River could have something to do with this.

We put our rucksacks down at José Martija, a small eatery. Almost every hamlet along the Camino has one of these bars. They're easy to recognise by the tables and chairs outside, and the rucksacks that are usually lying on the ground.

I'm beginning to enjoy this new routine of walking about six kilometres in the morning and then settling down to a café con leche and a tortilla de patatas. The Spaniards are also big on freshly squeezed orange juice.

After breakfast I see a red rucksack with a trekking pole and a pink hat on the ground outside the café. Could it be Rubí?! Did she decide to stick with the Camino Francés after all?

But then an old grey-haired guy picks up the bag, pole and hat and hits the road. I can only smile at my misplaced excitement.

Robert finds my confession very amusing.

* * *

Random moment in Puente la Reina: storks like to make huge nests in old church towers. And stand guard over them with the dignity of angels.

* * *

We are walking on one of the old Roman roads, a steep and stony dirt track. My rucksack is giving me hell today. I have to do something about it.

Near the town of Lorca we walk across an old bridge over the Río Salado. Picaud warned pilgrims in the *Codex Calixtinus* not to let their horses drink the water here, which apparently was deadly. And Basques were believed to be sitting on the other side of the river sharpening their knives, ready to slaughter any horses that had drunk.

At the Bodega del Camino in Lorca I become irrationally worried about the weight of my rucksack. But I can't find much to throw out. I do get rid of a few things, like my box of washing powder and the mosquito repellent I bought in Bayonne.

I realise I'm losing the plot when I throw away thirty of the fifty *Go* business cards too, as if that's going to make my rucksack any lighter.

* * *

Outside Estella I see this quote on a fountain: "Buen pan, óptimo vino, carne y pescado, y llena de toda suerte de felicidades." This was Picaud's medieval TripAdvisor review of Estella in the *Codex Calixtinus*: "Good bread, the best wine, meat and fish, and plenty of all good things." Estella is well known as a wine-producing region. The town is one of many that were established centuries ago because of the stream of pilgrims along this route.

Robert and I have already walked 25 kilometres today. My body feels better, at least. Robert's pace is slower than mine, which probably helped. But I am dead tired.

The first four hostels in Estella we enquire at are fully booked. I start getting despondent. It's not supposed to be so busy at this time of the year. June to August, the hot summer months, are high season for the Camino.

Fortunately we find a place to sleep at Albergue Rocamador. All the bunk beds are taken, but we can book a room with two single beds and an en suite bathroom. It does cost us twenty euros each, though.

One thing I've noticed so far is how clean and neat the albergues are. The night in Roncesvalles aside, though, I haven't stayed in any of the large municipal albergues. This will probably happen soon enough.

I enjoyed my walk with Robert today. His outlook on life's a bit absurd; like me, he's a great fan of Monty Python and John Cleese in *Fawlty Towers*. He can also poke fun at himself.

In the albergue's overheated laundry room an appropriately silly scene is playing out. We are too tired and lazy to do our washing by hand, and want to use the washing machine. But both the washing machine and tumble dryer are out of order. Two Spanish handymen are trying to fix them. We decide to sit and wait until they are done, in case someone else takes the gap with their own load of washing.

The handymen are priceless. The one is tall and thin, with grey hair and a cigarette behind his ear; the other one is dumpy. They look like Spain's answer to Laurel and Hardy.

And they are clearly not having much luck with the appliances. They frequently step back, look at the machines and literally scratch their heads. Then the tall guy turns to us and says, "Un momente . . ."

I go and buy us each an Ámbar Caesar Augusta beer (at €2,50, still cheaper than a boutique beer in Cape Town).

And so we sit, beer in hand, watching two old guys looking at a washing machine.

* * *

While the washing machine is being repaired, I walk to the pharmacy across the road. My little jar of Vaseline is nearly finished. I buy some more and, at the recommendation of the pharmacist – an attractive woman who speaks fluent English – a tube of Pedi-Relax, an "anti-rubbing foot cream, second skin effect".

My earliest memory of a pharmacy is of one in Plettenberg Bay. My uncle was the owner and he later expanded it into a toy shop. But he always had other plans and projects on the go.

I knew him as Uncle Boet. In the eighties he was my favourite uncle. For some reason he was always travelling to places like New York and Hong Kong. He often brought presents back for me. I may have been the first kid in South Africa (in Uitenhage, anyway) to have a fancy radio-controlled car that you could even set to 4×4 mode.

Or one of those woolly little dogs you could activate by clapping your hands; it would come to you, barking all the way.

No one really knew how Uncle Boet afforded his extravagant travels. I suspect nobody asked. Our family sometimes popped in for a visit on our way to Cape Town. He was always involved in some scheme or other. We heard later, for example, that he had ostriches in Namibia.

Uncle Boet had inherited the family farm near Uitenhage in the seventies after my grandfather died. He then started a sand-supply business. I remember visiting the farm with my grandmother and walking past huge bulldozers and pyramids of sand.

In the late eighties he got a brand new black Porsche. This was long before cell phones. One afternoon he came charging up to our house in Uitenhage in his Porsche, got on the landline and had an animated argument with someone. Uncle Boet could be something of a hothead.

Sometimes he would ask us to do him a favour, like bringing a few boxes of medicine he'd stored in my grandmother's garage in Uitenhage. I would help my father load the boxes into the boot of our car.

One Sunday in the early nineties, our family was having lunch with my grandmother. Uncle Boet was on a short fuse the whole time. Before we even got to dessert he jumped up and said, "Will you excuse me? I have to go and see Oupa Gqozo." He then raced off in his Porsche from Uitenhage to meet the leader of the Republic of Ciskei. No one knew why.

Uncle Boet was also a family man with a wife and two kids. He built himself a mansion with a palm-tree-lined driveway on a hill outside Plettenberg Bay. But somewhere along the line, karma or something caught up with Uncle

Boet. By the time my grandmother died in 1995, people were already gossiping about his business ventures. Shortly after that, it was big news in the local papers that he'd allegedly committed fraud amounting to millions of rand.

And then Uncle Boet just vanished. It later emerged he'd had close links with Mafia boss Vito Palazzolo. Palazzolo, who is whiling away his days in an Italian jail, lived in Franschhoek at the time.

Uncle Boet appeared on the Interpol website as one of a handful of South Africans with a "Red Notice" next to their name. I remember a newspaper reporting that he and Advocate Barbie's Dirk Prinsloo were both being sought by Interpol.

Interpol indicated that "possession of explosives" was one of the reasons they wanted to arrest and extradite Uncle Boet. To this day, not one of us knows what happened to him. There are all sorts of rumours that he's somewhere in Europe or the Far East. And that a spy sometimes travels to Cape Town to see how his two sons are doing.

While the police were investigating the case, a detective came to our house. He claimed that my uncle had stored more than just medicine in those boxes. My father and I may have been unwitting drug mules.

* * *

Supper at the albergue. We're sitting around a table with a Danish architect and two older guys from England, Ken and Ed. Ed is the man whose bag, trekking pole and hat I mistook for Rubí's earlier. Ken is a retired medical doctor who came to walk the Camino with his neighbour, Ed. Ken plans to walk only as far as Burgos, but Ed wants to press on all the way to Santiago.

I didn't pack anything to read on the Camino. Many people leave books they've finished reading at the albergues. Ken had picked up such a book that he now wanted to pass on to someone else. It was a book of essays by the Scottish philosopher David Hume, *Dialogues Concerning Natural Religion*. One of the essays in the book is "On Suicide". No thanks. I enjoy reading philosophy, but this looks to me like heavy reading for the Camino.

The time immediately after my break-up in November was tough. I hit rock bottom. Cruelly disillusioned, livid, heartbroken, confused. I'd sleep very badly; every morning, it felt like I was waking up in a car crash. This was my "long dark tea-time of the soul", to borrow a phrase from Douglas Adams.

I sat in my flat for a long time one night, staring at the TV. The TV was off. I stood up, fetched a knife from the kitchen and sat down on the couch again. It was the first time I'd done something like this. I looked at the blade for a long time, drew it along my arm, to my right wrist. Applied a bit more pressure. Hesitated. Waited. Stopped.

The memory haunts me. The Komodo dragon nearly bit me that night.

Shortly afterwards I read an article entitled "Jumpers" in an old *New Yorker*. It was about people who jump off the Golden Gate Bridge in San Francisco, and the few who survive.

Many of the survivors seem to have something in common: the moment they jump and start to fall, they feel enormous regret about their irreversible decision.

Day Seven, Tuesday 12 May
From Estella to Sansol
(28 kilometres)

Red wine for breakfast is probably not the best idea. But how often does one walk past a fountain of free red wine?

The Fuente del Vino at Bodegas Irache outside Estella has been a well-known stop-off for visitors since 1991. Robert and I join the queue with our water bottles. I heard the church clock strike eight just a few minutes ago.

There are two taps: one for red wine, the other for water. A notice reads: *Peregrino si quieres llegar a Santiago con fuerza y vitalidad de este gran vino echa un trago y brinda por la felicidad.* ("Pilgrim, if you want to arrive in Santiago full of energy and vitality, drink some of this wonderful wine and propose a toast to good health.") That's exactly what we do. The wine tastes great.

At the Hotel Irache I follow my daily ritual and order a café con leche, tortilla de patatas and naranja – orange juice.

* * *

I stop at a modest little stall at the side of the road and buy a small Camino pendant for four euros. It's very basic: a little block of wood with a yellow arrow and the words *Camino de Santiago*.

Robert starts to fall further behind, but I have a spring in my step today. I take a break next to a fountain along the way and wait for him to catch up. Here I meet two Germans, Sabine and Sebastian, who also met on the Camino and have been walking together for a few days. They look about my age.

Sabine did some volunteer work in Cape Town two years ago and has also visited Namibia. Sebastian was in the military but is now studying towards a business degree.

Robert joins us and takes off his shoes. His feet are shocking. I have seen a few blisters on pilgrims' feet, but this is next level.

He'll need to get help and shouldn't walk much further today. But he wants to keep at it and decides to walk in his slip-slops for the rest of the day. Even this doesn't help. When we stop at a caravan bar in the green wheat fields, Robert decides he's had enough for now. He phones a taxi to take him to Torres del Río.

I feel sorry for the guy, but I'm also relieved about his decision. Now I can walk at my usual pace to Los Arcos, about four kilometres away.

The food caravan has a loudspeaker and one old-school hit after the other blares across the wheat fields. ABBA's "Chiquitita", Bon Jovi's "I'll Be There For You" . . .

The other walkers sitting around don't seem too bothered, but I can imagine this soundtrack annoying a few purists.

Today, I choose silence. Time to hit the road. If I sit here one minute longer, Céline Dion might just start singing.

* * *

In matric I played right wing for the second rugby team. Every now and again I played a small cameo role as a substitute in the first team, but there was stiff competition: the top wings were our school principal's son, Gideon Goosen (disclaimer: he made the team purely on merit), and the lightning-fast Wylie Human.

Because I was the second team's resident nerd and only

CSA group leader, I always had to say the prayer in the locker room before the match when the captain said: "Guys, come, let's huddle."

One Saturday the big match was against our arch-enemy, the Daniel Pienaar Technical High School. I knew in the locker room already that this was going to be a rough day.

A few of the guys would sometimes party hard on the Friday night before a match (not me, I was the nerd), so it was not unusual to see them pulling boots on and rubbing Deep Heat in with massive hangovers. This was certainly the case on that particular morning, but Shaun, one of the flanks, had some extra magic: a little bottle of Livita, an energy drink similar to BioPlus. (This was some years before Red Bull.) Everyone guzzled a mouthful; Shaun had two. I got the shakes very soon.

When we formed our little prayer circle and I dutifully began with "Lord, thank you for –", Shaun interrupted me. "Sorry, I forgot something." We all waited, eyes shut and heads bowed, while Shaun fiddled, then pressed a button – and Céline Dion began to wail on a stretched tape:

Don't say what you're about to say
Look back before you leave my life
Be sure before you close that door
Before you roll those dice
Baby think twice

I pressed ahead with the prayer, with Céline Dion's "Think Twice" as soundtrack. By the time I said "Amen", half the team was sobbing.

To this day I don't know whether it was my inspiring prayer, Céline Dion or too much Livita, but we stormed onto the field that day like the wildebeest stampeding in *The Lion King*. Wildebeest on Livita.

In the first three minutes I scored a try, but then our team's wheels came off. We spent most of the match under our own goalposts.

* * *

Three kilometres from Los Arcos. I sit on a wooden bench and admire the view: wheat fields, vineyards and olive groves . . . the sky is criss-crossed with Boeing vapour trails. Busy airports. Busy lives. A week into the Camino I'm beginning to taste something of the freedom of life on foot.

An elderly man sits down next to me on the bench. We start with "Buen Camino" before he says "Bonjour". I indicate that I don't speak French, but that doesn't stop him. He gestures and spouts fine French truths. I have no idea what he's talking about, but I nod and play along in English.

Conversations like this can last surprisingly long. He reminds me of La Linea, that animated line-drawing TV character from the eighties.

A few walkers pass by. He points to each of them, then to me, then to himself. He smiles and hunts for the words: "Camino . . . Camino . . . eh . . . eh, one world . . . oui, oui, peace on earth!"

* * *

My first overseas trip was in September 2003, when I visited my friend Toast in South Korea. He taught English there for a year. This was long before we worked together at *Go*. The magazine didn't even exist at the time.

Those ten days in South Korea made for one of my happiest holidays ever. The annual Chuseok festival took place during my visit. It's a harvest festival. Most people travel to see their families, as we do at Christmastime. There are all kinds of traditions and rituals, like visiting the graves of family and ancestors and tending them.

During the Chuseok festival, Toast and I went to see a friend of his at her parents' home in Busan. We took a ferry to an island near there.

One evening we were socialising with some Koreans at the hotel. We didn't understand one another at all, but everyone was in a good mood and the soju flowed liberally.

In a gesture of intercontinental ubuntu, one of the Koreans embraced me and Toast and uttered what was probably the only English sentence he knew: "We are the world!"

* * *

I hunch down on the dirt road. Soaked through with sweat. Out of breath. Thirsty. Gatvol. There are no fountains and no shade along the eight kilometres between Los Arcos and Torres del Río. Today it feels like the sun is on a mission, and has its own agenda.

There's farmland all around me, green wheat fields stretching into the distance. On the horizon I spot a church spire. It must be in Sansol. But the damn tower won't get any closer. It starts to feel like a mirage, an unreachable oasis in the desert.

I've made a bad mistake.

Los Arcos was bustling, the restaurants on the square packed with people. I wanted to keep going. But I didn't fill my water bottle. Eight kilometres is not *that* far. Or so I thought.

I turn around and see two walkers approaching in the distance. The landscape is so flat that it's impossible to tell whether they're five minutes or half an hour away. I'll just have to push on. On with the corpse . . .

I eventually stumble into Sansol and follow the yellow arrows to the albergue. "Agua! Agua! Por favor!" I mumble as I get to the bar counter. People giggle at this sweaty oaf storming in and begging for water. I gulp down at least a litre and dissolve a packet of Rehidrat Sport in my tin mug.

That was a near thing – I could have passed out somewhere along that dirt road.

There are still a few beds available here, but Torres del Río is just a kilometre away and it sounds like a more interesting village – according to Brierley, a "quintessential pilgrim's village". It also has a church that, like the one in Eunate, is believed to have been influenced by the Templars.

To get there I need to walk down a steep hill. I need to be careful with my dodgy right knee. It's not my lucky day: all three albergues in Torres del Río are fully booked. I now have to clamber back up the steep hill to Sansol.

Thankfully Deshojando el Camino, the albergue in Sansol, still has room. There's also an ice-cold salt bath, like a paddling pool, where pilgrims can soak their battle-worn feet.

Here, I experience one of the more wholesome moments of my life: sitting with a few other pilgrims on the edge of the salt pool with a cold San Miguel in my hands, my feet soaking in the water, back from the brink of dehydration.

Archie from Glasgow is well into his sixties. But he has the most impressive calves, like a strong young first-team centre in high school. Archie has walked the Camino twice. Or three times. Or five. I don't know. He speaks so quickly and his Scottish accent is so thick that I struggle to understand what he's saying. I pick up the odd "wee", which I think means "small" rather than "us".

I do know one Scottish saying: "Whit's fur ye'll no go past ye." You cannot avoid what's going to happen to you. Just another way of saying "whatever will be, will be".

The two pilgrims I saw in the distance earlier this afternoon between Los Arcos and Sansol are also here at the salt pool. Celso and Luigi are two friends from São Paulo – fit, friendly guys who don't seem to have come to process any awful trauma on the road to Santiago. Which is fine; the Camino doesn't discriminate. I think of the late Hennie Aucamp's phrase "slegs vir almal" – "for everybody only". He uses it in another context, but the Camino is decidedly for everybody only.

I also meet three cheerful Italians: Alessandro, Antonio and Francesco. They're from different parts of Italy, and met on the walk in Spain.

Supper at the albergue offers a typical pilgrim's menu for eight euros. The starter is a choice between lentils, a basic tuna salad or pasta. The main course is chicken, pork or meatballs, with chips. The dessert is yoghurt, fruit or flan – a baked custard pudding. And, as usual, there's a bread basket. The menu includes a carafe of vino tinto (red wine). Not bad for about R110.

It may sound like a menu you can easily tire of, but it doesn't bother me. Each day's long walk leaves me ravenous in the evenings, especially as I don't go big at lunchtime.

The waiter – I suspect he is also the owner – is clearly in a good mood: he puts a full bottle of vino tinto on my table. Maybe he feels sorry for me. He was behind the bar counter when I staggered in on my last legs this afternoon.

I offer the woman at the table next to me a glass of wine. Marcella is from Manchester in England, and in her early forties. She is immersed in her iPad.

She runs a rental agency in Manchester. Despite being on holiday, she still needs to spend about two hours every day on office work and responding to emails. Whether an albergue has wi-fi or not is an important consideration for her.

I don't even want to think about how stressed I would be if I had to wrestle with a *Go* article in my evenings on the Camino. I'm finding it easier all the time to sit at a table in the evening without any digital distractions. And to be okay with it.

When I eat alone at work or at home, I want to keep compulsively busy – that's what smartphones were made for, after all. It's difficult for me to switch off, especially if there's continual stuff coming in on email, Facebook or WhatsApp. It gets addictive.

It has become very rare in modern life to not be permanently accessible. It's a luxury, even. Etienne van Heerden, once my editor at LitNet, often commented: "One has to work on one's scarcity." I like that idea a lot. This was in the days before social media; these days, it's becoming increasingly difficult to be "scarce".

Here Marcella sits, next to me in a small hostel in rural Spain, battling correspondence about tenants, payments in arrears and chancers' excuses. Wi-fi connects her with the digital world's never-ending demands, but in reality disconnects her from her immediate environment. And from herself.

I'm not judging. I understand Marcella's situation – but

had to mail my phone to an unknown address in Paris to realise it.

* * *

In the restaurant at Sansol we watch the televised match between Bayern München and Barcelona, playing in the semi-final of the UEFA Champions League. The Italians at the table are big soccer fans. They are especially passionate about Juventus, who face Real Madrid tomorrow night.

I only really get swept up in soccer fever when the World Cup is on. But it's fascinating to see how spellbound the spectators can get. I can identify, because I feel the same way about rugby.

One incident I'm not particularly proud of occurred the previous year at the Spur in Hermanus. My girlfriend and I (before she became my ex, of course) and her little daughter were sitting in the Spur's kiddies' section. The Springboks were playing Australia on the TV.

We didn't have a TV at home, so the Spur was a logical solution – the little girl could play and keep herself busy.

I behaved very well among all the parents and children . . . until the final moments of the game, when Morné Steyn didn't kick into touch. We were in the lead at that point. If only Morras had found touch . . .

When Rob Horne scored the winning try, I lost it. Like Rumpelstiltskin tearing himself in two, I threw a tantrum, banged my fists on the table and screamed "FUCK! FUCK!"

It went very quiet in the Spur kiddies' section. Uncomfortably quiet. I realised everyone was staring at me: mommies and their children. My girlfriend's eyes flashed.

And her daughter admonished me loudly: "Don't say 'fuck', Uncle Erns."

Day Eight, Wednesday 13 May
From Sansol to Logroño
(22 kilometres)

Something is wrong with my rucksack's front buckle, which clips shut across my chest.

I am deficient in many talents, the most conspicuous of which is handicraft. I pluck and pull at the buckle, but can't get it right. It's still pitch dark outside the albergue in Sansol.

"For fuck's sake! Just. Fucken. Sort. Yourself. Out!" I have a hysterical giggle at my desperate swearing in rural Spain. But I'll have to make a plan quickly. Walking a full day with a hostile rucksack is going to be tough. I want to cover 22 kilometres to reach Logroño today.

"Wait. Let me help you."

I jump at the voice next to me. It's Celso, the walker from Brazil who sat next to me at the salt pool last night. He produces two cable ties out of nowhere. Within a minute the buckle works perfectly.

* * *

I don't remember exactly what happened on my first day at Kabouterland Kleuterskool.

When my mom came to fetch me, the teacher didn't say, "Erns plays so nicely with the other kids" or "Erns colours in beautifully".

No, the feedback was less positive. Apparently she said:

"You need to take your child to the doctor. He's walking funny."

Well, if my preschool teacher could see me now, struggling outside Viana, she'd probably say, "See? I told you!"

My troubles began this morning about a kilometre outside of Sansol, when I passed through the little medieval hamlet of Torres del Río.

The little toe on my left foot began chafing so badly against my shoe that I could hardly stand on the foot without grimacing. Whether it's a blister forming or just a swollen toe, I don't know. Time will tell. But it's blooming sore.

I'm sitting on a rock feeling sorry for myself. I've taken off my shoes and socks. Things don't look good. The sore toe is very red. Two other toes on the same foot also look like candidates for blisters.

This is where it gets lonely. I don't see any walkers approaching. I can't phone or email anyone. I can't even fish for sympathy in a Facebook status update. And I have no idea what time it is. I have to think carefully to work out what day of the week it is.

Wednesday. My eighth day on the Camino. I have walked roughly 150 kilometres – not even one-fifth of the road to Santiago.

Years ago, I attended a Dwarf Festival in Standerton. It was a bit of a ridiculous weekend. About forty dwarves (their preferred terminology) attended the festivities – events included a march through the streets of Standerton, a Mister and Miss Dwarf competition, and dwarf wrestling.

One morning I was talking to a dwarf who had a hangover from hell. He said to me: "My battery is drawing amps." I didn't quite understand what he meant, but it looked like he was in agony.

I had a really good time with Marcella and the Italians last night, but I managed to evade a hangover. I think it's more my psyche drawing amps this morning.

My friend J.P. once gave me a card with one of those corny motivational messages on it, something like "Don't Ever Give Up". Inside he wrote: *When days are dark and friends are few / remember there's always someone worse off than you. – Schopenhauer (more or less).*

We can't spend too much time feeling sorry for ourselves in this life. I just have to plod on. In spite of the pain.

* * *

Jesus saves me. Not the historical or metaphysical Jesus, but a wonderful old Basque gent from San Sebastian with a short ponytail. He is 71, but does not look a day over 60. He is on his third Camino.

I manage to extract this basic biographical information from him with great difficulty as we walk the last seven kilometres to Logroño. Jesus hardly understands English, and I know literally only a handful of Spanish words and phrases. This does not get in the way of an animated discussion and mutual language lesson, though.

I point to a yellow arrow.

"Aha. Flecha amarilla," he says.

I give him a thumbs-up, as if to indicate "good luck".

"Aha. Tengo suerte."

Then Jesus points to my trekking pole.

"Walking stick," I say helpfully.

"Aha. Wal-king stick," he says.

Then we both have a laugh at this interaction. This pleasant exchange with Jesus makes me focus less intensely on my sore toe. It quickly feels better.

Jesus also teaches me the Basque words for a pretty girl: "Neska polita". Just a pity that, now we're getting to Logroño, we're leaving the province of Navarre behind, where a few Basque words would have come in handy. We're heading for the province of La Rioja.

I see this graffiti as we cross a bridge: "If Jesus was alive today, he would have walked."

* * *

Random observation in the Albergue Santiago Apostol in Logroño: the Danes have the best genes of everyone on the Camino, hands down.

The albergue itself, however, is less impressive. It's lit like a Home Affairs office. The guy on the bed next to mine is German. "I grew up in East Germany." Deeply introverted.

The poor man has huge insect bites, all grouped together: on his back, right arm and above one knee. These can only be from bed bugs, the Camino's most notorious goggas. Bed bugs, or chinches in Spanish, are invisible to the naked eye. They live in mattresses and are a Camino reality, whether you stay in a dirt-cheap municipal albergue or an expensive guesthouse.

There's all kinds of advice on how to sidestep them. You're not supposed to put your rucksack on your mattress, ever. Or lie on the mattress without your own sleeping bag or sheet. Some pilgrims always put their rucksacks in a black refuse bag before they put them down in the sleeping quarters.

Some albergues provide disposable fitted sheets and pillow cases, for even more peace of mind. But I still wonder how often the mattresses are washed properly – especially given the daily flow of pilgrims looking for a place to sleep.

Before the Camino, I treated all my clothes, my sleeping bag and my rucksack with a spray called HHL Vital Protection. It was quite a business – on the chaotic day before my departure, my friend Sophia was on the deck outside the *Go* office spraying my underpants, while I was at my desk rifling through my Slagtersnek notes.

There are two things everyone warns you about before the Camino: blisters and bed bugs. Well, I'm in Logroño and have so far been spared both. May my luck hold.

* * *

Logroño is the capital city of La Rioja. I'm at a restaurant on the Plaza del Mercado – a square full of shops and places to eat. Across the way is the Catedral de Santa María de la Redonda – an imposing Gothic cathedral with two tall spires.

The clock has just struck three. I have a café con leche and listen to the doves coo on the square. A father and son share an ice cream. At the table next to mine a man says in a strong European accent: "What the fuck am I supposed to do?"

I have no advice to give him.

Today was a difficult day, especially before I started walking with Jesus. My toe is feeling better, but now my legs are aching – it's as if the pain is moving along a circuit through my body. But I'm very lucky not to have any blisters yet.

So far I have walked roughly 160 kilometres. My bag still feels about three kilograms too heavy. I consider mailing my sleeping bag and some of my warm clothes to Paris, or even Cape Town.

As far as my digital detox is concerned: I am astounded at the high premium that pilgrims place on wi-fi – the second they've checked into the albergue they're all on their phones. I don't miss my phone, nor Facebook, nor WhatsApp. I am gradually beginning to understand how little one needs them. If my laptop and phone never make it to Paris, so be it.

My Camino has been much more social than I expected so far. I guess it was a bit naïve of me to imagine that I would be able to walk alone and in silence for forty days on one of the most popular pilgrim routes in the world. Especially since I'm a full-scale extrovert who gets a lot of energy from interacting with others.

I also enjoy seeing a familiar face again from time to time, someone I met on an earlier part of the Camino. Earlier this afternoon I bumped into Joe from the USA here on the square. I last saw him outside Beilari, the albergue in Saint Jean, when he and Bill were praying together. Joe was sitting on a bench on his own, eating an ice cream with a huge smile on his face. I said hi and asked how things were going. He gestured all around and laughingly said: "It's the Camino!"

I have walked long distances on my own over the past two days and have enjoyed it very much. Perhaps I should try to find a balance between solitude and companionship. Or no, it's rather that I should try to have fewer expectations, worry less about outcomes over which I have no control anyway. And this applies to everything on the Camino: from where I'm going to sleep to whom I'm going to talk to or walk with.

"I knew I would find you!" somebody says, right near my table. I jump with fright. It's Robert, my Camino doppelgänger! He tells me he stayed over at Torres del Río last night and walked to Viana this morning. But then the blisters got the better of him again and he took the bus to Logroño. He wants to stay two nights in Logroño to give his feet some time to recover.

I feel even sorrier for him now. Robert is highly motivated and wants to walk every step of the Camino, to immerse himself in the whole experience, but his feet thwart him again and again.

* * *

Toast loves sending postcards, especially if he is travelling far away on *Go* stories. I'm always surprised when I receive a postcard from some distant place. In a time of WhatsApp and other instant messaging, the honest postcard, written by hand, with a licked stamp up in the top right corner, is almost an artefact, something from years gone by.

I'm still sticking to my resolution not to touch a smartphone or computer during my Camino. But I would like to send a few postcards. Logroño is the first city since Pamplona where I've seen the yellow post boxes with the word *Correos* (Spain's PostNet, I imagine).

Robert and I buy postcards at a little shop.

Postcard to Sophia

Hola Soph! This is such a tiny postcard that this message feels like a tweet. It is Day 8, I have already walked 165 km and you may only receive this once I'm back at the office already, but anyway: the Camino is real, fucken intense and a hell of a test for body and soul. I'm enjoying intothemild hugely and not battling (yet) with blisters. You have to come and do this! Keep well. Erns xxx

I gasp myself awake, breathless. I hear the people in the other bunk beds shifting around uncomfortably. "Are you okay, peregrino?" a voice asks in the dark. "Yes, I . . . I think so. Sorry," I reply.

That was a doozy of a sleep apnoea episode. My heart is racing. I didn't use the nasal plasters tonight. I roll onto my side and listen to my heartbeat, which is still very fast. Too fast. My heart has to work overtime when my oxygen supply is cut off like this.

I can still hear other pilgrims moving restlessly. I must have woken quite a few people. Not a good feeling. People walk far every day. They're tired. No one wants to be yanked out of sleep by the desperate gasps of what must sound like a Loch Ness monstrosity coming up for air.

I start to feel real anxiety. Should I have listened to the specialist and bought a CPAP device? What if this gets worse? Will I have enough energy to get through the days? I still have hundreds of kilometres to walk.

Am I putting my own life in danger?

Day Nine, Thursday 14 May
From Logroño to Nájera
(30 kilometres)

Something between Kingsley Holgate and Gandalf from *The Lord of the Rings* . . . that's what Marcelino Lobato looks like, one of the "faces" of the Camino.

He sits alone at his stall, Ermita del Peregrino Pasante, outside Logroño. This morning's first five kilometres were difficult. I had to haul myself through Logroño's extensive suburbs and keep my wits about me to follow the yellow arrows. (How's it going to feel to be back in Cape Town and find my way around without yellow arrows?)

Marcelino walked the Camino for the first time in 1972. It must have been very different in those days: less commercialised, fewer brand-name clothes, fewer people. Over the years he has appeared in many books and brochures on the Camino.

His stall offers free food: apples, cherries and dry biscuits. And there is a container marked *donativo* – for donations.

This Camino stalwart with the intense gaze doesn't speak much English, sadly. He stamps my Credencial. I give him a friendly nod and I go on my way.

Today I'm walking on my own. A few Danes I met at the albergue are a little way ahead of me, but I deliberately hold back a bit. Sometimes I just want to walk and listen to my breathing, my footsteps and the tick-tock, tick-tock of my trekking poles. For it to become a walking meditation, constantly bringing me back to the present moment.

* * *

The landscape on the way to Nájera reminds me of the Boland. I see blue mountains in the distance and walk on dirt roads between rows and rows of vineyards. But what is different from the Boland is the soil: deep red here in La Rioja.

Shortly before the Camino I read an article on *The Guardian*'s website called "Why the modern world is bad for your brain". A neuroscientist wrote about our addiction to technology and made the point that multitasking is a myth.

I like multitasking and I'm often working on a number of projects at the same time – the greater the variety, the better.

But the article warned of the "cognitive cost" of this: you think you're multitasking, but your brain is switching frantically from one task to the other. This perpetual loss of focus makes you much less productive than you think.

Smartphones and social media fuel this fire: every email, Facebook message or WhatsApp that arrives distracts you. You need to make new decisions about how and when – and even whether – you are going to respond. This quickly becomes so addictive that your brain regards this loss of focus and the instant hit of new messages as a kind of "reward".

The article refers to a rat study: When the rats in the study pressed a lever, a part of their brain that regulated dopamine levels got activated. According to the article, this is the same part of the brain that is activated when you win at a gambling table, sniff cocaine or have an orgasm. You get a dopamine hit whenever you are "rewarded" with new messages on your smartphone.

The rats enjoyed this dopamine reward so much that they wanted more and more. They kept pressing the lever, and even stopped eating and sleeping.

The result? They eventually dropped dead.

Walking through the vineyards of La Rioja, I'm far removed from all the little levers that compete for our attention in modern life.

Perhaps walking is the best way to cure us of this digital dependence. The illustrator Maira Kalman writes: "The ability to walk from one point to the next point, that is half the battle won. Go out and walk. That is the glory of life."

I drink a café con leche and eat a banana and a bocadillo at a little café in Ventosa. I have already walked twenty kilometres today, mostly through vineyards and, here and there, an olive grove. I saw the odd red poppy and blue cornflower along the road.

A demanding ten kilometres to Nájera lies ahead. The walking is particularly enjoyable today. The toe that had me almost in tears yesterday still hurts, but I'm used to it now. The Camino tests your pain threshold in so many ways. I'm finding that the best way to deal with the pain is simply to keep walking. On with the corpse.

The Catholic legends fascinate me. According to my guidebook, there have been frequent bloody conflicts between Christians and Muslims through the ages in this part of La Rioja. According to the legends, Roland, the renowned Christian knight and nephew of Charlemagne, defeated the Muslim giant Ferragut here, just outside Ventosa. The story reminds me of the Bible's David and Goliath: Roland killed Ferragut with a stone from his slingshot. The legend claims that Poyo de Roldán, a hill outside Ventosa, is the very stone Roland used to vanquish the giant.

* * *

There's a wall just beyond the river Yalde, four kilometres before you get to Nájera. On the wall is a long poem written in Spanish and German by Eugenio Garibay Baños, a priest from Nájera. The words are touching:

Dust, mud, sun and rain
is the Way of Saint James.

160

Thousands of pilgrims
and more than a thousand years.

Pilgrim, who calls you?
What hidden force attracts you?
It's not the Field of the Stars,
nor the grand cathedrals.

It is not the courage of Navarra,
or the wine of the people of La Rioja
nor the seafood of Galicia
nor the countryside of Castile.

Pilgrim, who calls you?
What hidden force attracts you?
It's not the people of the Way
nor their rural customs.

It is not their history and culture
or the cockerel of Calzada
nor Gaudí's palace
nor the castle in Ponferrada.

I see it all in passing
and it is a joy to see it all
but the voice that calls me
I feel much deeper still.

The force that drives me
the force that attracts me
I cannot explain it.
Only the One above knows.

Nájera is a quiet town at the foot of dramatic red sandstone cliffs – the name has Arabic roots and appropriately means "place between the rocks".

In the last five kilometres before reaching the town, I encountered my friend Jesus from San Sebastian. After walking nearly 25 kilometres in silence, it was nice to talk to someone again. Jesus mentions that he has booked at Puerta de Nájera, a private albergue next to the river with 32 beds.

You can't book in advance at the municipal albergues and monasteries, but many walkers phone private albergues, guesthouses and hotels to reserve accommodation before their arrival. You can also arrange for your rucksack to be ferried from hostel to hostel, but this also needs to be booked in advance.

I can understand that this is good for planning and peace of mind. But for someone without a phone it can get very frustrating to find most hostels fully booked when you arrive in a town. You have to make an early start and reach your destination at about two o'clock, when most albergues open.

I try to find a spot in Puerta de Nájera. The albergue looks full of character. I join the queue in the lobby, with seven people ahead of me.

When I'm second in line, the hospitalero announces: "Completo! Completo!" I'm dispirited – I was *so* close.

My only other affordable option is the municipal albergue. On the way there I bump into the friendly Italians, Francisco and Alessandro, whom I met at the albergue in Sansol. They want to sleep for a few hours somewhere in Nájera and then walk through the night to Santo Domingo de la Calzada. I wish them luck but think to myself, like Obelix in the *Asterix* books, "These Romans are crazy!"

The commotion at the municipal albergue reminds me of an average afternoon at Home Affairs. We are almost 100 people, making a winding queue in the dining hall in the hope of getting a bed for the night.

It occurs to me that I'm waiting more patiently than usual. I'm usually making a plan to get to the front of the queue by now, or to bypass it altogether through some shortcut. After nine days of walking, the impulse to do this has weakened. The Camino provides.

Accommodation is free, or on a donativo basis. My guidebook suggests that I donate at least five euros for a night in this kind of albergue.

"Please wait patiently, there are enough beds!" the hospitalero calls out over the din. I immediately recognise her accent as South African.

Anna Kapp is from Durban and is working for a few weeks at the albergue in Nájera as a hospitalero. After her husband's death two years ago, she started hiking regularly, and came to do the Camino – which has since called her back to serve other pilgrims.

It's nice to speak a bit of Afrikaans again. Anna mentions that a few South Africans have passed through over the past week, including a gent who turned 70.

The dormitory is intense and jam-packed: ninety bunk beds in one room, pushed up against one another with no partitions between the mattresses – you could literally spoon with the man or woman lying next to you. And you have no control, of course, over who might creep into the bed next to yours . . .

Opposite me (not on the same bunk bed) is Candy, an eighteen-year-old from Canada. She's also walking the

Camino on her own. She is trying to load airtime onto her phone to let her parents know she is safe. "They are stressing so much, I keep telling them it's okay, I'm fine, and I'm enjoying it," she says.

She has finished school and wants to travel and see more of the world before deciding what to study. I am surprised every day by the variety of reasons why people decide to undertake the pilgrimage to Santiago. Fitness, the beauty of nature, hope of spiritual growth, to process a loss ... Everyone's reason is valid, and none ranks higher than any other.

Again, I perform my rituals: shower, change into my clothes for the evening, wash some clothes by hand and hang them outside.

A large man is busy in the communal kitchen. This albergue does not have a restaurant, but pilgrims can prepare something themselves in the kitchen.

I sit in the dining hall and weigh up my options. A nap is on the cards. I could explore the town, maybe get something to eat, or just relax here and write a few ideas in my Moleskine diary. Today's thirty kilometres was the furthest I've walked in one day. I am tired, but feel much stronger and fitter than I did ten days ago.

Just as I'm getting up to go and find something to eat, the large man comes out of the kitchen into the dining hall.

"Hola! Would you like something to eat?"

He sets a plate of food in front of me: meatballs with creamy cheese sauce, cabbage and potato. Bernardo is a chef at a Spanish restaurant, Casa Conzuela, in Berlin. He has rustled up a huge pot of food from leftover vegetables that pilgrims left behind in the fridge. All he had to buy was the meat.

Bernardo dishes up a few more plates and hands them out to the people in the dining hall. What a generous gesture. Another of the Camino's gifts, even in such a cramped albergue.

Humans are complicated creatures – capable of shocking ideas and atrocious deeds, but also of showing one another immeasurable goodwill.

It strikes me that Bernardo's spontaneous gesture has made him part of a centuries-old tradition of care and charity on the Camino. Of giving, without expecting anything in return.

* * *

On the washing line outside the albergue hangs a T-shirt with the words: "Be humble, you may be wrong."

* * *

A Korean man stumbles into the albergue, blind drunk. I have just brushed my teeth. Anna and her staff try to deal with this; it doesn't seem like he booked a bed earlier in the day. And no one knows where his rucksack and shoes are. The poor man looks like he is about to collapse. He mumbles something, but nobody understands.

But it's not like the Camino to turn away anyone in need, especially not from a municipal hostel. Anna decides to find a place for him to lie on a mattress somewhere on the dormitory floor, before he falls out of a bunk bed and makes an even greater spectacle of himself.

I feel sorry for the guy. What's his story? What brings him to this place, all the way from South Korea? And why have the wheels come off for him tonight?

When he shuffles past my bed ten minutes later with the help of two hospitaleros and another pilgrim, he steps on one of the bags next to the beds. I hear something crack. Candy's scallop shell, the one she's carried for 200 kilometres from Saint Jean, lies in pieces on the ground.

She's already fast asleep.

Day Ten, Friday 15 May
From Nájera to Santo Domingo de la Calzada
(21 kilometres)

Walking for the sake of walking. That's what I'm doing this morning, with the little town of Santo Domingo de la Calzada my provisional destination.

The day's walk starts with a steep hill outside Nájera, through a pine forest and past a few vineyards. About 100 of us left the town at the same time. I'm walking alone once again. The pilgrims spread out quickly, especially when the landscape opens its arms with green fields stretching into the distance on all sides.

Sometimes two or three bicycles pass us – people ride mostly in groups. I usually hear the wheels and make sure I'm not in the middle of the road, but more often than not the cyclists ring their bells anyway or call out "Hola!" or "Buen Camino" before they pass. This can be an irritation; sometimes, I catch myself feeling a bit superior to the cyclists. But then I remind myself: the Camino belongs to everyone.

I'm very relieved that the Camino does not feel overcrowded. Not yet, anyway. I'll have to see what it's like when I eventually reach Sarria, about 100 kilometres before Santiago de Compostela. But that's literally weeks away.

I wonder how Candy reacted this morning when she saw her flattened scallop shell. And how serious was the

Korean's hangover? Does he have any idea where his ruck-sack is?

When my thoughts stray, I calmly bring them back to my immediate environment: the narrow dirt road stretching almost to the horizon, the sounds of the birds, the tick-tock of my trekking poles, my footfall, the voices of the pilgrims in the distance.

I focus only on what I'm experiencing in the moment. Years ago I read an article in the *New Yorker* about a remote tribe in the Amazon, the Pirahã. The Pirahã are completely geared towards living in the moment. When someone walks away, out of sight, they use the word "xibipio", which means that person has "gone out of experience". The article also mentions that the Pirahã regard the dancing light of a candle as something that constantly "goes in and out of experience". On the Camino I try consciously to remain "within the experience". I hope something of this mindset survives when I am back in Cape Town.

I repeat my mantras to focus my thoughts while I'm walking: "Ultreia", "On with the corpse" and "Caminante, no hay Camino". Initially I repeated them in my thoughts, but now I say them out loud, especially when I'm walking long distances without any other pilgrims near me. I don't want to alienate people with my little habits.

For some reason the title of a Breyten Breytenbach poem pops into my head as a new mantra: "Is klaps par gel te nar." I have no idea what it means, but the words fit the rhythm of my trekking poles exactly.

For the next three kilometres or so, until I get to the village of Azofra, this is all I do: walk through farmland and say aloud, "Is klaps par gel te nar".

* * *

I walk past a wooden post with the words *A Santiago 581 kms* on it and a yellow arrow pointing ahead. A long road to the famous cathedral still lies ahead.

On the hilltop I see two young guys – in their twenties, I'd say – sitting at a table next to the road. On the table there are bananas, sweets, biscuits and oranges. They also have cans of cool drink in a cooler box. Scribbled on a piece of cardboard are the words: *We haven't job. Spain: 60% younger unemployment. (Pay what you want.) Good Way!*

I support them with three euros for some freshly squeezed orange juice. I have heard about Spain's economic crisis and unemployment rate of over twenty per cent, more than double that of other European countries such as Portugal and Italy.

There is also a picnic spot here with an absurd road sign: a stick figure sitting on its haunches with a red line drawn across it, and the words *Prohibido Defecar / Don't Shit*.

* * *

I am eight kilometres from Santo Domingo de la Calzada. Cirueña wins the prize, hands down, for the strangest village so far. The Rioja Alta golf course and clubhouse are completely deserted. There's a whole suburban development here – houses, tall blocks of flats, a park for children to play in – but not a single soul in sight. Everything is completely empty, with *Se Vende* signs in the windows . . . for sale.

It feels like something from Cormac McCarthy's *The Road* or Andrew Niccol's *The Truman Show*. A modern ghost town made of cement, probably built a decade ago, when developers were more optimistic about Spain's economy. Yet it seems people have never lived here. After all the glorious vineyards, it's sobering.

The village does have an "old" part with a church, a few houses and an albergue, but I head for Santo Domingo de la Calzada. This post-apocalyptic concrete jungle makes me nervous.

* * *

At high school one of my more eccentric Afrikaans teachers, Joe Cloete, awakened a love of creative writing in me. In my matric year he compiled an anthology of haikus, *Deur die oog van die son* (*Through the Eye of the Sun*), which consisted mostly of contributions from learners. Haikus were among the first poems I attempted to write.

Near Santo Domingo de la Calzada a new haiku occurred to me:

almost like the song
I will walk five hundred miles
to Santiago

* * *

After the municipal albergue in Nájera, I want to find less crowded accommodation in Santo Domingo de la Calzada. Fortunately, I'm in time to find a bed at Abadía Cisterciense, a seventeenth-century convent.

I give five euros to an elderly nun who speaks only Spanish and comes across as a bit stern. There are 33 beds in five rooms. The convent has a cosy refectory with a fireplace, a terrace and a lovely garden.

I shower, catch a siesta (one of my most enjoyable discoveries on the Camino) and head off to explore the town. I take my washing with me in case I find a laundry. It's cloudy and I don't want to risk my clothes getting a second soaking on the washing line.

Santo Domingo de la Calzada (Saint Dominic of the Road) is named after Domingo García, a priest who did groundbreaking work in the eleventh century: Not only did he build a pilgrim's hospital, but he was a road builder too. He built many of the local roads and bridges to ease the pilgrims' journey to Santiago.

The village centre is gorgeous: it has the same authentic medieval feeling as the old part of Pamplona, with narrow streets, little restaurants and an impressive cathedral that anchors the village.

But what makes the village truly unique is the legend of the Miracle of the Rooster.

In the Middle Ages a German pilgrim called Hugonell walked the Camino with his parents. When they stayed over at an albergue in Santo Domingo de la Calzada one night, the owner's daughter fell head over heels in love with the young Hugonell.

But Hugonell did not feel the same way about her. This enraged the girl and she decided to take revenge. Before Hugonell and his parents left, she hid a silver cup in his bag. She then claimed that Hugonell had stolen it. The poor boy was found guilty and hanged, which was the punishment for theft in those days. His parents were shattered, but continued their walk to Santiago.

On their return journey they wanted to visit the grave of their son, but they found Hugonell hanging on the gallows, still full of life! He asked his parents to tell the mayor of the village that a miracle had occurred in Santo Domingo, which brought him back to life.

The parents went to the mayor, who was having lunch. When he heard that Hugonell was still alive, he exclaimed:

"That boy is as much alive as these two roast chickens we are about to eat!" At that moment the two roosters came to life before their very eyes and started crowing.

To this day there is a saying in the village: "Santo Domingo of the Way, where the roosters crow after being roasted."

The village seized the opportunity to use this legend to boost tourism. Several restaurants have a rooster in their logos, and shops sell rooster memorabilia.

The strangest tradition is the chicken coop inside the cathedral, where a hen or rooster is always kept in honour of the legend. It apparently bodes well if you hear the rooster crow while you're inside the cathedral.

* * *

I bump into Robert again. He had a good rest in Logroño and gave his feet a chance to heal. He is ready to start walking again tomorrow.

There is a private albergue in the next village, Viloria de Rioja, which sleeps only ten pilgrims. It is supported by Paulo Coelho and Robert has gone ahead and reserved accommodation for the two of us for tomorrow night. We are both Paulo Coelho fans.

We have a beer at La Gallina, a popular rooster-themed bar. Sabine, the German girl I met earlier, is sitting with us.

Sabine and I are both curious about the chicken coop in the cathedral and decide to go and have a quick look. There's a big village festival on the go, and the cathedral is packed; you can follow the proceedings on the many TV screens inside. A weird contrast: centuries-old architecture meets brand new flat-screen TVs.

The church service is in Spanish, unfortunately, so neither of us can follow along. "Where's the rooster? I want to see the rooster!" Sabine calls out and we both start giggling uncontrollably. How ridiculous, to go looking for a chicken coop in a cathedral.

Just as we are about to give up, we both hear the rooster crowing at the top of its voice. I am thrilled – a bit of good luck is always welcome.

* * *

The Abadía Cisterciense may be a convent full of nuns, but the refectory is lively. The fireplace is crackling away – for the atmosphere more than anything, as it's not cold outside.

I see Claire again, the American girl I met at the station in Bayonne. She introduces me to Manuel, a friendly Italian from Savona who restores frescos during office hours.

We sit around a table drinking beer and red wine and eating dry doughnuts. Marcella, whom I last saw in Sansol, is also here. At least she's not preoccupied with her iPad tonight. The two British gents from Estella, Ed and Ken, are also here.

Spanish, Italian and English reverberate around the table. It could just be the wine, but I'm starting to pick up more and more Spanish words and phrases.

* * *

Random thought in the middle of the night: if you listen patiently for long enough, a dormitory full of snorers begins to sound like the deep guttural throat-singing of Buddhist monks, the faintly out-of-tune white noise of dreamland.

Day Eleven, Saturday 16 May
From Santo Domingo to Viloria de Rioja
(14 kilometres)

Robert and I meet again early in the morning for coffee at La Gallina. There are a few newsflashes on the TV in the bar. I feel very far removed from the outside world. From news.

There's been another big earthquake in Nepal. I hope my friend Sam is safe. After the previous earthquake she went there to help and take photos.

B.B. King has died at 89. A great spirit. My love of the blues began in an unusual way. At university I used to correspond with Koos Kombuis by email. It was just typical fan mail and I sometimes sent contributions to his *Ons Klyntji* magazine. After my first break-up I thought I'd send him a long email telling him the whole sorry tale.

Koos sent a short reply with a quotation: "It was a bad time for love, but a good time for the blues."

Claire also came to join us at La Gallina. We had a very pleasant evening chatting and laughing at the nuns' albergue. I hope I'll meet this genial American again, perhaps in two days' time at San Juan de Ortega.

* * *

My left arm is itching like mad this morning. I find four bite marks neatly grouped together on my elbow. I tell myself it was a mosquito, but I know I'm kidding myself: despite all my precautions, the bed bugs have had a party somewhere, perhaps between the nuns' sheets.

* * *

Before Robert and I hit the road, we visit the Santo Domingo de la Calzada cathedral and the adjoining museum. Robert is eager to hear the cock crowing in the coop for himself, but this morning the thing keeps quiet.

We stand in front of the imposing golden Renaissance altar, several storeys high and populated with angels and mythological beings depicted in the finest detail. The altar dates back to 1537.

But what amazes us even more is a vast Lego exhibit behind glass in a quiet corner of the cathedral's museum, without any context or explanation.

It's a scale model of a medieval village, with a cathedral, pilgrims and crusaders. All in Lego. Even a Lego reconstruction of Jesus' crucifixion. I find this very strange.

* * *

Today is the shortest walk of my Camino. Robert's blisters seem to have healed nicely and we're walking at the same pace, but we're both lost in our own thoughts. I keep thinking about Claire.

Am I in love yet again?

For kilometres on end we don't say a word. All I hear is the rhythm of our footsteps on the dirt road and the tick-tock, tick-tock of my trekking poles.

We leave La Rioja behind and enter a new province – Castilla y León. Wheat fields replace the vineyards of La Rioja. The bush around here is full of sunflowers and I think of a Gert Vlok Nel song: "Maar hy't swaar gesterf soos 'n sonneblom. En sonneblomme kom aaklig om" ("He died full of woe like a sunflower. And sunflowers die a horrible death").

God knows why predominantly sombre lyrics keep

coming to mind in landscapes that would keep postcard photographers busy for ages.

We pass a couple holding hands. It looks like new love. A Camino romance, mad love among the sunflowers.

* * *

On a wall in a bar in Viloria de Rioja: "Cada encuentro, es un encuentro consigo mismo" ("Every encounter is an encounter with yourself").

* * *

The married couple Acacio and Orietta are our hosts at the private albergue Acacio & Orietta. He's from Brazil, she's from Italy.

A few years ago Acacio walked the Camino himself and came across an old stone building in the hamlet of Viloria de Rioja. He knew immediately that he wanted to open an albergue on that spot.

But he had only 50 dollars. He asked his friend the writer Paulo Coelho for help. Since Coelho's book *The Pilgrimage* was published in 1987, it has played a significant role in the revival of the Camino. Paulo helped Acacio out and is still the spiritual godfather of the albergue.

The smell of incense hangs heavy in the room and soothing harp music plays in the background. There's a gift shop with some of Paulo's books, and photos on the wall of his visit to the albergue. I buy *Veronica Decides to Die*, one of his books that I have always wanted to read.

Acacio actually looks a bit like Paulo. I think most pilgrims who book a room here secretly hope he'll be at the albergue himself to give readings from his books come evening. On the way here Robert and I joked that the albergue might harbour a Paulo Coelho sect. The last thing I need is weird rituals or something like Stanley Kubrick's *Eyes Wide Shut* behind closed doors in rural Spain. All just silly flights of fancy, luckily.

Acacio's smile widens when he hears I've interviewed Paulo. He immediately googles the link to the interview on LitNet. "Let me tell Paulo that you finally came to the Camino, after all these years," he says, and starts typing an email.

Judit, a fitness instructor from Budapest, arrives at the albergue in the late afternoon. She helps me and Robert with some stretching exercises, something I've neglected so far. Judit looks like an Eastern European version of the former tennis player Amanda Coetzer.

It was *The Pilgrimage* itself that inspired Judit to come on the walk. She's been working luxury cruise liners for years and has criss-crossed the world. She came to walk the Camino to reflect on her current relationship. She also wants to try living at a slower pace.

The Camino tested her almost from the outset. "I was in such a hurry when I started. I was almost running across the Pyrenees and hurt my Achilles badly. But it really forced me to rest and take it slow," she says.

I'm happy I got to visit this unique albergue. Acacio and his wife are two special people. Long after the delicious communal supper, we're still talking at the table.

"All you need for the Camino is your backpack," Acacio says, "and an open heart."

Day Twelve, Sunday 17 May
From Viloria de Rioja to San Juan de Ortega
(33 kilometres)

After my shortest walking day yesterday, my longest one lies ahead today. I want to push all the way through to San Juan de Ortega, where there's only a historical monastery with a church and one albergue.

But the monastery is a secondary concern. What I really want is to see Claire again. She mentioned in Santo Domingo de la Calzada that she was aiming to overnight there.

After breakfast at Acacio & Orietta, Robert and I walk a hard eight kilometres. Even though Judit has only recently recovered from her Achilles tendon injury, she stays a little way ahead of us.

At the village of Belorado we drink from a fountain. It's still early on this Sunday morning. The village is deserted. I look up at a balcony and see an older Spanish woman, dressed in black, who quickly draws the curtains. She must have been keeping a beady eye on us through a gap in the curtains. Another art film scene. All that's missing are the subtitles.

* * *

A second haiku occurs to me outside Belorado:

every mile is
a syllable on the Way
to Santiago

* * *

At Villafranca Montes de Oca, Robert calls it a day. I don't know how he manages it – there are ten blisters on his feet. Either he's wearing the wrong shoes, or his bag is still way too heavy. Both, maybe.

He's going to call a taxi and see if he can get a place to stay in Agés, a few kilometres beyond San Juan de Ortega. We seem to have a way of bumping into each other, so I may see him again in Burgos. "See you later, brother from another mother!" he says as we say goodbye.

Judit and I walk the day's last twelve kilometres through a forest of pines and oaks. At a picnic spot outside town there is a sombre monument – a stone obelisk – commemorating the hundreds of people who were executed near here during the Spanish Civil War and buried in a mass grave.

On the monument are the words: "No fue inútil su muerte, fue inútil su fusilamiento" ("His death was not in vain; his execution was futile").

It's easy to forget how much blood has flowed through the ages – even relatively recently – near the Camino.

* * *

San Juan de Ortega's Romanesque church and monastery has been a haven for pilgrims since 1142. I don't see any modern buildings. The red and blue umbrellas at the bar aside, the place probably didn't look very different in the Middle Ages.

The albergue is fully booked, but the hospitalero offers me a mattress on the floor, which I readily accept. And as I go to put my bag down, Claire comes down the steps. She's on her way to mass.

It's my first mass on the Camino. The service is in Spanish, with lots of readings. But we've each received a little book with the text in Spanish and English.

The Pilgrim's Blessing at the end is very moving: "Be for them on the road companion, guide at the crossroads, breath in fatigue, defence in the dangers, shelter along the way, gentle breeze in the heat, shelter before the cold, light in the darkness, consolation in disappointments and firmness in its purposes, so that, with your guide, arrive unharmed at the end of his pilgrimage . . ."

Everyone who attended the mass receives a little pendant of the cross of San Juan de Ortega.

* * *

Claire and I have dinner together. It's the tradition here to have a bowl of garlic soup as a starter after the mass.

Claire is 24 and lives in Richmond, West Virginia. She is a devout Catholic. Her sister walked the Camino a few years ago. Until recently Claire worked on a farm project ensuring that low-income communities have access to healthy food. She loves music and writes her own songs, some of which she has recorded.

I'm a bit infatuated again . . .

Day Thirteen, Monday 18 May
From San Juan de Ortega to Burgos
(25,6 kilometres)

I couldn't find my orange trekking pole anywhere this morning. At most albergues you leave your trekking poles and shoes in the lobby or in the passage outside the rooms. There are usually shelves for the shoes and a holder for the trekking poles. Since my trekking poles didn't match, no one could have taken one by accident. It's not the end of the world – I should be able to buy a new one quite easily in a city like Burgos. But still, it upsets me a bit. I search the rooms and the area outside of the albergue with care.

Near the church I spot a middle-aged woman with a trekking pole – *my* orange one! The woman, who doesn't speak English at all and says something in what sounds like Danish, is very surprised when I point this out. But she returns the pole immediately. I don't think she was being malicious – probably just an oversight on her part.

* * *

In the bar in Agés the owner, who is both chef and waiter, scurries around like someone from a Spanish version of *Fawlty Towers*. He's dripping with sweat and curses and almost loses his temper when yet another person orders a tortilla de patatas. It seems his wife fell sick this morning, and now he has to do everything himself. All that's missing from the scene is for a waiter like Manuel in the TV series to say, "Aaah, si si!"

* * *

The Atapuerca caves, one of the most important archaeological sites in Europe, are not far from Agés. The most ancient human bones in Europe – up to 900 000 years old – were found there. I want to visit the caves, but they're three kilometres to the south of the Camino. I stick to my route. Ultreia!

All morning I sing aloud while I walk. Bonnie "Prince"

Billy's dark ballad "I See a Darkness" is at the forefront of my mind. It fits today's trekking pole rhythm perfectly, especially if I sing the song slowly.

And that I see a darkness
Did you know how much I love you
Here's a hope that somehow you
Can save me from this darkness

* * *

I sit outside the impressive cathedral in Burgos admiring the centuries-old sculptures and allegorical representations. Some of the panels are gruesome, showing sinners being devoured by demons or dragged into the pit of hell.

I think of Linda's theory about demons and fairies. Linda is a friend of mine from Wellington. She reckons we all have fairies and demons. When your fairies take a smoke break, your demons emerge. When this happens, you have to look each demon in the eye, give it a name, and then wrestle it until you're done. Then your fairies come back from their smoke break, because you've done what you had to do.

* * *

At a pharmacy in Burgos I buy ointment for the bed-bug bites. Fortunately, there are no new ones, but those that are there already still itch. It's a huge irritation.

There's a scale in the pharmacy. You can weigh yourself for twenty cents.

I now weigh 86,6 kg. I've walked off about five kilograms in two weeks!

Thoughts in a bunk bed in Burgos

I think the time has come for me to go rogue on the Camino. I can't help thinking that I'm neglecting my own personal journey.

Kilometres of the Meseta wheat fields lie ahead: a remote and mostly monotonous landscape where the villages are quite far from one another.

I want to get away from everyone for a while, put some distance between me and all the people I've met so far and spend more time doing my own thing. I'm sure I'll meet Robert again somewhere along the way, and that's okay too.

I don't need to overthink things, but it will be good to walk on my own again for a while, or I'll lose myself in the otherness of things and especially in the camaraderie. Not that that's a bad thing – I am on leave, after all. On holiday. But maybe I've gone too far "into the mild" these past few days.

I mustn't be too hard on myself either. That happens so easily. When you just walk like this, without the usual distractions, you can't help becoming more aware of your thoughts, and patterns especially, and ways of doing things.

Like how I'm often too accommodating of others at my own expense. Earlier this afternoon, when I finally sat down outside the cathedral after a long and busy day, I yearned for silence. Time on my own. I wanted to sit for a while, in council with my thoughts. I'd hardly opened my notebook when Robert arrived. It was good to see him again, but I fell in with his plans and the rest of the day was no longer my own.

Jeez, I can be neurotic. Like a Woody Allen, but without his sense of humour. Ouch.

I think another Camino lesson lies ahead: to reclaim my own space.

MESETA

"Walking, ideally, is a state in which the mind, the body, and the world are aligned, as though they were three characters finally in conversation together, three notes suddenly making a chord. Walking allows us to be in our bodies and in the world without being made busy by them. It leaves us free to think without being wholly lost in our thoughts."

– Rebecca Solnit, *Wanderlust*

Day Fourteen, Tuesday 19 May
From Burgos to Hontanas
(32 kilometres)

I leave Burgos at the crack of dawn, feeling a bit like I'm getting a cold again. It's chilly and raining. Not one of the most pleasurable mornings on the Camino.

I'm wearing my fleece but I wonder if I shouldn't have put my thermal underwear on. Too late to fret about it now. All I want is to make it out of Burgos's busy streets in one piece and hit the Meseta.

I'm curious about the landscape between Burgos and León that stretches for some 200 kilometres – a part of the Camino that many Americans apparently prefer not to walk because it's so monotonous.

At one of the pedestrian crossings on the outskirts of Burgos I meet Nozomi, a doctor from Japan. She is dressed entirely in purple: purple raincoat, purple rucksack, purple slacks, purple trekking poles and purple shoes. Purple is her look, and it suits her.

I, on the other hand, would need to avoid this look. I'd just resemble a Boere version of Barney the purple dinosaur.

Again, the Camino takes a different course to the one I planned so earnestly in bed last night. Nozomi and I walk at the same pace and she is pleasant company. Who knows, it might be a good thing to be walking near a doctor if this cold of mine gets out of hand.

She tells me about her life in Japan, her strict parental home, and that she wants to travel for a year now that she's finished studying. Later, she might specialise in plastic surgery.

But most of the time we just walk, and that's good, and enough. Nozomi also has two trekking poles so we tick-tock, tick-tock, tick-tock the day's first few kilometres away.

Later we talk rugby a bit. In October the World Cup will take place in England and Wales, and South Africa is playing a group match against Japan. In 2019, of course, Japan hosts the competition.

I've been thinking about making a plan to go to the tournament in Japan for a long time. To see what can happen when sushi, saké and shosholoza meet.

"Erns, do you pray rugby?" Nozomi asks.

I have to suppress a grin. But Nozomi is onto something. After all, rugby is a religion in South Africa.

* * *

Nozomi and I rest in a bar in the village of Rabé de las Calzadas. I can only hope that the trinity of freshly squeezed orange juice, café con leche and tortilla de patatas helps this cold. Claire and the Italian guy Manuel, whom I last saw at Santo Domingo de la Calzada, join us. Two of Manuel's friends, Juan Antonio and Emerius, both from Spain, also sit at the bar.

I stick to my rituals: every time I stop for at least a quarter of an hour, I take off my shoes and socks and rub a thin layer of Vaseline on each foot before putting them on again.

I enjoyed walking the first ten kilometres with Nozomi today. She's good company. But now I want to walk on my own for a while. I don't make any grand announcements. I pick up my rucksack and walking shoes and say: "I'm heading off. See you guys along the Way. Buen Camino!"

Only time will tell whether I'll see any of these lovely people again. It's highly likely, as we do walk at a similar pace. The only way to break away entirely from a group of pilgrims would be to get thirty kilometres ahead of them by bus or taxi. That would be drastic, and unnecessary, though. But I still keep thinking how each interaction with somebody along the Camino could be the last time we meet.

There's a steep hill about a kilometre beyond the village. A young Korean woman walks by, greets me and starts chatting. Daria is originally from Seoul, but is a maths teacher in Frankfurt these days.

She tells me that a book about the Camino by the Korean writer Kim Hyo Sun has done so well over the past few years that thousands of Koreans have travelled to Spain, more than 10 000 kilometres away, to walk it. Many Koreans, almost a third of the population, are also Christians.

Daria is fitter than I am and climbs the hill quickly and energetically. I want to walk on my own for the rest of the day anyway, so this suits me fine.

On the hilltop, there's a stunning vista waiting for me: the Meseta in all its glory. Kilometres and kilometres of green wheat and oat fields as far as the eye can see, on either side of the narrow dirt road that passes through the village of Hornillos del Camino and beyond to the horizon, where a few wind turbines keep watch on a ridge. On the dirt road miles below, I see Daria walk on, doggedly.

I find this stripped-down, simple landscape extremely beautiful. I cannot understand why pilgrims would choose to take the train or bus from Burgos to León.

I planned to overnight in Hornillos del Camino, but today I want to walk further than just twenty kilometres.

The next village, Hontanas, is eleven kilometres away.

A light breeze picks up. I think back to Day Three, when Rubí and I watched the wheat fields rolling like waves in the wind. The scale of what I'm seeing around me now is incomparable to what we saw outside Pamplona. I hope it's going well for Rubí, wherever she's roaming on the Camino del Norte.

* * *

Ever since I heard of the Camino I've wanted to lie in a wheat field. Here's my chance. In the Meseta, somewhere outside Hontanas.

I see absolutely no one else, just the green, undulating wheat fields and the dirt road. That's all. I drop my trekking poles and rucksack on the ground, walk a few metres into the wheat field and fall flat on my back, arms wide. A soft landing between green sheaves.

I close my eyes and listen to nature: cicadas, birds, the rustling wind.

Joseph Campbell wrote: "If you follow your bliss, you put yourself on a kind of track that has been there all the while, waiting for you, and the life that you ought to be living is the one you are living."

This is what bliss feels like.

Once, when I was on the road outside Carolina in Mpumalanga on assignment for *Go*, I saw a road sign with the word "Geluk". I immediately turned off onto the dirt road to find this place called Happiness. If Happiness is a destination, I want to go, I thought, tongue in cheek. I couldn't find it that day, though. In any event, it used to be the name of a farm that had since been subdivided into several plots.

But here, in this moment, blissful and on my back, I

realise: happiness is a place along the way. It does not await you at the cathedral in Santiago, or in the arms of a lover. Happiness is not a reward for the outcome of some or other project. Happiness is here and now. The words of the Buddha against the wall of the albergue in Saint Jean prepared me for this: "There is no way to happiness. Happiness is the way."

I have no idea how long I've been lying in the wheat field – three minutes, or thirty. I'm yanked from my meditative bliss by a worried cyclist standing over me, peering down and asking, "Are you okay?" He must have seen my trekking poles and bag lying in the road and decided to investigate.

"Thanks for asking, but I'm more than okay," I answer with a smile. "I'm happy."

* * *

You get completely obsessed with your feet when you walk the Camino. I have never been so intensely aware of mine in my life. The daily care, the Vaselining, the forensic investigations into blisters, current or imminent . . .

I'm sitting in the bush, cutting my toenails. Years ago, I walked past the old Dorp Street Theatre Café in Stellenbosch. Gert Vlok Nel was sitting on the stoep, cutting his. We talked a bit. I don't remember what we spoke about, but at one point he said, "Erns, we have to unlearn love."

I've come close, Gertjie, but I don't think a single one of us has managed it yet.

* * *

Entry in Moleskine diary

There are two kinds of men in the world. One gets a massage by two girls at the same time – the Thinking Man's Prom Queen (neck, back and backside) and a hot Japanese doctor thinking of specialising in plastic surgery (thighs, knees and calves). The other kind sits and watches, then writes about it in his diary later.

Day Fifteen, Wednesday 20 May
From Hontanas to Boadilla del Camino
(27 kilometres)

Last night I dreamt about J.P. This is his third appearance in my dreams.

The first dream was in 2013, when I was seriously considering resigning from my job to study psychology full time. In the dream we were in a little village – presumably a university town such as Grahamstown or Stellenbosch – where J.P. led me to an old, almost medieval-looking house. We climbed up a wooden ladder to the attic, a small room with a low roof. J.P. was holding a lit candle in a candlestick. In the attic he pointed to bookshelves groaning under the weight of all the books.

My second dream about J.P. was also in 2013. I'd made an appointment with a new therapist, Peter, in Rondebosch. J.P. knew Peter. The night before the appointment I dreamt I couldn't for the life of me find the therapist's house. I realised I was going to be late for the appointment. In the dream J.P. led me straight to the right address.

Last night, in Hontanas of all places, in a small dorm with three old guys from Brazil, I dreamt about J.P. again.

He leads me to an American dude in a township, where a strange ritual is being performed: a kind of tomb is being built of fleshy-looking bricks to commemorate dead people. You sit at a machine and use a mouthpiece like at the dentist. Then you drink a concoction made of the ashes of your parents – your father and your mother – which have been mixed into an orange fluid. You swallow it and start to vomit. The bricks are made of the puke. So you first need to process them yourself. In the dream J.P. or someone starts vomiting and I also retch and rush to the bathroom . . .

It cannot be a coincidence that I dream such things on the Camino. I would really like to discuss this with Peter. I'm assuming it has something to do with psychic purification. Rather than representing the rejection of my parents, it may indicate an initiation or coming of age, of me finding my own voice and feet.

* * *

I leave Hontanas early in the morning. My cold is getting worse: my throat is sore and my head feels swollen.

I still intend to walk alone today. Robert mentioned in Burgos that he could meet me in Castrojeriz, but I don't want to make too many plans or create too many expectations.

I see a fox among the red poppies in the field. It feels like a nature scene from a Disney movie.

* * *

My first visit to a movie theatre was a disaster. My father and I went to the old Protea cinema in Uitenhage to watch the Disney version of *Snow White*. Everything went well until the scene when the evil mother-in-law changes into a terrifying banshee. During this animation transformation I squealed like a pig, so much so that my father had to put me on his hip and leave.

I still haven't seen the end of *Snow White and the Seven Dwarfs*.

* * *

Graffiti outside Hontanas: *This is not Hollywood. Go home you "The Way" tourist. Greenland was here.*
Also: *James I miss you. Danila.*

* * *

One of the more ridiculous Camino images: two Koreans, en route to Castrojeriz, carrying a huge box, in addition to their rucksacks. The box is full of packets of noodles – their whole group's staple while in Spain.

* * *

In Castrojeriz I bump into Claire, Nozomi, Manuel, Juan Antonio and Emerius. They're a really nice group of pilgrims so I decide to walk with them for a while, in spite of my plans.

I'm relieved that my infatuation with Claire has left me. It was like a fever – a Camino crush – that appeared from nowhere, but is now under control.

Looking back over my life, I see that these fits of love-sickness have been pretty common. In a corny Afrikaans love song I wrote at university I tried to articulate the dilemma: "Verward oor die eise wat die werklikheid stel / verward oor die grens tussen lover en pel" ("Bewildered by the demands of reality / confused about the boundary between lover and pal").

This is what the Camino does: in the absence of distractions, your issues flash along the way like glittering Las Vegas billboards. Especially here in the Meseta.

* * *

In Castrojeriz I teach my walking companions to sing "Shosholoza". I explain the basic details, that it was originally sung by miners, that the "stimela" mimics a steam train and that the song became a sort of second national anthem during the 1995 Rugby World Cup.

And so we walk, singing through the streets of Castrojeriz, an American, an Italian, a Japanese, two Spaniards and me: *Shosholoza / Kulezo ntaba / Stimela siphume South Africa.*

* * *

At Boadilla del Camino we decide to overnight at the Albergue Putzu. It's been a long, hot day with almost no shade among the wheat fields of the Meseta. I've walked 27 kilometres.

The village is tiny – only about 140 people live here. It's a typical Camino village: a small church, a village square and a few streets with old houses on large plots. But Albergue Putzu is unusual. It looks like someone's home.

There are also no other pilgrims – just a man with an intense look in his eyes in blue overalls spattered with white paint. The man and Manuel have a long discussion in Spanish. Is he a worker? Is the place closed for renovations, perhaps?

The man keeps casting quick glances in our direction and it sounds as if he is asking lots of questions.

Manuel comes to report back. The name of the man in the overalls is Serafin and he is the owner. But he doesn't take in just any walkers and personally decides who gets to overnight in his albergue. We are apparently welcome for the night, but he suggests we have a look at the other albergues in the village before we decide.

It's difficult to take Serafin's measure. He looks a bit headstrong, like someone with a temper. The long conversation with Manuel was presumably an "interview".

The other two albergues are both fully booked, and so we walk back to Serafin. Suddenly, he's shed the menacing attitude he had earlier.

"Welcome to my house, peregrinos. But for tonight this is your house," he says.

It feels nothing like an albergue. There's a large room, an extension to the house, with sixteen bunk beds and a bathroom with showers, but the rest is all Serafin's private domain. We have the whole place to ourselves.

Nozomi and I have a long discussion while showering (in two showers next to one another) about my cold, her conservative family and the freedom and growth that she is experiencing on the Camino. She's concerned about how she will reconcile these two worlds once she returns to Japan.

In the lounge Claire is playing the guitar. She starts with Leonard Cohen's "Hallelujah" and we all sing along.

* * *

August 2003. My friend Vicky and I are in my Volkswagen Chico on the way to Green Point to see Amanda Strydom's cabaret *State of the Heart*, with Leonard Cohen's "Hallelujah" playing on the car's CD player: "Yeah and I've seen your flag on the marble arch, but listen love, love is not some kind of victory march, no it's a cold and it's a very broken hallelujah . . ."

"I want this song played at my funeral one day," I remark.

"That could work," she says. "But let's not go there."

I was 23 years old and still working as content manager at LitNet in Stellenbosch. I had to proofread and publish letters on the LitNet letters page, SêNet, and encourage debates and discussions behind the scenes. This was long before comments sections and trolls on the internet and social media. At about that time I was also starting to write regular articles and do interviews.

Johannes Kerkorrel's suicide on 12 November 2002 generated an explosion of letters and tributes on SêNet. Amanda Strydom, a very good friend of Kerkorrel's, wrote a tribute and we corresponded regularly.

After the performance Vicky and I visited Amanda in a flat in Green Point. Amanda played her new album, *Verspreide Donderbuie [Scattered Showers]*, on the hi-fi. She recorded Kerkorrel's "Hoe ek voel" ("How I feel") on the new album and, in her own song "Ek het gedroom" ("I dreamt"), she took leave of her beloved friend in a most moving way.

We drove back to Stellenbosch in the early hours of the morning. About ten kilometres outside the town, we were involved in a serious collision with a bus. (I found out later that the bus driver's surname was Tyres . . .)

The back of the Chico was completely crushed – just a few centimetres away from where the impact of the collision had knocked our seats. Amazingly, we both survived and stumbled out of the wreckage with only a hard bump on the head.

One voice rose up above the post-crash admin and clearing up. Leonard Cohen kept singing from the battered Chico's CD player, just as he'd done before and during the accident: "Hallelujah, hallelujah, hallelujah, hallelujah."

Etienne van Heerden later described this as my mock funeral.

In a surprising turn five years later, Leonard Cohen began performing again at the age of 74 and announced a world tour. I transferred my salary directly to my overdrawn credit-card account, booked flights, and travelled to the Big Chill festival in the north of England, where Cohen was performing. In a crowd of 30 000 people, I hung on every word of this charming gentleman with his fedora, tailored suit and deep baritone voice.

Towards the end of his performance, as the sun was going down, he sang "Hallelujah". Thousands of us in the audience sang along with him. It was a sacred affair.

I stood there thinking of the car accident, immensely grateful to be alive and watching Cohen perform, "with nothing on my tongue but hallelujah".

* * *

The evening at the Albergue Putzu develops a momentum of its own. Manuel makes spaghetti bolognaise. Serafin joins us and makes sure our glasses stay fully charged with red wine. Dinner is an absolute feast – the Italian knows how to serve a pasta dish.

We play guitar, sing, laugh and dance until late into the night.

"No vino, oh, oh! No camino, oh, oh, oh, oh!" Manuel sings to the tune of "Volare" and we all sing along. "Cielito Lindo", too, which the hospitaleros sang in Roncesvalles.

I hear Claire sing one of her own folk songs for the first time. Her lyrics are striking: honest, raw and unpretentious. She should make a career of this.

Juan Antonio grabs the guitar and plays a lovely Spanish melody. He suggests we compose a song together: he plays the melody and everyone gets a chance to sing a verse in their own language that sums up their experience of the Camino.

I'm at least a bottle of wine down, and have to think on my feet:

ek stap nou die Camino	I'm walking the Camino now
ek soek antwoorde	I'm seeking answers
en vrae	and questions
en ek wandel en ek	and I'm wandering and
wonder	wondering
oor die dinge wat	about the things
my pla	troubling me

Serafin is an intense guy. He walked the Camino himself years ago – his Compostela certificate is framed on the wall. But he hates how commercial the Camino has become over the years.

"The Way is all about money nowadays. Money, money, money. All these stupid tourists, they don't know what The Way is about. They have no clue. They are tourists, not pilgrims."

By midnight we are all hungry again. Juan Antonio prepares a Spanish potato dish and serves it on a huge tray.

We each take a fork and polish off every single morsel on the tray. "Now you are eating like true pilgrims!" Serafin laughs.

Later he calls us all together to look at a painting on his wall. It is Serafin's reinterpretation of Pieter Bruegel's *The Blind Leading the Blind* – this famous painting shows how a group of blind men stumble and fall down in some rural village.

Serafin launches into a long monologue – half English, half Spanish – on the painting. The blind men are pilgrims, the church in the background looks like the church in Boadilla del Camino. And the shed in the painting is Albergue Putzu.

* * *

It was naïve of me to think the red wine would help cure my cold. It didn't. We only made it to our bunks after two.

Nozomi feels sorry for me and gives me some or other powder to dissolve in water, Japan's answer to Grand-Pa. She feels my forehead, stands back and makes her diagnosis: "Erns, you looks ba-a-a-d!"

Day Sixteen, Thursday 21 May
From Boadilla del Camino to Villalcázar de Sirga
(20 kilometres)

My morning routine (even with a proper hangover and a cold):

- Go to the loo, wash my face and brush my teeth.
- Fold my sleeping sheet, put it in its Ziploc bag and se-

cure it with an elastic band, stash it at the bottom of my rucksack.
- Pack my rucksack.
- Put on walking pants and long-sleeve shirt. Wear slip-slops.
- Walk back to bathroom for anti-blister ointment. Fill water bottle.
- Fetch walking boots from shelf at entrance to albergue.
- Sit outside, rub feet with Vaseline.
- Apply sunscreen.
- Put on ankle socks, then long socks and walking shoes.
- Fetch trekking poles.
- Have a quick coffee and croissant.
- Hit the road.
- Ultreia!

* * *

Today I need to make a plan about this cold, before it upgrades itself to flu or worse. I have started coughing, too.

Last night's party was great fun, but not the best medicine. Nozomi's Japanese powders haven't kicked in yet. The first six kilometres to Frómista are a real slog. Frómista apparently has one of the most impressive Romanesque churches in Spain, the Iglesia de San Martín. But I don't want to look at churches today. I need a pharmacy.

I buy Spanish cough mixture: Grintuss. On the bottle – featuring a picture of honey – there is a note about its calming effects: "Protege la mucosa calma la tos."

The Afrikaans word "tos" describes exactly how miserable I feel.

* * *

I've had worse coughs when I've been away. During my Kilimanjaro expedition in 2006 I nearly coughed myself into a coma.

The night I realised I was not going to make it to the summit due to altitude sickness, I lay in my tent coughing and wheezing. One of the guides, Theodolus, came to sit with me. I was so flat I couldn't even zip up my sleeping bag.

In the midst of a violent coughing fit Theodolus held a spoon in front of my mouth and shouted "HONEY, FUCK OFF!" This nearly scared the cough right out of me. Only once I'd tasted it did I realise that all he'd said was, "Honey, for cough."

* * *

I'm walking with the same group as yesterday. We are all a little less perky after last night's partying, but still laughing and singing and talking our way through the Meseta.

To the tune of "Country Roads" we sing:

Take me home, Camino
To the place where I belong
Santiago, Finisterre
Take me home, Camino.

I also teach them my favourite Xhosa word: "isimuncumuncu", which means "sweet things".

We find a bed for the night at the municipal albergue in the village of Villalcázar de Sirga. The hospitalero is Mike, from Michigan. He is in his sixties and manages the place on his own. He looks serene and satisfied with life.

While I'm hanging up my washing, I meet Mary from Quebec. She's a flight attendant, probably in her early thirties. She's very attractive, and looks a bit like the actress Juliette Binoche.

Mary gives me an unsettling glimpse into the challenges of walking the Camino alone as a young woman. "It's like I'm running the Camino. I'm just busy getting away from men who won't leave me alone. I have a boyfriend back home, I'm not here for romance," she says.

Spaniards and Italians are apparently the biggest culprits. Mary sometimes walks up to forty kilometres a day just to put some distance between her and the Camino Casanovas.

Day Seventeen, Friday 22 May
From Villalcázar de Sirga to Calzadilla de la Cueza
(23 kilometres)

We all wake with a fright when Mike, still foggy with sleep, opens the door to our room and walks in. "What's the time?" he asks.

I can see through the window that the sun is already high. We were supposed to be out of the albergue before eight.

"Half past eight," Emerius says cautiously.

I prepare to be told off, especially after last night's childish pyjama party in our room. Before we went to sleep Emerius and Manuel had a pillow fight and got up to all sorts of antics.

Hospitaleros are usually not at all amused when walkers don't behave themselves.

"Oh, well, so it is," Mike says with the kind of serenity you just can't buy. "Come have something in the kitchen, I'm boiling eggs," he proposes, then shuffles off to the kitchen, still wiping the sleep from his eyes. I'm intrigued by this tall American from Michigan (he would have made a good lock in club-level rugby) holding the albergue fort on his own.

We eat hard-boiled eggs for breakfast and pack our bags for the day ahead. But my cold is no better – I feel worse than I did last night, in fact.

I ask Mike's advice. He's mopping the floor. I'm my neurotic self.

"Sorry Mike, but I'm really battling with a cold. What should I do? Should I stay in bed or only walk to the next town? Do you think a day's rest will help? I was hoping to be in Sahagún in two days' time . . ."

He gives me just one look. "Walk it off," he says, and continues mopping. Deep Zen.

Who am I to argue with Mike?

* * *

I take leave of this group of Camino friends for the moment. I want to take it easy today. If I get to Carrión de los Condes after six kilometres and still feel this rough, I'm going to find an albergue or guesthouse and vegetate there for the rest of the day.

In the end, I persevere. Later, I walk the Via Aquitania, a Roman road that has been in use for over 2 000 years. It's a long and mercilessly straight road of almost twelve kilometres with hardly any shade and no facilities.

But I labour on with Mike's advice as my new mantra: Walk it off. Walk it off. Walk it off.

* * *

Walking along the Via Aquitania I think about my smart-phone for the first time in three days. I didn't go completely cold turkey, like in the movie *Trainspotting*. No imaginary babies crawling along the albergue's ceiling. But having no phone on the Camino *was* a bit harrowing at first.

Now I can very easily imagine life without one.

* * *

How many consecutive times can you sing Bonnie "Prince" Billy's "I See a Darkness" before it gets dangerous?

* * *

At the Albergue Camino Real in Calzadilla de la Cueza, the first little hamlet after the long Roman road through the Meseta, I decide to call a halt. Thanks, Mike – I've walked it off.

Someone's left a book of essays in the dormitory – David Sedaris's *Let's Explore Diabetes With Owls*. I love reading his work in the *New Yorker*. The book is heavy, but I'm going to cart it along for a few days to read.

Day Eighteen, Saturday 23 May
From Calzadilla de la Cueza to Sahagún
(22 kilometres)

Colin and Caleb remind me of W.O. Kühne's *Huppelkind* stories. I saw them last night at the albergue in Calzadilla de la Cueza. Colin is 76 and is walking the Camino with Caleb, his thirteen-year-old grandson.

I have seen many combinations of people on the Camino: young people in love, old married couples, families, groups of friends . . . but this is the first time I've met a grandfather and grandson en route to Santiago.

We walk together for about six kilometres on a dirt road heading towards Sahagún. The landscape is flat, bare and grey. The Meseta around here still looks very much like the Free State countryside. But more Clocolan than Clarens.

Interestingly, the grandfather sets the pace, and even I need to walk a bit faster than usual to keep up. Colin mentions that he has been active throughout his life and has always enjoyed hiking. I can see that. He has strong, sinewy legs. Wally Hayward legs. He is an experienced traveller. Even at his age he still regularly does missionary work in places like India and Pakistan.

Caleb seems to be a quiet, decent child. Not someone who sneaks out and gets up to mischief while grandpa is asleep in the evening.

Both of them write a daily blog about their Camino on an iPad. Colin is very surprised to hear that I am on a digital detox.

"That must take tremendous courage and discipline, Ernest. Don't you miss contact with your loved ones, though?"

Yes, naturally I miss them.

I calculate whether I'll be able to walk the Camino with a grandchild one day. The numbers are not in my favour. Unless I see my way clear to doing so in my eighties.

Strange how sad this thought makes me this morning. Maybe I long for the kind of connection I see between Colin and his grandson. And the fact that they're having such a major experience together, sharing it in the moment.

But there's something else in this Spanish no-man's-land that's stirring something in the depths of my psyche this morning. Colin reminds me of Uncle David.

I got to know David Evans, or Uncle David, in 2004 in Stellenbosch.

I was 24. It was a confusing time in my life – has it ever really been otherwise? The old Black Dog of depression was nipping at my heels. I enjoyed my work at LitNet very much, but was always in trouble for missed deadlines and late projects.

My so-called love life was ridiculous: if you were to publish *Bridget Jones's Diary* in braille and force someone who is not blind to read it, it would have been easier to understand. I had perfected the art of running after unattainable women like a headless chicken – especially those who were desperately unhappy in other relationships. I wanted to rescue *and* screw every broken-winged dove.

I was also excessively worried that I might have been the oldest virgin in the Western Cape.

My friend Reinette suggested that I go and talk to David, her uncle. He was a psychologist with a doctorate in theology. We immediately connected. He was in his mid-sixties at the time, a wise, gentle man. Carl Jung was one of his main influences.

David was short and gnome-like, and with his beard and pocket watch he looked like a traditional Jungian therapist. He was a keen cyclist and puffed away at his pipe on his bike.

David believed in Socrates' maxim: "The unexamined life is not worth living." He not only believed this, but lived it. He had the humility of a Socrates, in the sense that he knew he did not know.

We usually met on Tuesdays. I wish I had kept a diary or even recorded those sessions. I would have had more than enough material for a book about all his wisdom about life.

He would sometimes just sit back and exclaim, full of wonder, "Isn't life fascinating?" This was both a question and a confirmation.

One of his favourite movies was *Zorba the Greek* and he often quoted from it: "Life is trouble. Only death is not. To be alive is to undo your belt and look for trouble."

In February 2013 Uncle David drowned at Puntjie near Witsand. No one knows exactly what happened, but his fishing boat must have capsized.

His family asked me to write a little piece about him for the funeral notice. I wrote about a green postcard he had on his wall.

On the postcard was a quotation from Goethe: "The point of life is life." Just that. We often talked about the postcard. He would say, "You know the point of life is life. It's as simple as that. And if you look for something else you're missing the point." And we'd both laugh.

At the funeral his daughter Sarah gave me the postcard as a keepsake. It's the only thing on the wall above my desk in my Green Point flat.

Day Nineteen, Sunday 24 May
From Sahagún to Mansilla de las Mulas
(39 kilometres)

A thought while I'm brushing my teeth: I've been without my iPhone for nearly three weeks. I try to remember the PIN . . . but it's gone. I'm not the least bit worried.

* * *

Outside Sahagún there is another long and ancient Roman road, the Via Romana. At nineteen kilometres it is considerably longer than the Via Aquitania I walked two days ago. Augustus Caesar himself is said to have travelled here.

* * *

I'm thinking about all sorts of things today. This may have something to do with the mention of Augustus Caesar in Brierley's guidebook; I remember asking my Sub A teacher who performed Mary's caesarean in the stable at Bethlehem.

For a long time my rucksack has been a burden, but now it's become an ally. It's so liberating to know that what I'm carrying on my back is enough. There is no excess baggage.

I think of all the boxes in my flat in Green Point. All that stuff. Clothes, newspapers, magazines, paperwork and things I've been accumulating for years. How much of that stuff do I really need?

* * *

Random thought along the Via Romana: You can always walk further than you think. And you can always think further while you walk.

* * *

Entry in Moleskine diary

Walked almost 40 km today. I am totally buggered, but body and mind played along. Had breakfast this morning with Colin and his grandson Caleb from Canada. I'm actually too tired to write now; too tired to think. Is it really that bad? I am probably laying it on a bit thick, but there's a massive difference between walking 30 km and 40 km. True that. Now I'm sitting in the sun at a municipal albergue in a little town 18 km from León, having walked about 480 km so far. Today I walked the last few kilometres of the Via Romana with Claire. When we arrived at the albergue, we booked literally the last two beds. I also bumped into Alessandro, the Italian guy I last saw a few weeks ago. And met a Camino friend of Claire's, Timna, here. She is from Tel Aviv. My shoes are beginning to fall apart – a bit worrying – I'll have to make a plan in León. I think I'm going to have an orange now. Tonight there's risotto on the menu. I need to find something to do with my hands, like the man sitting opposite me carving something out of wood.

* * *

I was probably the worst woodwork pupil in the history of Laerskool Handhaaf in Uitenhage. I had a lovely woodwork teacher, but he'd often make me stand outside in the corridor – I was just too inept, a danger to myself and the other kids.

Once, I think it was in Standard 3, I actually managed to make a little boat out of a piece of wood. But my happiness was short-lived. When the teacher thrust a chisel into my hand and asked me to make the boat look a bit older and battered, within seconds there were three bits of boat on the table.

I stood in the corridor for the rest of the period.

Day Twenty, Monday 25 May
From Mansilla de las Mulas to León
(18 kilometres)

Graffiti outside León: *Wat maak wij met de rotten appels, mij lief?* – What should we do with the rotten apples, my love?

* * *

Entry in Moleskine diary

I could get used to life in Spain. It's just after half past three, I'm sitting in León behind the huge cathedral, very impressive city, I'm sitting on my own for a bit, walked about 18 km today, that's more or less 500 km in 20 days, of which I rested for one day so technically walked 500 km in 19 days. That's an average of 25 km per day, so right, that means precisely 20 days of walking left and I'm planning to walk about another 500 km: 300 to Santiago and then another 200 km to Finisterre, Muxía and back. Holy crap. León intense. Cathedral overwhelming. Met Alessandro, Claire and Timna again this afternoon. And another girl from Hungary, Bridget. She is also a fitness instructor. Also saw Sabine and Sebastian and the Brits Martin and his wife. My shoes will apparently be okay for another 500 km. Walk it off.

* * *

My parents have been married for nearly forty years. As is probably the case with all couples who have made a life together for decades, they've taken the crises, frustrations, boredom and forks in the road with the good times.

My father is an eternal optimist with an inborn enjoyment of life and an easy-going nature. He avoids conflict and tries to see and point out the good in others. My mother is a dynamo – always busy, and quick in thought and deed. She is also more sceptical about people and can be anxious. They butt heads every now and then, but never for long. They understand and tolerate one another's foibles. I don't think either can imagine a life without the other.

I suspect I've inherited a solid combination of my parents' strengths and quirks.

When it comes to their three children and four cats, their love and care are unstinting. Over the years my parents have sacrificed a great deal – too much, maybe. It's a pity they didn't travel more – they haven't been overseas together since their honeymoon in 1976, despite their best intentions and plans.

I hope the two of them will get to walk through a cathedral like this one in León one day.

A church played a large part in the start of my parents' relationship, actually. They are the same age and were in the same year at Hoërskool Brandwag in Uitenhage, but they didn't really know each other back then. My father was an extrovert, very sociable and a top sportsman. He earned Junior Springbok colours in amateur wrestling and wrestled in Europe and the USA while still at school.

My mother grew up on a farm outside Uitenhage and was more of an introvert. She excelled in music and played the piano, flute and accordion, among other instruments. In high school she was in a choir, Die Vrolike Vinkies (The Happy Finches), which recorded LPs and toured in Germany and Belgium.

One evening in June 1973 my father was on his way to a drive-in in Port Elizabeth with his girlfriend and her younger brother. He was 20 at the time and had been in a relationship with this girl since high school.

On the way to the drive-in a truck with no lights ran a stop street and hit my father's Volkswagen Beetle. The fuel tank exploded and the Beetle burst into flames. A fireman who happened to be driving behind them tried to pull all of them from the wreckage.

My father's girlfriend was killed in the accident and her brother died shortly afterwards in hospital. My father sustained serious burns, especially to his face and upper body. His next of kin started making funeral arrangements, but he clung to life and started on the long road to recovery with superhuman determination.

He was in the intensive care unit of the Provincial Hospital in Port Elizabeth for almost two months, then continued receiving intensive medical treatment, including plastic surgery. The doctors and nurses did not want him to see himself, so they removed all mirrors from the ward. He had to use a spoon or the LP records of the time to see his reflection.

Additional surgical reconstruction happened later at the Brenthurst Clinic in Johannesburg under Dr Jack Penn and his son John, who had previously treated burn patients in Hiroshima and Korea.

When my father could eventually carry on with his life, he attended prayer meetings at the Dutch Reformed Church North in Uitenhage regularly. My mother was the organist and recognised my father's voice when he prayed, but she couldn't place him. My father remembered her from their school days and went to say hello after one of the prayer meetings. She got such a fright when she saw him that she grabbed her sheet music and ran out of the church.

She phoned him later to apologise. They couldn't stop talking; within six months they were engaged.

On my parents' matric photo, taken five years before this reunion, my father sits cross-legged in the front row. Next to him is his girlfriend. And next to her is my mother.

* * *

Postcard to my parents

Monday 25 May 2015, 10 p.m. (still daylight here)

Hello Ma and Pa!

I'm sitting in a small square here in León in Spain in front of an incredible cathedral! (see photo) with over 1 800 m² of stained-glass panels inside, built in the 13th century.

Walked 500 km so far, almost exactly halfway because I'm going to walk further, over 1 000 km in 40 days. I'm safe, losing weight and thoroughly enjoying it all. The Camino is good for me. I miss you and hope all is well.

Much love, Erns

Day Twenty-one, Tuesday 26 May
From León to Villar de Mazarife
(22 kilometres)

I have now been walking for three weeks. Roughly 500 kilometres behind me. I have lost even more weight since Burgos – I can feel it in my clothes. Even when I look in the mirror when I'm brushing my teeth, I can see my cheeks look a little less chubby, despite my not holding back on the bread and starch at mealtimes. And every day, some-where along the Camino, I've had a beer, usually by late afternoon or evening. I think I'm turning into a bit of an epicure. Sorry, Tim Noakes, but screw banting. I'll walk myself thin.

This simple lifestyle is addictive. Get up in the morning, brush teeth, put on walking clothes, drink a café con leche, eat a croissant, walk, walk, walk, stop for a tortilla de patatas, drink another café con leche and a glass of freshly squeezed orange juice, walk, walk, walk, stop and eat a tin of tuna or order a bocadillo for lunch, walk, walk, walk, find an albergue, shower, wash clothes and hang them up to dry, have a siesta, drink a beer, get something for supper, read or talk, brush teeth, sleep. Do this for a month and your life will change, I think.

* * *

Today I'm walking with the Italian, Alessandro. We hap-pened to set out at the same time from the monastery in León, and we walk at the same pace.

Over the past few days I've handled the runaway thoughts better. When something comes up, it's as if I can create a natural distance between it and me – say to myself, okay, I am now thinking such and such. I take note of it. And I let it go. Ah, now I am thinking such and such. I take note of that too. And I let it go.

Walk, walk, walk . . .

We walk past the Casa de los Botines, an imposing mod-ernist palace designed by Gaudí. Alessandro is 39 and lives with his fiancée on a smallholding in the mountains near Verona. He needed a break from his job in packaging and courier services. He calls me Luigi – I think I remind him of one of the tubby plumbers in the Super Mario Bros. computer game.

"I want out, Luigi," he says. "The job is killing my soul. This here is freedom, how life should be."

He teaches me an Italian sentence: "Cosa stai facendo?" It means "What are you doing?" But if you say it slowly with hand gestures like a mumbling Marlon Brando in *The Godfather*, the phrase takes on a quite different kind of intensity.

I tell Alessandro about my visit to Verona almost three years ago. In September 2012 I spent four days in Italy with my father. We travelled all the way to Verona to see Leonard Cohen perform during his *Old Ideas* world tour. That was my second Cohen concert after the one in England in 2008.

It was my father's first overseas trip since his honeymoon in 1976. When I was a child he introduced me to Cohen's music with songs such as "Suzanne", "Bird on a Wire" and "So Long, Marianne", which played regularly in my parents' home.

Shortly before the concert Cohen had turned 78 and was busy with a world tour of 120 concerts across the whole of Europe, the USA, Canada and Australasia. This particular concert was held in the Arena in Verona, a Roman amphitheatre built in the year 30 AD. It's older than the Colosseum in Rome. The afternoon before the concert, a huge cloudburst over the city almost ruined the evening – concerts in the Arena are usually cancelled in such heavy rain. It looked like we were going to end up on the wrong side of life's Duckworth-Lewis calculation. But we were lucky: the weather improved in time.

For over three hours Cohen and his ten-piece orchestra entertained and consoled us in an ancient arena where lions and gladiators chased one another around centuries ago. It was very special to share this experience with my father. We spent a few carefree days in each other's company, sparing no expense.

I often think of Cohen's words towards the end of his concert as he bid the audience farewell: "And may you be surrounded by friends and family. And if this is not your lot, may the blessings find you in your solitude."

* * *

It takes a good two hours of energetic walking to escape León's bustling city centre and outskirts. There are noticeably more pilgrims here than I've seen over the past few days. León is a little over 300 kilometres from Santiago de Compostela and it's a popular starting point for people who have only two weeks or so to walk the Camino.

The wheat fields of the Meseta are now behind us. There are snow-capped mountains on the horizon. We walk through fertile farmland. Red soil. Green hills. Blue and yellow wildflowers grow abundantly.

Alessandro and I talk about this blissful way of living. He is concerned about what will happen after the Camino: "But I'm worried, Luigi, I'm worried that I will just go back to my old life and be old Alessandro again after a few weeks."

To what extent can one really change? How quickly do we relapse into old patterns and habits when we get back to the life we know?

These questions keep us busy on the way to Villar de Mazarife, where we plan to find an albergue. We don't have the answers. And while it's good to be aware of the challenges awaiting us after the Camino, it's useless to speculate about them now. We'll just have to live the answers to our questions.

Something red in the grass at the roadside catches my eye. It's a small memento in the shape of the Canadian maple leaf, something you'd hang on a rucksack. On the back there is a name and address: Bill Innes – the Canadian with whom I started the Camino!

For the umpteenth time something small and inexplicable has happened along the Camino: that I of all people should spot and pick up this memento belonging to Bill. This means that he is probably not too far ahead.

Half an hour later I catch up with Bill and hand him his maple leaf. It is a happy reunion. He is very surprised to see me again and didn't even realise it had come off his bag. Bill looks considerably thinner than three weeks ago. He tells me that he had a serious case of shin splints, but that he's much better now.

This is another of the Camino's gifts: to reunite with pilgrims whose path crossed yours earlier. Each interaction is significant. And as soon as someone steps beyond your field of vision, "out of experience", you have no guarantee that you will ever see them again.

I forget so easily that this also applies to life itself.

* * *

The Albergue Casa de Jesús in Villar de Mazarife is a colourful place with a large area for socialising – a lawn with tables, chairs and white beach umbrellas.

There are graffiti, poems and names all over the walls inside. Someone wrote "My Camino Friends", followed by a long list of names. I see a sketch of a pilgrim gazing into the distance, with the words "Tu pasado no determina tu futura" ("Your past does not determine your future").

Alessandro and I have walked the 22 kilometres from León in under four hours. I think the last time I was this fit I was in high school. We are among the first pilgrims to arrive here today and secure a room with four bunk beds. I shower, hand wash my clothes, hang them up to dry outside and enjoy the usual siesta. But I sleep for much longer than I intended to and wake up late in the afternoon.

In the meantime Robert, Sabine, Sebastian, Claire and Timna have also arrived. The albergue is now much fuller – pilgrims are camped out, relaxing all over the lawn. Some are reading or writing in their diaries, others lying asleep on the grass.

Damon, a young American from Washington, joins us with his guitar. He is only twenty years old and on his gap year. From here he wants to travel to Thailand and India. I saw him in León playing his guitar near the cathedral. He's carrying it with him all the way along the Camino.

We have a spontaneous jam session. Claire and I and Damon take turns to play the guitar and sing songs such as "The Boxer", "It Ain't Me Babe" and "Hallelujah". Damon plays brilliantly and sings songs by Dave Matthews and Jack Johnson.

Later some twenty pilgrims sit with us and somebody makes sure our glasses stay full of vino tinto. I sing a few Afrikaans songs that I wrote more than a decade ago. Later I sing "Hillbrow". Claire quickly learns the chorus and sings along.

I realise how much I have neglected playing the guitar and singing over the past few years. It was always a great passion of mine, especially when I was still at university. I'd never have guessed that I'd have to travel so far to rediscover this and find my "voice" again.

Claire also sings some of her original songs. She has a beguiling voice and her lyrics are moving and beautiful – it's as if all of us listening to her hold our breath while she sings:

Well I have heard, have heard the sparrow sing
and I have reason, reason to believe
these bodies are not all they will be
these bodies are not all they will be

Damon listens attentively. "I've tried to write my own songs, but I can't seem to get it right," he says.

"Has your heart ever been broken?" Claire asks.

"Uhm, no, I don't think so," he replies.

Claire smiles. "Just wait. It will come."

* * *

Bridget, the other Hungarian fitness instructor I met briefly in León, is also here at the Albergue Casa de Jesús. Before dinner she shows me a few yoga moves on the lawn. I'm naturally clumsy; my preschool teacher was right. And I've hardly ever been able to touch my toes.

But I attempt to master Warrior One and Warrior Two. Bridget is not impressed with my posture in general. "Don't stand like a piece of shit!" she commands in her heavy Hungarian accent.

We have dinner together at the albergue and order from the pilgrim menu: the usual trinity of a tuna salad, pork chops and chips, and yoghurt. Tommy, another Hungarian whom Bridget met on the Camino, sits downs with us. She asks him to guess what country I'm from. He gives me one look and says: "That's easy. Polski."

When Tommy hears I'm from South Africa, he begins singing J.M. Coetzee's praises, especially his book *Boyhood*. I didn't expect this – usually Madiba, Oscar Pistorius, the Springboks (especially among pilgrims from New Zealand and Australia) or Johnny Clegg are the first associations people have with the country.

Bridget tells us she has already found the answer she was looking for on the Camino. She is currently in a relationship with someone in Budapest, but it's not serious. Her former boyfriend lives in Auckland. They last saw one another two years ago, but remain in regular contact.

"I realised that I really want to be with him," she says. "My family doesn't know it yet, but I plan to move to Auckland in October. I might as well stop walking now."

* * *

Our jam session resumes after dinner and carries on late into the night. Most pilgrims have already gone to sleep, but we sing as if nobody around the table has to walk over twenty kilometres tomorrow.

Robert tells us about a word that's very difficult to pronounce correctly: *Oachkatzlschwoaf.* It's a slang word in Austria that means "squirrel's tail". Apparently Germans in particular really struggle to pronounce it. The urban legend is that you get Austrian citizenship if you pronounce it perfectly for the customs officials.

We hold *Oachkatzlschwoaf Idols,* with Robert as the only adjudicator. Each person around the table gets a turn to say the word. Not one of us, it seems, is getting Austrian citizenship, but Timna gets an honourable mention for effort.

Later, Robert gets talking to an interesting character –

Benni, also from Austria. Benni is in his forties and wears an orange headscarf. He literally plays with fire by juggling flaming skittles on the lawn. Years ago he studied art in Vienna. These days he "lives" on the Camino. He walks from albergue to albergue and basically lives from hand to mouth, selling sketches to make a living.

Benni seems content with his way of life. I wonder what it must be like to pass all your days among pilgrims like this. With skittles and sketches to feed your body and put a roof over your head.

It's dark, so it must be after ten. No one's come to shut us up yet, luckily. I play Bruce Springsteen's "Tougher Than the Rest". I mess the chords up a bit – it's been such a long time since I last sang it. Until very recently I thought I'd never play this beautiful ballad by The Boss again. Or even listen to it.

It was our song, me and my ex-girlfriend. It can be impossibly hard to get away from strong associations, especially if a song is charged with specific memories.

Nostalgia can be a bugger, a misty mirror. Milan Kundera warns in *The Unbearable Lightness of Being*: "In the sunset of dissolution, everything is illuminated by the aura of nostalgia, even the guillotine."

But tonight, here at an albergue in Villar de Mazarife, I sing my heart out. The song will always have the aura of nostalgia, but now I'm creating a new memory for "Tougher Than the Rest". What happened has happened.

Sing it off. I probably sound like a half-drunk soloist in a choir of cats. That's okay, too.

Meanwhile, Benni has started painting a picture of a medieval bridge on one of the walls. We don't have water at the table, so Benni dips his brush carefully into a glass of red wine to "clean" it before he carries on painting. He is upset that somebody wrote the words "God is gay" on the wall. "I want to change that," he says.

Later, he wants to play the guitar, too. He says he knows only one song and launches into "Always Look on the Bright Side of Life" from the Monty Python film *Life of Brian*.

We all sing along – an appropriate conclusion to a party on the Camino that I could never have foreseen:

> If life seems jolly rotten
> There's something you've forgotten!
> And that's to laugh and smile and sing,
> When you're feeling in the dumps,
> Don't be silly chumps,
> Just purse your lips and whistle – that's the thing!
> And always look on the bright side of life
> Always look on the bright side of life.

Day Twenty-two, Wednesday 27 May
From Villar de Mazarife to Astorga
(31 kilometres)

We drank an inordinate amount of wine last night, but I feel surprisingly fresh this morning. Before we set off, Robert and I each write something on the wall of the albergue. He goes for "*Oachkatzlschwoaf*"; I write "Walk it off". On the outskirts of the village we take a group photograph. Robert sets the timer on his fancy camera and triggers it with his cell phone.

Sebastian, Sabine, Timna, Claire, Alessandro, Robert. I'm going to miss these people a lot. We'll always have this shared experience. This is something else about the Camino that hadn't occurred to me before: how important and precious these interactions are, how quickly one makes friends on the long road to Santiago.

Also: how wonderful it is to share something with someone, in the moment. Like when Claire leaves the main road as we walk through a town to smell a flower and encourages us to do the same.

I find myself in a group again, which is good – for the moment. This can change at any time if someone feels they want to walk alone. No expectations, no judgement. There is no right or wrong way to walk the Camino. There is only the way *you* walk it. Shouldn't life away from the Camino also be like this?

* * *

We walk in a group, but not as a sociable band. Everyone walks with their own thoughts, usually about fifty metres apart.

After three weeks of walking I'm beginning to cherish the silence. To be as present in the moment as possible and to tune in to all my senses as keenly as possible: to listen to my breathing, the bird sounds, my footsteps and the rhythm of my trekking poles; to look, mostly just in front of me at the white dirt road, often dead straight up ahead but sometimes taking a turn or meandering; to smell spring around me, and taste the saltiness of a drop of sweat.

Sometimes, when the road stretches out long and straight, I close my eyes for a few seconds while I walk. Thoughts come and go. Sometimes a memory, a fantasy, the words to a song, a line of poetry. Other times, purely practical things. How much further to walk today? Where am I going to sleep? I try not to fixate on anything.

I greet every idea with "Buen Camino" just the same as I acknowledge pilgrims along the route.

Robert's starting with blisters again. He's already on his fourth pair of shoes. His courage and determination are remarkable. I designate him the Camino's undisputed Mister Blister.

* * *

In Santibáñez de Valdeiglesias I sit in the town square eating an orange. It is enough. Annie Dillard wrote: "How we spend our days is, of course, how we spend our lives."

* * *

"Welcome to paradise!" a man calls out from a little stall next to the road. We still have about seven kilometres to Astorga.

The last two hours of walking were tough, but took us through some of the most beautiful and tranquil landscapes I have seen on the Camino: forests, initially, holm oaks, then scrubland; and then, up the flanks of a steep hill, arable fields.

On the front of the stall are the words "La llave de la esencia es presencia" ("The key to the essence is presence"). There's a hammock, too, and a building that looks like an old barn. David, the owner, is tanned and shirtless, and has a ponytail. The name of his little stall is La Casa de los Dioses (The House of Gods). He offers fruit juice, bananas, grapes, biscuits, jam and even Nutella.

David tells us that he used to live in Barcelona, but for the past five years he has been here every day of the year, summer and winter. He serves the pilgrims full-time and lives here without electricity, internet, a phone or any kind of vehicle.

And everything at his stall is free! There is a little box for donations, which he uses to buy the refreshments he sells. "Money is only for buying. But life is sharing. Give for nothing, it's the best," he says. David makes a fist. "You take . . . freedom gone."

I eat some biscuits with Nutella, drink watermelon juice and lie in the hammock. Claire picks up a guitar and plays two of her songs.

David talks non-stop to passersby and shares bits of wisdom about "surrender" and "sharing". As we say goodbye, he gives each one of us a hug and says: "Have a good life."

* * *

I'm lying in the municipal albergue in Astorga. All seven of us have found a place to sleep, in a room with bunk beds.

I've walked well all day, but now my legs are stiff and sore. It was easy to tell the pilgrims from the locals earlier this evening, on the town square. You just had to look for the ones who were limping.

Pain has taken on a new meaning for me on the Camino. You are often much stronger than you think, and can usually walk through the pain.

But I have a more urgent worry that has nothing to do with pain. Potential pain, maybe, which will probably be over very quickly . . .

Sebastian is sleeping on the bunk right above me. His bed is creaking, and his mattress bends the wooden slats. If his bed were to break, the whole shebang – Sebastian included – would come crashing down on me. Death by bunk bed is hopefully not my fate tonight.

Day Twenty-three, Thursday 28 May
From Astorga to Rabanal del Camino
(21 kilometres)

Sebastian and I are walking together this morning. His bed held up last night, mercifully. Interesting guy, this former German soldier. We share an interest in psychology and philosophy. Our conversation revolves around the word "enough". I tell him one of my favourite stories that I read on the Brainpickings website.

The writers Kurt Vonnegut and Joseph Heller once attended a billionaire's party. Kurt asked Joseph how he felt about the fact that the billionaire made more money in one day than all the royalties he, Joseph, had received over the years for his bestseller, *Catch-22*. Joseph said it didn't worry him at all, because he had something the billionaire did not.

"What could that be?" Kurt wanted to know.

"The knowledge that I have enough," Joseph answered.

* * *

There's a cat prowling around the municipal albergue in Rabanal del Camino. A Persian job.

I am a cat person, probably because I grew up with cats in my parental home. The first cat I remember is a white Persian, Boeboe, that my father bought my mother in 1976 as a wedding present. Boeboe had a good innings and the last of his nine lives ended in 1991.

There's a joke doing the rounds about what your name would be if you were a character in a porn movie. Use the name of your first pet and your mother's maiden name. Mine is a hit: Boeboe Rens.

I wouldn't call myself a cat whisperer, but I do seem

to be able to win most cats over quite quickly. We do, in fact, have someone in our family who can apparently communicate directly with cats. The gent with this special gift comes for Christmas lunch every year. I have seen him paging through a *Go* magazine and then beginning to "meow" when our overweight tortoiseshell cat waddles into the room. The cat answers him, and so they to and fro for a bit.

During one Christmas lunch, the same guy, while eating Brussels sprouts and without any context whatsoever, remarked, "I last saw a fruit bat in 1965." I didn't get to hear the rest of the story: my brother and I had to excuse ourselves to finish our laughing fit in the bedroom.

The Camino cat responds when I click my fingers and settles on my lap. Robert takes a few pictures. "Erns, you look just like a Bond villain with the cat on your lap!" he says.

* * *

I like weird stories. Hunter S. Thompson wrote: "When the going gets weird, the weird turn pro."

In my twelve years as a journalist with various publications – LitNet, *Insig*, *Huisgenoot* and *Go* – I have done quite a few weird stories.

Like when I went undercover to expose a far-right youth camp in Limpopo. Or drove around in a pink Greyhound bus with a child star and her parents. There were also the 24 hours I spent in the company of an eccentric long-distance truck driver and freelance evangelist.

But by far the weirdest story was about a cat. It was written during my stint at *Huisgenoot* (I worked there for 64 issues). One Sunday evening in 2007, I received an unforgettable SMS from a friend: "My wife's aunt's neighbour's wife breastfeeds her cat. Do you want to do a story?"

A week later a lady photographer and I were on our way to a little house near a mine in the platinum belt. There we met the 57-year-old woman – she was a grandmother several times over – who let her black cat "drink" from her.

She told us the cat had been a birthday present from her husband ten years ago. The cat may have been taken from its mother too early, because one night it crept up the woman's nightgown and began to suckle. Two days later, at the ripe old age of 46, the woman could breastfeed again. Apparently the woman kept producing milk for another five years. She said the cat could "suck till the foam would fly".

We had to get photos, of course. I waited outside while the photographer took pictures of the woman and her cat in the bedroom, but I did take a peep on my way past . . .

These photos shocked the *Huisgenoot* editorial board to such an extent that they never ran the story. This was a relief.

I'll never forget driving away from that house. The cat was sitting next to the driveway, licking its lips. The cat that got the cream.

Day Twenty-four, Friday 29 May
From Rabanal del Camino to Molinaseca
(26 kilometres)

A humble wooden post with an iron cross on top: the Cruz de Ferro, about eight kilometres outside Rabanal del Camino, is the most famous beacon along the Camino Francés, apart from the cathedral in Santiago de Compostela.

It is believed that there used to be an altar to the Roman god Mercury here. But since the eleventh century the Cruz de Ferro has been a place for pilgrims to put a stone or leave something behind. These days, pilgrims still leave stones or mementos – photos, notes, even items of clothing.

I write the words "Walk it off" on my piece of fabric with the South African flags on it, and wrap it around a rock.

* * *

Timna and I walk together until we get to Molinaseca. I tell her about an interview I did a few months ago with the adventurer David Grier. David had run a full 4 008 kilometres in 93 days, from the foothills of the Himalayas to the southernmost point in India.

Somewhere along the route he had a discussion with an old man, who said to him: "You will find nothing you are looking for in India. The answers you seek are already within you. But India could be the catalyst."

I think the same applies to the Camino. And you need to be patient with the questions as well as the answers.

The poet Rainer Maria Rilke expressed this well in his *Letters to a Young Poet*: ". . . have patience with everything unresolved in your heart and try to love the questions themselves as if they were locked rooms or books written in a very foreign language. Don't search for the answers, which could not be given to you now, because you would not be able to live them. And the point is, to live everything. Live the questions now. Perhaps then, someday far in the future, you will gradually, without even noticing it, live your way into the answer."

From Molinaseca to Villafranca del Bierzo
(31 kilometres)

Today Sebastian and I leave Molinaseca together. I tell him one of my favourite Zen Buddhist anecdotes.

A Japanese girl had become pregnant and the Zen master Hakuin was claimed to be the father. Her parents were furious and confronted the master. All he said in response was, "Is that so?"

After the child was born, the girl's parents brought the infant to Hakuin so that he could look after it. He took care of the child very well. But a year later the girl admitted the truth: The father was not Hakuin, but a young man who worked at the market.

The parents went to fetch the child from Hakuin and apologised profusely and asked for forgiveness.

Hakuin gave them the child and again said only, "Is that so?"

* * *

Near Villafranca del Bierzo we meet Timna. Sebastian tells us a bit about his time as a soldier and Timna mentions that during her military service in Israel she was trained as a sniper. You're surprised every single day on the Camino.

Later Timna and I discuss music. We are both very fond of the *Into the Wild* soundtrack, especially the song "Rise" by Eddie Vedder. She looks for the song on her phone.

As we walk into town, we sing:

Such is the way of the world

You can never know
Just where to put all your faith
And how will it grow?
Gonna rise up
Burning black holes in dark memories
Gonna rise up
Turning mistakes into gold

Day Twenty-six, Sunday 31 May
From Villafranca del Bierzo to La Faba
(25 kilometres)

I have no idea what the time is. A watch or alarm clock would be handy right about now. I arranged to meet Timna and Claire at six. The challenging, steep Dragonte route lies in wait for us today.

Brierley describes the Dragonte as "remote and poorly waymarked" and for "seasoned pilgrims only". But today, the three of us are ready for adventure.

I try to slip out of the room as quietly as possible with my sleeping bag, rucksack and clothes. Four other pilgrims – including Sebastian – are still fast asleep. It must still be way too early. Otherwise I would have heard bags being zipped up, or people whispering as they got ready to walk.

In the bathroom I wash my face and brush my teeth. A Korean man comes in, fuzzy with sleep. He gets a fright, but then gives a friendly nod. He looks very much like the guy who stumbled dead drunk into the albergue in Nájera.

I catch sight of his watch. Half past three. No . . . it can't be! I doubt I'll be able to fall asleep again. Time to lie awake for a while . . .

I remember a night in De Akker, years ago. It might have been during the Woordfees. I was living in a flat next to the BP garage in Dorp Street, opposite De Akker.

This legendary bar was my living room. A few good friends and I spent many evenings – even nights – there. As my friend Liezl always said: "I found and lost my mind at De Akker."

That evening, Andries Bezuidenhout came to our table to say goodbye after a performance at the Hidden Cellar on the top floor of De Akker.

"Sleep tight, all of you. I'm off to go and lie awake . . ." he said, and walked through De Akker's saloon-type doors with his guitar case.

* * *

Timna and Claire and I are standing at the turnoff to the Dragonte route, weighing up the pros and cons of going that way. It is half past six and the sun's going to rise any minute now. Claire and Timna are a bit nervous about taking this route. But I'm in the mood for an adventure. What could possibly go wrong?

Already there are troubling signs. Last night in a bar someone showed us a newspaper report about two pilgrims who got hopelessly lost on the Dragonte. It took a rescue operation to find them. And at our albergue the woman at reception just shook her head when she heard our plan and said firmly "Malo! Malo!" (which basically means "very bad idea").

A car drives past. The driver stops, reverses, opens the window. I already know what's going to happen. He waves his arm in the direction of the Dragonte and shouts: "Malo! Malo!" Then he points passionately to where all the other pilgrims are walking.

"Okay, if I see a dead cat up in the road I'm turning around," Timna says as he drives off.

Fortunately we don't see a dead cat. But less than fifty metres on we come across an enormous dead snake in the middle of the road. It's presumably been hit by a car and is lying there covered in thick blood.

Timna stops immediately. "That's it." Claire is also reluctant. I'm not particularly superstitious, but have to admit: this is deeply weird.

We choose the route over Alto Pradela instead. I'd rather not attempt the Dragonte on my own. Next thing my name's misspelled in an obituary in a Spanish community newspaper.

Out of nowhere comes Tommy, the Hungarian J.M. Coetzee fan, whom I last saw at Villar de Mazarife, walking with another guy. They are ready to take on the Dragonte.

Tommy literally steps on the snake without realising it! He cannot understand why we won't join them. We show him that he's standing on a dead, bloodied snake. He looks down and laughs. "In Hungary a dead snake means good luck!"

* * *

I have my usual tortilla de patatas for breakfast at the Albergue Camino y Leyenda in Trabadelo. Most mornings I start looking for a breakfast spot after eight kilometres, but today I've already walked twelve.

I have no idea how the Dragonte route would have tested us, but the steep Alto Pradela was enough of a challenge. I haven't seen Timna and Claire again, and think I'll be walking solo more often from here on in.

It's time to move on alone. I really enjoy company, but if I walk with a group for too long, it starts to feel too comfortable – easy, even. It gets in the way of my own Camino.

On the Camino, you don't owe anybody an excuse or explanation. Each person has his or her own journey to follow. I like the fact that "groups" form organically and dissolve organically.

On the albergue wall someone has written: *Welcome to today, another day, another chance, to feel free.*

And: *If you really want to do something, you will find a way. If not, you will find an excuse.*

Day Twenty-seven, Monday 1 June
From La Faba to Triacastela
(27 kilometres)

I walk into the province of Galicia. The landscape has changed dramatically over the past two days and is now much greener and more mountainous, with forests and hills that put one in mind of the Scottish Highlands. In fact, Galicia has a proud Celtic heritage stretching back to the Iron Age.

The mist rolls in over the mountains and for the first time in weeks I wear my fleece against the cold. I am walking alone, with no other pilgrims in sight. It's one of the few times on the Camino I've itched for a camera.

When I find myself in such a magical landscape, I start thinking almost automatically about camera angles and potential double-page spreads in *Go*. It feels so good to remind myself that whatever I am seeing now, I can simply enjoy in the moment, without the pressure of making it into a photo for the magazine. Then, I can walk on to the next vista around the corner.

O Cebreiro is an iconic little village on top of a mountain. These first five kilometres from La Faba have been a hell of a steep climb.

The entire village is covered in mist. It looks as if most of the pilgrims who stayed here overnight have already hit the road. It's a pastoral scene: a few dogs lazing around, cows mooing, the smell of dung on the breeze. There are several traditional pallozas – round stone cottages with thatched roofs that show how the Celts lived centuries ago.

The church at O Cebreiro is apparently the oldest surviving one along the Camino and has been a refuge for pilgrims since the ninth century. I sit for a few minutes inside this pre-Romanesque building. It's much more modest than some of the other churches I've visited.

Next to the church is a bust of Don Elías Valiña Sampedro (1929–1989), who used to be the parish priest. We modern pilgrims owe him a huge debt of gratitude. In 1971 he published the first pocket-sized modern guide to walking the Camino, *Caminos a Compostela*. And the yellow arrows to mark the route were his idea. In 1982, he tried to make the Camino more user-friendly by painting these arrows all along the route. Sampedro and his tins of paint drove the Camino Francés flat in his Citroën GS. He had some helpers, but did most of the painting on his own.

In the province of Navarre, where there is often tension with the Basque population, he was stopped by a Spanish policeman who wanted to know what he was doing: "I am organising a huge invasion!" he announced.

If you look at the stream of pilgrims following his yellow arrows these days, it's clear the priest was not far off the mark.

* * *

I enjoy walking through the Galician hamlets – stone cottages with a tractor where the car should be, chickens running around, cows mooing, and lazy Alsatians sleeping on their sides right across the road. They're on full-time siesta and refuse to budge an inch. I have to step over one a number of times.

The mist keeps rolling in. A life-size statue of a medieval pilgrim emerges, holding onto his hat as if battling stormy weather. I enjoy these statues and monuments, silent witnesses to the Camino's rich history and the millions of pilgrims who have walked – for whatever reason – to Santiago de Compostela through the ages.

The past two days' climbing has been rough. I have never been as walking fit as I am now, but my legs still feel sore and stiff today. And my energy levels are low. This morning the yoghurt and muesli and pancakes with banana were a nice enough breakfast at El Refugio Caminarte, but I miss my daily tortilla de patatas.

Near Alto do Pollo, the highest point in Galicia at 1 330 metres, I haul myself into the Bar Puerto. Time for a second breakfast. There's a large vending machine full of oranges that automatically squeezes fresh orange juice. I immediately feed it my coins, and order a tortilla de patatas and café con leche.

Renewed, I set off on the long and steep road down the mountain to Triacastela. I walk slowly, and zigzag like Timna showed me.

My right knee is no longer painful, as it was before the Camino. But I must still be careful – there's a week to go before I get to Santiago, and I'd like to walk even further. Preferably with no aches and pains.

The views over the mountains and the lush green vegetation that reminds me of the Garden Route are astounding. I would never have thought the Camino had such a rich variety of landscapes.

When my friend Le Roux and I hiked through the Fish River Canyon in 2014, he spoke of "panorama fatigue". I suspect the term is his own invention. It refers to the kind of psychological fatigue that sets in when you are exposed to a profusion of breathtaking new vistas and panoramas over a short period. It's almost too much for your brain. I'm starting to wonder if a kind of panorama fatigue is going to hit me somewhere in Galicia.

One of the hospitaleros at El Refugio Caminarte told me of the Albergue Ecológico El Beso outside Triacastela. It's a small, environmentally friendly albergue with only sixteen beds. I used the landline at the albergue this morning and booked a bed at El Beso under the name André. The friendly man on the other end of the line told me he could keep a place for me until two this afternoon.

I was baptised André-Erns Hendrik, but as far back as I can remember I've been called Erns. I can't pronounce my r's properly, though, which often leads to confusion during telephone conversations. I hear "Hi, Owens" or "Okay, Alice" practically every day. So whenever I reserve something, whether it's a table at a Cape Town restaurant or a bed at an albergue in Spain, I use "André".

Le Roux and I have agreed that one day we will write each other's obituaries. We have been threatening to start for a long time and then to send each other what we've come up with, bit by bit, because most people never get to read their own obits. Le Roux has already come up with the first sentence of mine: "His taxi name was André."

* * *

The church bell rings three times as I walk into Triacastela. I didn't know it was so late. I hope my bed at El Beso is still available.

"I saw your brother in the pub around the corner!" somebody shouts in my direction. It's an Englishman, Jacob from Southampton, sitting at a little table with a café con leche. The "brother" he is referring to can only be Robert. I don't want to socialise right now, and choose to keep my distance.

El Beso is only one and a half kilometres beyond Triacastela, but I'm buggered when I get there. Maybe I drank too little water. I think the last time I felt this exhausted was at Şansol, near Los Arcos, when I was close to dehydration.

"André," a tall, friendly man says as I stumble into El Beso. Marijn is from the Netherlands and owns the albergue with his Italian wife Jessica. I am so happy he kept a bed for me that I want to hug him.

El Beso is exceptionally environmentally friendly. I'm even given an eco-friendly soap to use in the shower. And outside I come across Timna and Anna, a Dutch woman I met yesterday at La Faba. They've also decided to sleep here.

For a solid hour and a half after showering and doing laundry, Timna, Anna and I lie in hammocks suspended between centuries-old trees. I look up at the treetops. A light breeze rustles the leaves. In the distance I hear something like rapids in the river. A dog barks, then barks again at its own echo.

I read a bit more of David Sedaris's book, chat with Timna and doze off for minutes at a time. After a long first day in Galicia I cannot think of a better way to relax.

When I clamber barefoot out of the hammock to go and eat, I step on a clump of thorns. One of the thorns breaks off in my flesh, so deeply that I can't dislodge it with a needle. I'll have to sort it out later.

There are eight of us around the dinner table on the stoep. Marijn and Jessica eat with us, and I meet a charming German woman in her forties, Katrin, who is recently divorced. And a Dutch social worker, Rob. Given that

Anna is also from the Netherlands, I tell the group (in English) the two Dutch jokes I know:

They say the Dutch are too honest to be polite. Afrikaans people are too polite to be honest.

When an Afrikaans baby is born, his first word is usually "Mamma" or "Pappa". A Dutch baby's first words are almost always "Volgens mij!"

These usually get Dutch people laughing heartily, and luckily it's the same with Rob and Anna.

Supper is a vegetarian feast: broccoli pasta with vegetables and salad, and Tarta de Santiago (Galicia's renowned almond cake) for dessert. The vegetables are all from the albergue's garden. Marijn provides three bottles of red wine for the table.

The couple's one-year-old daughter has just started walking. While Jessica plays with her, Marijn tells us their remarkable love story. In 2011 they were both walking the Camino. They were strangers. On what was the last day of the walk for them both, they met near the lighthouse at Finisterre just before sunset. That very same night they became a couple.

A few months later Marijn went by car to fetch Jessica in Italy and they embarked on a road trip along the Camino. As they drove past a dilapidated farm building outside Triacastela, they decided: We're starting an albergue here.

Shortly afterwards they bought the property, moved in and started renovations. In 2013 the Albergue Ecológico El Beso opened its doors.

"I wouldn't want any other life than to be here with my family," Marijn says. "This work makes me so happy. To meet new pilgrims every day, feed them well and to see them leave with a smile."

A refuge born out of love. El Beso means "the kiss".

* * *

Near my bed in El Beso I pick up a book, *The Idle Traveller*, by Dan Kieran. I've heard of Kieran; he was on the staff of *The Idler*, a British journal with philosophical essays known as "literature for loafers".

The book is falling apart, unfortunately, and many pages have gone missing. But this paragraph captures something of the journey on which I find myself:

"There are certainly no more compelling travelling companions than the inescapable thoughts and feelings of your own soul. Travel with a friend and his or her presence secludes you from the way your brain delves into itself when you are in an unfamiliar place and wholly alone. When you travel alone your identity slips away, especially if you do it slowly and go a long way. You speak very little, which in itself is quite meditative. Your thoughts are free to roam into the often-neglected parts of yourself. The transition can be uneasy at first, but soon there is great comfort in what is lost."

Day Twenty-eight, Tuesday 2 June
From Triacastela to Barbadelo
(22 kilometres)

"SNORRRING!"

I wake up with a start and a grunt. Katrin, the German lady who sat with us at the dinner table, is standing right up against my bed. She is wearing a white nightgown. Just as well I met her last night, or I might have mistaken her for a ghost with a thick German accent.

She thumps the mattress with her hand.

"You are SNORRRING!"

It's the dead of night. I hear other people shifting around in their beds. Katrin returns to her bed, about three metres from mine. I hear someone sigh from another corner. I turn on to my side, feeling a bit guilty about falling asleep again. Maybe I should get up for my Provent plasters, but that might wake even more sleepers.

A few hours later I get up, feeling very tired. I feel a bit like the Valiant Swart song: "Woke up this morning, and God knows the devil was there." Or rather, the German was there.

Katrin isn't finished with me yet. She storms the break-fast table where Timna, Anna and I are sitting with our yoghurt.

"I didn't sleep at all last night because of your snoring," she says, still furious.

I try to apologise between gulps of yoghurt, completely on the back foot. "I'm sorry, I didn't keep you awake on purpose."

"You should go see a doctor, you really have a prob-lem," she snaps back.

"Yes, I have a medical condition."

Timna stares at her yoghurt. She hasn't said a word. Her bed was right next to mine.

"Did you not sleep either?" I ask carefully.

She shakes her head, makes no eye contact. It seems that on the Camino you can even lose friends in your sleep.

"Shame, poor you," Anna says and smiles.

I want to get away from the albergue and start walking as quickly as possible. As I finish packing, Timna appears by my bed and lifts her arms. For a moment I think she wants to high-five me. But then I see something written on each palm. "In silencia" on the left and "Gracias" on the right. Now I understand why she said nothing this morning. She is not angry with me for snoring – she just wants to walk in silence.

I say goodbye to the owner, Marijn, and tell him about the German woman who shouted at me.

"They're good at that," he says with a little laugh.

* * *

Today I intend to walk about eighteen kilometres to Sarria. From then on things will get busier, so I must appreciate this quiet road through the woods outside El Beso.

Most people who walk the Camino set off from Sarria, because it is the largest town near the 100-kilometre point – the minimum distance you need to cover to get a Compostela certificate.

The thorn I stepped on yesterday by the hammock is irritating. Not as bad as the thorn of old in the apostle Paul's flesh, though.

Timna is walking a short distance ahead of me and stops every now and again to take a photo, but I respect her request for silence and do not try to make conversation. I once went on a "silent" hike with friends over two days near Alexandria in the Eastern Cape, and I found the experience really meaningful.

"Speak only if it improves upon the silence," Gandhi said. If you think carefully about this, there is often very little left to say.

Timna beckons me closer, however, when she sees a sign at a turn-off reading: *Alquimia. Minerals.* We follow the path and walk in silence until we get to a house in the woods that's also an art gallery.

It reminds me of the Owl House in Nieu-Bethesda, but

without the depression. The artist, Antonio Bello, gives us a friendly greeting in Spanish. He looks like a shaman or druid (without the customary long white beard). Somebody who would be at home in an *Asterix* book.

His English is a bit sketchy, unfortunately. I would love to have talked to him about his art. Antonio's paintings are full of esoteric and mystical elements – circular patterns, geometric forms and mandalas.

On the top floor there is a darkened room with cushions and a candle, where pilgrims can meditate. I sit cross-legged on one of the cushions for a few minutes.

Antonio also has a large collection of crystals. "You choose," he said with a smile as I was looking at a basket with crystal pendants. I select a light-green crystal. "Amethyst." He presses his hand to his heart. "Healing energy."

It's twenty euros, but I pay gladly. Now I have another pendant to go with my yellow Camino arrow and the San Juan de Ortega cross.

* * *

Two kilometres before Sarria I see Robert, Alessandro, Sabine and Sebastian sitting at a bar. We hug like old friends.

I last saw them four days ago. In O Cebreiro Robert bought himself a trekking pole – more like a walking stick – with a carved squirrel on top. The squirrel has an enormous curly tail – *oachkatzlschwoaf.*

It looks like Robert's ready to start a sect. He refers to himself as the "Bearer of the Holy *Oachkatzlschwoaf* Stick".

Sabine, armed with a needle, quickly helps me remove the thorn, which had lodged itself deep in my foot. I remain amazed at how regularly help turns up on the Camino exactly when you need it – small gestures of goodwill.

It's always a pleasure to bump into familiar people. These four Camino friends are evidently going to walk all the way to Santiago de Compostela together, maybe even to Finisterre.

I detect no resentment about my decision to break away. I do my own thing now. Peace to all.

* * *

I want to get away as soon as possible from the hustle and bustle of Sarria. The old part of the town, along the Rúa Maior, is packed with albergues on either side of the road.

I walk past a busy restaurant and hear a laugh. It can only be Timna's. She is with a handsome Spaniard, eating octopus and talking enthusiastically.

She blushes a bit on seeing me, given this morning's pledge of silence. "I got hungry and my friend from earlier on the Camino invited me for lunch," she says. "I had to break my vow of silence. It would have been bad manners, you know." She doesn't have to explain; I would have done the same.

I keep focused and walk a beautiful forest path to Casa Barbadelo – an albergue that looks more like a hotel, with big lawns and a swimming pool. There are dorm rooms here with bunk beds, but I decide to treat myself for a change and pay fifteen euros for a room with only three single beds and an en suite bathroom.

I spend the afternoon at the pool: order sangria, read some of David Sedaris's book, jump in the pool now and then. As it should be, on holiday. It feels like I've taken a break from the Camino. Purist pilgrims would likely not approve, but that's their problem.

I don't even want to think about the tantrum Serafin from Albergue Putzu would throw if he could see me now: next to a swimming pool, sangria in hand, tapping my foot to Tina Turner's "Simply the Best" that's blaring from the loudspeaker.

Day Twenty-nine, Wednesday 3 June
From Barbadelo to Portomarín
(19 kilometres)

Somebody takes my hand while I'm waiting to pay for my café con leche at Casa Barbadelo. It's Katrin, the German woman who was so angry about my snoring yesterday.

The till is busy, the place is packed. But Katrin goes on her knees in front of me and says loudly: "I am so sorry I was rude to you yesterday. This morning someone told me that I also snore at night. And he also could not sleep."

It looks like she's going to burst into tears. I give her a hug and say thank you, everything's okay.

* * *

The landscape stays green and luxuriant, with an abundance of trees. Typical rural Galicia, with lots of hamlets and hórreos – barns made of stone for storing wheat – along the road.

There are noticeably more pilgrims and bicycles. It's summer and the Spaniards are starting to walk the last 100 kilometres to Santiago de Compostela in droves – often in groups of six or more. They can get nice and loud when they want to.

Most of their shoes and rucksacks are brand new. Many

people walk with small day packs. Some of them don't even have rucksacks at all. I suspect the taxis are properly busy carting bags from one albergue to the next.

I try to see this as just another phase of my Camino. Getting crabby about all the new pilgrims won't help.

At Mercadoiro, about six kilometres outside tonight's destination of Portomarín, I see Robert, Alessandro, Sabine and Sebastian again. I'm walking nice and fast today and don't want to slow down, but I take a quick photograph with them.

I have a strong feeling I won't see them on the Camino again. They want to get past Portomarín by tonight and reach Santiago de Compostela a day earlier than I plan to.

Buen Camino, friends.

* * *

I cross the long bridge across the Miño River to Portomarín, a little town on a hill with a big dam.

The guidebook tells the interesting history of the place. Portomarín dates from the Middle Ages, but the whole town would have ended up underwater when the dam was built in 1962. The town was moved to higher ground; some of the historical buildings – including the Romanesque church of San Juan – were moved stone by stone.

I find a place to sleep at Albergue Ferramenteiro – a hypermodern albergue that overlooks the river, and has a spacious dormitory and room for 130 pilgrims. But I could kick myself for not reading about the albergue Casa Banderas sooner. Three kilometres before Portomarín in the hamlet of Vilachá, it is owned and managed by a South African!

I find a spot to sit high up on the steep steps, look out over the bridge and the dam, and write in my diary.

Entry in Moleskine diary

To whoever might read this one day: don't believe everything you read – here and elsewhere – too easily. Words are weapons, words flutter, words jump around all over the place but seldom speak the truth. The moment you put something into words, it becomes something more and something less, something else. And too quickly I get lost, at a loss for words, think and overthink, try with words to make sentences and sense of this shifting whirlpool that the word life tries to capture.

* * *

I'm sitting on the terrace of the Restaurante O Mirador in Portomarín. I look out over the dam and the road I must walk tomorrow. From here I can see the yellow arrow on the route marker at the little bridge pointing in the direction of Palas de Rei. I have just eaten a substantial bowl of cauliflower soup and half a bread roll. My glass is full of red wine, the pork chops and chips are ready, and the waitress looks cuter each time she hurries past. I'm about to finish David Sedaris's book.

I'm extraordinarily satisfied, and committed to the here and now.

Day Thirty, Thursday 4 June
From Portomarín almost to Palas de Rei
(19 kilometres)

There is a dense mist hanging over Portomarín this morning. The pilgrims walking ahead look like ghosts.

Ghosts that mainly speak loud Spanish.

* * *

Entry in Moleskine diary

I'm at Iglesia de Vilar de Donas, just over two kilometres off the Camino route. There's an ancient Romanesque church from the fourteenth century, but the roots of the little church apparently date back to the tenth century, there are statues of medieval knights and a beautiful crumbling fresco behind the altar. It's a very peaceful spot, just a pity about the guide who is speaking at the top of her voice in Spanish to two Spanish (I presume) pilgrims.

Note to self: Next time learn Spanish properly before taking on the Camino.

* * *

I'm taking it particularly easy today. I find a place to stay at Casa A Calzada, a small albergue with space for only eight people. The next big town, Palas de Rei, is about six kilometres away. Tomorrow I'll have to walk further than I'd planned, but that's okay.

Ron from Toronto, in his sixties, is one of the other pilgrims at the albergue. He is walking the Camino with Linda, a former colleague.

Ron and I have a broad discussion about karaoke. He is absolutely fanatical about it and loves travelling to major cities specifically to experience their karaoke culture.

"It's all about the energy," he says to me. "Energy is the secret. Don't sing slow dance songs when people want to party." His favourite is Robert Palmer's "Doctor, Doctor" and Creedence Clearwater Revival's "Travelin' Band". And when there are young people in the audience, the Beastie Boys' "(You Gotta) Fight For Your Right (To Party)" is always a hit.

Ron plans to travel to Barcelona after Santiago de Compostela and spend the night at a karaoke club there, before catching a 5 a.m. flight back to Canada. I'm not sure what Linda thinks of this plan.

I have sung karaoke only once, at a club in Busan in South Korea. The Koreans are very keen on karaoke. That was the same night a typhoon called Maemi struck the city. While Maemi blasted Busan and South Korea all the way onto CNN, I sang the Kansas tearjerker "Dust in the Wind":

> Now, don't hang on, nothing lasts forever but the earth
>   and sky
> It slips away, and all your money won't another minute
>   buy
> Dust in the wind
> All we are is dust in the wind

I doubt this will make it on to Ron the karaoke pilgrim's top ten any time soon.

Day Thirty-one, Friday 5 June
Near Palas de Rei to Arzúa
(34 kilometres)

At the little town of Casanova I meet a couple from Texas who are walking the Camino all the way from Saint Jean with their 18-month-old baby.

Along a forest path I come across a message that Robert and the others left for me on a sheet of paper wedged under a rock: "Keep walking Luigi! *Oachkatzlschwoaf!*"

A man ploughing a field by hand reminds me of a poem, *Musée des Beaux Arts,* by W.H. Auden that I memorised some months ago. The poem was inspired by Bruegel's *Landscape with the Fall of Icarus*, where Icarus plunges to earth from the sky and the rest of the world simply carries on with life.

Life is very much like this. The psychotherapist Sheldon B. Kopp sums it up well: "Life is mainly simply inevitable."

I find a bed for the night at the Albergue Don Quixote. Cervantes's story about the legendary figure who storms the windmills is something I must still read.

Day Thirty-two, Saturday 6 June
From Arzúa to Monte do Gozo
(36 kilometres)

I reach Monte do Gozo by late afternoon and immediately stretch my calves and hamstrings against a wall. Counting yesterday's 34 kilometres, I have covered 70 kilometres in two days.

The sore muscles no longer bother me. Every pain I en-

counter is yet another meeting, another intimate acquaintance along the road. "Buen Camino, ankle. Buen Camino,
calf." I wish you well. My body feels completely different
from how it felt after the first few days on the Camino.
Eish, that was more than a month ago.

The cathedral of Santiago de Compostela is less than
five kilometres from here. I didn't plan to make it as far as
Monte do Gozo today.

Most people follow the route in the Brierley guide and
walk as far as O Pedrouzo, the last big town before Santiago and about twenty kilometres from the cathedral, on
their second-last day. If you start walking early the next
morning, you should easily make it to the cathedral before
the midday mass starts.

When I left Arzúa this morning, I wanted to walk on my
own, for as long and as far as possible. These last few days
before Santiago can be a tremendous challenge if you want
to walk in silence – there are so many people here who
want to walk the last 100 kilometres for a Compostela certificate. But by this time I'm used to the chattering of the
groups of cheerful (mostly Spanish) walkers.

I'm anything but alone on the route, but I don't talk to
any other walkers. Except to wish them "Buen Camino" in
passing. And I don't get lost in thought while I'm walking;
actually, I try to think as little as possible.

All I focus on is my breathing and the rhythm of my trekking poles on the ground, like a metronome on a piano.
When a thought or a question or a wish comes to me, I take
note of it and let it go.

Because I'm walking, first and foremost. And that's
enough. What will be, will be. Walk it off. Ultreia! You can
do this a surprisingly long time.

Graffiti seen along the road: *Jill, before we finish I want to tell you every step with you was better. I love you.*

By the time I get to O Pedrouzo I'm not in the mood for busy albergues. Or walking with masses of people tomorrow morning. Brierley's guidebook warns: "As we get nearer the city, asphalt and crowds begin to take over as busloads of pilgrims join the route for the one-day into Santiago. If you are making for the pilgrim mass at 12 noon be prepared for large crowds and try and create an air of compassionate detachment."

So I just keep on walking through O Pedrouzo, for another fifteen kilometres, to Monte do Gozo. The name means "Hill of Joy", because this was the first place where the medieval pilgrims could see the town of Santiago de Compostela and specifically the cathedral's two prominent spires. Here, they could joyfully exclaim that their pilgrimage was almost over.

* * *

My pants are getting dangerously loose. At a guess, I must have walked off at least another four kilograms since I last stepped on a scale at a pharmacy.

Today is a Saturday, but that's purely academic. The days of the week haven't mattered for hundreds of kilometres.

Tonight I'm sleeping at the Monte do Gozo Xunta, a massive albergue that can accommodate 400 walkers. It looks as if it was designed by someone with serious OCD and hardly any imagination. The cement buildings stand in a row, like barracks or prefabs. As if somebody thought they could coin it, here on the hill, by going to no trouble for the throngs of walkers who want to overnight five kilometres from the cathedral.

This aesthetic deficit and the clinical architecture must

count against the Monte do Gozo Xunta: tonight only two of the "barracks" are open. Fewer than thirty people are overnighting here, at a cost of only six euros.

There is a monument on the hilltop commemorating Pope John Paul II's visit in August 1989. It was World Youth Day and the Pope said mass here at Monte do Gozo. I remember seeing him on TV as a child, at about that time. In my little world in Uitenhage the Catholic Church was enough of an oddity, never mind the Pope.

The monument is modern, with several panels: representations of the Pope touching a pilgrim on the shoulder and another where he is blessing pilgrims outside the cathedral in Santiago. There is also a panel depicting St Francis of Assisi, who is believed to have walked the Camino from 1213 to 1215 and passed by here.

* * *

Entry in Moleskine diary during dinner, Albergue Polski

Wow, this is really good beer. 1906 Reserve Especial. Right: the 8-euro dinner was lentil soup (tinned lentils), three hefty meatballs on rice, 2 big slices of fresh bread, a carafe of red wine and a gluten-free chocolate mousse – okay, so I crossed the line with the sweet tooth, but really, I'm not going to judge myself about this.

I have just looked in this journal at what I threw into that plastic ball a month ago at Josele's tree in Saint-Jean-Pied-de-Port: "To learn to love myself, be present, know my worth, walk the earth."

These were not necessarily bullet-point goals, but I think I'm much closer now than I was a month ago. I do think I've let many things go over the past month, and

have been challenged a lot about how I think, act, some-
times anticipate things, old patterns of thinking and doing
... If you spend so much time on your own, in the absence
of so many of the routines and distractions of daily life, it's
a requirement, I think, to have some insights. It was like
that for me, anyway. I want to judge less, especially myself.
Live more in the moment. Be more spontaneous and crea-
tive. Have fewer expectations of anybody: family, friends,
colleagues and myself. Really try to live it and understand
it when my therapist Peter says "don't invest in any out-
comes". Perhaps this increases your capacity for surprise,
I don't know, but I like the idea of being surprised. By
other people, but also by myself.

* * *

After supper at the Polish albergue I walk to the lookout
point where you can see Santiago de Compostela from
Monte do Gozo. There's another statue here, of two pilgrims pointing to the cathedral with outstretched arms.

Santiago is a large, sprawling city. It's already dusk; I
really have to look for the silhouette of the two cathedral
spires in the distance. I am very nearly there.

Day Thirty-three, Sunday 7 June
From Monte do Gozo to Santiago de Compostela
(5 kilometres)

The four other walkers and their bags in the room wake
me. Just as I've got used to the symphony of snores (and
sometimes contribute to it without realising), I've long
found the rustle of plastic bags and a sound of a travel

mug or something tinkling to the floor reassuring rather than frustrating, and maybe even something I'll miss when all this is over.

There is a tradition among pilgrims of leaving their shoes at Monte do Gozo and walking the last five kilometres to the cathedral barefoot. This tradition apparently goes back to the very beginnings of the Camino.

I have a lot of time for rituals, but can't see this happening this morning. My Camino does not end at the cathedral: I want to walk for another full week to Finisterre and Muxía.

I set off. How will it feel to reach the cathedral? The place where millions of mortals arrive, and have been for more than a thousand years, after a long and exhausting pilgrimage?

On my journey through Spain, images of the cathedral have often flashed through my mind. I'd feel the emotion start welling up in these moments. I don't cry easily or often – sometimes, I wish this were different – but if I shed a tear or two at what's regarded as the burial site of the apostle James, so be it.

It is a bright, crisp morning with little traffic on the busy highways near the route. I started at a good pace, and see no other walkers.

About two kilometres before the cathedral my coffee addiction kicks in. The albergue didn't have a café or vending machine. It's not even seven in the morning, but I do find a little shop where I can have a quick café con leche.

CATHEDRAL AND FINISTERRE

"I have two doctors, my left leg and my right."

– G.M. Trevelyan

I walk onto the square and stand before the western facade of the world-famous cathedral.

My trekking poles clatter to the ground. I look up and burst out laughing. Not a giggle or a reserved chuckle, but a roar of laughter that echoes across the quiet square.

Because the facade of the cathedral – and the whole of the spire to the right – is covered in scaffolding! If it were not a Sunday morning, Spaniards in hard-hats would probably be sitting all over it. I have walked more than 800 kilometres through Spain to arrive at a massive building site: they are busy with restoration work, as is so often the case with historical buildings in Europe.

Have I walked into a Monty Python movie? Is John Cleese going to appear on the square any minute now, do one of his funny walks, tap me on the shoulder and tell me it's all just a big joke?

Then two words come to me: under construction. The cathedral is under construction. It is undergoing a process of renovation, recreation, renewal. A process that is perpetual.

And the same applies to me. I am also under construction, in a process of change. This is not the final destination. Tomorrow I take to the road again and continue my Camino to Finisterre.

If all goes well, in seven days I'll be back at the "building site", with a grand total of 1 025 kilometres in forty days behind me.

It's not about the destination, anyway. It's the walk that matters.

The church bell rings seven times. People are starting to gather on the square. So many emotions. As Gert Vlok Nel sings in a different context: "Ek het sommiges gesien huil, ek het enkeles hoor sing, miskien oor die mixed feelings wat om om te draai bring" ("I saw some crying, I heard a few singing, perhaps about the mixed feelings that turning back brings").

I think about the pilgrims of the past, who walked to this very spot hundreds of years ago from faraway places all over Europe without the luxury of trail-running shoes, K-Way rucksacks and ATM cards that work anywhere.

Those poor pilgrims couldn't just catch a bus or hop onto a plane to get back to their homes and families. They just had to turn around and walk back.

I ask a friendly woman from Portland, Oregon, to take a photograph of me in front of the cathedral. This is one moment that should be preserved for posterity.

The cathedral is open. At the entrance I press a coin into a mumbling beggar's hand. It's cool, low-lit and silent inside. The extravagant altar – the extravagant *everything* – is astounding. There are plenty of security guards, and boxes for donativos.

Over the centuries pilgrims have performed all sorts of rituals here in the cathedral at the end of their pilgrimage. One of the traditions is to gently head-butt a statue of the apostle. Jeez, these Catholic traditions! I look for the apostle, but don't find him.

Another tradition is to climb the steps behind the altar to a large golden statue of the apostle James in a little room, give him a hug, and then say something to him. What does one say to an apostle? Especially if you're not a Catholic and aren't walking the Camino for religious reasons?

I climb the steps to the apostle. It must be a pinnacle of Baroque art, this shiny James surveying the cathedral from his booth. But I can't help thinking the poor apostle looks a bit kitsch – Catholic excess meets Las Vegas.

He looks like he's trying to say something, but can't. I give the cold, gold apostle a hug anyway and whisper the three words that made the most sense to me on the Camino: "Walk it off."

* * *

Just to the left of the steps to the apostle is an entrance to the crypt, the Sepulcrum Sancti Iacobi Gloriosum. As opulent as the rest of the cathedral, the silver Romanesque sarcophagus reminds me of the Ark of the Covenant in the Indiana Jones movie.

I'm standing at the final resting place of James the Apostle. Or alleged resting place. Pope Leo XIII declared it to be authentic in 1884, but how can we ever really know? Not that it matters now; I'm sharing the tradition of the millions of pilgrims who have stood here. In the hope of forgiveness, a second chance, a new leaf turned over.

A woman stands next to me. She sinks onto her knees and starts to sob. How many tears of joy, relief and heartache must this room have seen?

I think of my grandmother, Ouma Charlotte, who sat in the parking lot in Port Elizabeth reading from the Book of James while I was being born.

We were very close. She was only 72 when she had a stroke in 1995. She lived for another two weeks, but was partially paralysed. She could say nothing but the word "yes". While she was still in hospital she kept trying to say something, but couldn't form the words. Until one afternoon, when my mother and aunt were standing next to her bed.

In her normal voice, as clear as it had been before the stroke, my grandmother said only one sentence: "You have to keep believing."

* * *

I can already smell the incense. It's a good sign. The Botafumeiro – an enormous censer – hangs above the altar. The cathedral has room for a thousand people and is packed. The Sunday-afternoon mass is about to begin.

I'm in the eighth row from the front. It's a good thing I found a spot an hour early. People are noisy and restless. A woman at the microphone in the front is trying her best to maintain some order: "Silencio, por favor . . . Shhhhh . . ."

The Botafumeiro ritual is not performed at every mass. But if you're lucky you get to see the censer swing through the whole cathedral at a hell of a speed, a tradition believed to have started here in the eleventh century. The original aim of the swinging censer was to conceal the stench of the dirty pilgrims and disinfect the air during epidemics.

Times have changed. Many of the pilgrims sitting here this morning have already had a shower today. I reckon the ritual is just a tourist spectacle these days.

The mass is conducted entirely in Spanish. I hear "el Señor", which means "Lord", a lot. During the service I notice a pilgrim on his knees next to a confessional, mumbling a prayer or a confession. He is still wearing his walking clothes and boots. What would he be confessing here in the cathedral in Santiago?

Perhaps he's just getting some kneework in. As one of my grandmother's friends often says to my mother when she bumps into her in church in Uitenhage, "Kneework, Winnie, kneework." This same aunty later had to have a knee replacement.

The priest drones on in monotonous Spanish. Just as I start falling asleep, there is a commotion. The Botafumeiro sinks down, all the way to the altar.

While a man in ecclesiastical dress lights the incense, the organ begins to rumble. A choir led by a soprano sings the "Hymn to St James".

Eight men in brown uniforms manipulate the Botafumeiro's rope. They are not priests or monks, but tiraboleiros – porters specially trained to send this huge censer, more than a metre and a half in length and weighing 80 kilograms, down the length of the cathedral. At first it slowly swings back and forth, but as the tiraboleiros gather momentum and pull the rope more rhythmically, the censer picks up speed. Within a minute it is swinging dangerously fast, with the mighty organ and choir of voices as a soundtrack. Smoke billows from it, filling the cathedral.

The tiraboleiros know their stuff. If the censer came loose and landed in the crowd, there'd be casualties. Another item on Timna and my Ways to Die on the Camino list: Death by Botafumeiro.

I'm not a churchgoer, but cannot remain unmoved by this magnificent tradition. I observe the awestruck pilgrims watching it through their smartphones, taking photos and videos. Hundreds of smartphones point upwards, trying to capture something of this extraordinary ritual. I understand the need to preserve a moment all too well, but after more than a month without a phone or camera it makes much more sense to me just to sit and watch.

* * *

The Pilgrim Office, where you receive your Compostela certificate to prove that you have completed the Camino, is just around the corner from the cathedral. The queues can be long, but today I'm lucky – there are only ten people ahead of me. The atmosphere is festive. The pilgrims take photos, laugh and talk.

"Where did you start walking?" is a question I often hear. When someone answers "Saint Jean", the response is usually "Oh wow!" or "Really?" It sounds like most of the pilgrims waiting with me started near Sarria.

In the days before the Compostela, a scallop shell was evidence enough that you had walked the Camino – a shell you could pick up yourself near Finisterre and take home. But in the thirteenth century the church started issuing the Compostela, an official document proving that the apostle had forgiven your sins.

I think of Angie from New York. Where on the Camino could she be now? I saw her outside Pamplona four Sundays ago. I recommended that she walk no more than twenty kilometres a day, and that she makes sure she gets enough rest.

The admin at the counter is quick and painless. The official looks at the stamps in my Credencial to confirm that I have walked more than 100 kilometres. On a form, I need to give the reason why I walked the Camino: "Religious/Spiritual" or "Non-religious". If you choose "Religious/Spiritual", you get a Compostela, and for "Non-religious" you get a Certificado – a more general certificate.

I select "Religious/Spiritual". If the Camino has awakened anything in me, it is a sense of wonder and the mystical. It's less a church- or religion-related sense than a sense related to life itself. A type of secular conversion.

The Compostela is in Latin: "Capitulum hujus Almae Apostolicae . . ." And my name appears in at attempt at Latin on it: "Dominus Andreum Ernestum Henricum Grundling."

"Oh my God!" I hear as I step out of the office. I recognise the voice immediately. It's Angie! Angie from New York! How on earth is this possible? We hug and the tears flow freely.

I can only interpret this meeting near the cathedral as a significant coincidence, or synchronicity – it cannot be accidental. I never thought I would see Angie along the Camino again. It was supposed to have taken her at least two more weeks to complete the walk.

We have dinner together at the Hospedería San Martín Pinario. Angie tells me she walked as far as Burgos, but her shin splints were so bad that a doctor booked her off for a week. After that she walked again for a few days and then decided to take a bus to Sarria. Over the past ten days she walked very slowly and calmly all the way to the cathedral. And tomorrow she will take the bus to the Finisterre lighthouse.

Later, she takes a few photos of me in front of the cathedral. As we say goodbye, we hear singing a little way from us: "Ay, ay, ay, ay, canta y no llores."

Sing, don't cry. Like that first morning at Roncesvalles, and now once again. Full circle in Santiago.

The Camino provides.

Day Thirty-four, Monday 8 June
From Santiago de Compostela to Vilaserío
(33 kilometres)

I'm really looking forward to the Camino Finisterre. Only ten per cent of pilgrims who reach their destination at

Santiago de Compostela walk for another three days to "the end of the Earth". Most people who want to visit the Finisterre lighthouse take the bus from Santiago de Compostela.

Last night I slept at Albergue Roots & Boots. I could see the cathedral from my bed.

This morning I have a tortilla de patatas at Café Tertulia, to the west of the cathedral and near the albergue. Here I see Timna again, who is also on her way to Finisterre.

We walk together for the rest of the day. There are lots of trees and hamlets along the way. For a long while we walk through an oak forest. We cross the River Tambre on a striking medieval bridge that's over 100 metres long.

We talk about things like her life in Israel, the country's recent history and conflicts, and aspects of the Jewish faith such as the Talmud and Kabbalah. As we talk I become aware once again of the significant role of Israel in my life growing up, because of the stories in the Children's Bible. The first stories I ever heard were set in Israel. I'd love to go there one day.

* * *

The Camino Finisterre has no shortage of myths and legends of its own. At Chancela de Abaixo, about a kilometre before the little town of Negreira, we pass the sturdy stone walls of a fourteenth-century manor house.

Brierley's guidebook – the one dealing specifically with the Camino Finisterre – tells the sad story of a caretaker who lived here many centuries ago. The owner went on a Crusade against the Moors and left his son in the care of a woman. On his return, he learnt that his son had drowned in the River Tambre.

The owner decided to decapitate the caretaker as punishment. Just before the axe came down, the caretaker's husband knelt beside her and so they were both decapitated.

It is believed the couple are buried somewhere in the surrounding pine forest. According to local legend, the sounds you hear when the wind blows through the pines are the sighs of their final embrace.

* * *

Timna and I walked long and hard today, but the kilometres flew by. Most pilgrims spend the first night of this Camino in Negreira, but we wanted to walk a bit further. We stay overnight at the Albergue O Rueiro in Vilaserío.

A John Deere tractor rumbles past with a load of hay. A lazy Labrador lies at the bar. The birds are having a concert; some cyclists are carbo-loading before continuing on their way. I sit on a little veranda and drink an Estrella beer.

Life is good.

Day Thirty-five, Tuesday 9 June
From Vilaserío to O Logoso
(24,6 kilometres)

Today I'm mostly walking alone again.

I like the balance I've found on the Camino between spending time on my own and with other pilgrims.

Timna read in a brochure about a new albergue, O Logoso, near a river just beyond Olveiroa. There are only twenty beds, so she has booked for us both for tonight.

I really like Timna. I don't know if it's yet another in-fatuation. But I'm not going to let this run away with me and definitely don't want to try anything impulsive. She's very independent and focused on her Camino. We're good friends and that's probably enough.

Maybe I've learnt something on the Camino after all: to be less concerned about outcomes. And to accept reality for what it is. In the moment. To waste less energy on all kinds of possible scenarios or yearnings.

While I'm turning this over in my mind, an idea strikes me like a gong: Forget about "what if"; stick with "what is". It sounds easy, but I think I'm onto something here.

I've experienced so much pain and disappointment by focusing on – even clinging to – "what if" thoughts. It is a dismally human thing to do: to wish that things had turned out differently. To think "If only I had . . ." or "If only she had . . ."

I have a new challenge now: not to escape into "what if", but to remain anchored in reality – in the "what is".

* * *

I have almost reached O Logoso and think about November 2014 once again. I nearly lost my mind after that break-up. I paced up and down in my flat's tiny lounge for nights on end, runaway thoughts on repeat. Not unlike a traumatised zoo animal patrolling the bars of its cage.

My perspective on that time, and that crazy pacing in my flat, is different now. The idea of the Camino hadn't occurred to me, but maybe that pacing prepared me sub-consciously for the real walk that would happen here in Spain a few months later.

While I was completely lost in the "what if" back there

in my flat, I engage more calmly and consciously with my thoughts here on the Camino.

I have come across the Latin expression "Solvitur ambulando" ("It is solved by walking") before. Now, I am living it.

Day Thirty-six, Wednesday 10 June
From O Logoso to Finisterre
(30,6 kilometres)

Today I am walking to the "end of the Earth". By sunset I want to be sitting on a rock at Cabo Finisterra, near the lighthouse that looks out over the Atlantic Ocean. The holy place of the pagans of days gone by. And the place where the Celtic druids erected an Ara Solis – a stone altar in honour of the sun.

Cabo Finisterra is my final destination, at the sea. Where I literally cannot walk any further. The cover of Brierley's guidebook to the Camino Finisterre shows him seated and gazing at a perfect sunset over the sea. It's a prospect that has idled in my mind for a long time.

Last night I enjoyed a delicious meal with Timna, Jacob and Anna. They are still busy packing for the day. It will be great to see them again at Finisterre, maybe even at the lighthouse. But I don't think any of us feel we need to arrive there as a group. If it turns out that way, I hope it happens spontaneously. We each have our own appointment with the end of the world.

The Camino Finisterre is an opportunity to integrate the lessons you've learnt and the experiences you've had en route to Santiago de Compostela, but without overthinking things. The last time I wrote a proper entry in my journal was outside the cathedral – three days ago. But this doesn't worry me.

As David Sedaris writes in the book I read earlier on the Camino: "It's not lost on me that I'm so busy recording life, I don't have time to really live it." At the moment I just want to walk and *live*, and trust that the unfathomable psychic processes are running their course.

I leave O Logoso and set off alone. Two ponies are grazing calmly outside the albergue. I enjoy Galicia immensely. All the little hamlets between the woods, the ancient hórreos, the mothers and daughters who seem to be farming together and drive the cattle along at the tops of their voices . . . this part of the world differs dramatically from the Pyrenees, the Meseta and the landscape before O Cebreiro.

It also helps that at present only a few pilgrims walk the Camino Finisterre. The silence is most welcome, especially after the few days from Sarria to Santiago de Compostela with those huge groups of Spaniards.

It's also very good for my fitness and weight to keep on walking. I just have to watch that my pants don't start hanging below my butt like a hip-hop singer's.

I walk past a hamlet called Hospital, which has been providing medical services to pilgrims for centuries. The little village was once completely destroyed by Napoleon's troops.

The road forks at a route marker: left to Finisterre and right to Muxía. I keep left. If all goes according to plan, tomorrow I'll be able to walk from Finisterre to Muxía, the fishing village where the Virgin Mary is said to have appeared to the apostle James.

An unsightly factory belching clouds of smoke unexpectedly comes into view in the distance to my left. Another reminder of humankind's endless capacity for destroying nature.

The factory reminds me of a book I was given in the eighties: *The Wump World*, by Bill Peet. This book was far ahead of its time. It's about the Wumps – cute, woolly creatures – who live in Wump World. They eat green grass, swim in crystal-clear rivers and pools, and are not threatened by anybody.

But one day the Pollutians arrive in huge steel spaceships. And it's not long before they start building cities and factories and highways. The Wumps scurry off to seek refuge in caves. Wump World eventually becomes so polluted that the Pollutians can hardly breathe the sooty air, and so they rise up against their leader. He just sends his spaceships off to look for a new world. When all the Pollutians have left for their next destination, they leave behind a Wump World that will never be the same again.

We, of course, are the Pollutians of the Earth. But we have nowhere else to go.

* * *

For twelve kilometres I walk through a higher-lying heath with wonderful views of the mountains and valleys. Every now and again there's a cross by the roadside – some clearly older than others – with cairns left by the pilgrims.

I fill my water bottle at a fountain near the little church in San Pedro Mártir. There's a bench at the fountain you can sit on while you rest your feet in the water. Like many of the fountains along the Camino, this one is said to contain holy water that will cure your aches and pains. I am grateful that I haven't had a single blister yet.

The view of the Atlantic Ocean that Brierley writes

about must be really close now. About two kilometres further along I see a route marker painted green. Someone has painted "TO THE END" on the sign in red.

For the first time in five weeks I see the sea: Spain's Costa da Morte, the rocky "Coast of Death", where many ships over the centuries have gone to their watery graves.

I take a deep breath. Emotions well up.

It is a truly powerful sight. I look out over the bay and the coastal villages of Corcubión and Cee. And beyond them, far beyond Corcubión, the peninsula runs out at Cabo Finisterra.

* * *

Although I last ate at O Logoso this morning, I hurry through Cee and Corcubión. I want to press on to Finisterre, find an albergue in time, and make sure I reach the lighthouse, about three and a half kilometres outside of town, by early evening.

But before I get to Finisterre, I take a footpath through the shrubbery down to the beach. Playa Talón is a secluded beach with turquoise water in a sheltered bay. Rough, rocky cliffs loom on both sides. It suddenly feels like I'm somewhere near Nature's Valley in the Eastern Cape.

I am the only person on the beach. The temptation to run into the ocean stark naked is great, but I see a few pilgrims coming along the ridge. So I wear my running shorts.

The water is freezing but wonderfully refreshing. I taste the salt and plunge deep into the surf. This is probably the closest I will get to an adult baptism.

A line from a Sheila Cussons poem occurs to me as I dry myself: "Ek het meteens onthou dat ek gelukkig is" ("I suddenly remembered that I'm happy").

Playa Langosteira is a bright white beach, two kilometres long, stretching all the way to the little town of Finisterre. Even though the swim cooled me down, it's still very hot. I buy an almond-flavoured Magnum at a little stall – my first ice cream in Spain and hands down one of the most delicious ever.

The beach is central to the legend of the Camino Finisterre. It is believed that James preached at Playa Langosteira and tried to convert the pagans here. There is even a story that, as a young man, Jesus himself came to preach here during the eighteen "lost years" of which there is no record in the Bible. Some of the druids at Finisterre may even have mentored him.

This is also where the pilgrims in the early years of the Camino would pick up scallop shells before the long journey back home.

I take off my shoes, walk along the beach and look for shells in the shallow water. There is an abundance of scallop shells, smaller than the one on the back of my rucksack. I would much rather give a few people back home a scallop shell from Finisterre each than blow euros on souvenirs from the myriad tourist shops in Santiago de Compostela.

My grandmother always had a large seashell in the lounge of her Uitenhage flat. I would often lie on the carpet and press the shell to my ear – you could hear "the sea" in it, apparently. I would later learn that these were simply background noises resonating within the shell. But I still prefer the idea that it's the sea, and that in these shells I'm taking a bit of ocean from the Finisterre soundtrack home with me.

The municipal albergue has beds for only 44 pilgrims and is already fully booked. But it is the place to get your Finisterre certificate, similar to the Compostela, as proof that you have walked all the way to Finisterre. The Fisterrana is a simpler certificate, with a lovely picture of the sun setting over Cabo Finisterra on it. Unlike the Compostela, its wording is in Galician.

I bump into Anna and Timna outside the albergue, where they've also come to fetch their Fisterranas. We find a place to sleep at Albergue Finistellae, higher up in the town, for twelve euros each. From here it is only two and a half kilometres to the lighthouse.

I shower, throw my dirty clothes into the washing machine and enjoy one of my last siestas in Spain.

* * *

We have supper at the Restaurante El Puerto in the harbour. The Englishman Jacob and two other pilgrims I met at O Logoso – Hans from Holland and Anette from Denmark – join us.

It is an eminent seafood restaurant. Galicia is renowned for pulpo, or octopus. But I play it safe and order pork. The last thing I need at the end of the Earth is an allergic reaction.

When I was still at school, my parents used to treat me after prizegiving every year to a meal at the Prairie Eagle Spur in the main street in Uitenhage. Year after year, I would order the surf and turf and end up vomiting horribly later that night. My mother claimed it was because I ate too fast – until once, years later, I ended up in hospital on a drip after a small plate of calamari.

Luckily my allergy is limited to molluscs – mussels, oysters, squid and snails. I can eat prawns and other shellfish to my heart's content.

What I would really love to order now is sushi, but I haven't seen this anywhere along the Camino. Forty days without sushi. I feel about sushi the same way that Esau in the Bible felt about a pot of lentil soup – right now I would sell my birthright for a plate of salmon roses.

Anna finds this hysterically funny. "I'm going to have to tell my friends back home that there's a South African that misses sushi more than his phone."

* * *

We set off as a group to Cabo Finisterra, but soon spread out along the tarred road. I'm walking out front at a stiff pace. I feel ecstatic, as if the adrenalin is rushing through my veins. It's just after half past nine. The sun will set in about 45 minutes.

Just before the lighthouse I see the last route marker. A simple concrete beacon with *0.00 km* written under the Camino shell. At last!

There's also a white peace totem planted next to the lighthouse with the message: "May Peace Prevail On Earth".

Pilgrims perch like dassies on the rocks, all eyes turned west, where the sun is already hanging low on the horizon. A few sit together, others prefer being alone. I can hear talking, but nobody is noisy.

I understand why the pagans and the Romans thought the earth ended right here at the furthest point of this peninsula. Especially if you are convinced that the earth is flat. Because everywhere around me, as far as the eye can see, is the sea – infinite and unfathomable – reaching to the horizon.

All of us who had supper together are now here on the

rocks. Anette asks me to take a picture of her as she throws her trekking pole into the sea.

I would also like to leave something behind. In Cape Town a consultant at Media24, Evelyn Howard, gave me a small piece of rose quartz to take with me on the Camino.

At work I have a monthly appointment with Evelyn. We've walked a long and meaningful road together. Initially, I went to see her for help with time management and career development. But over time she began to play a much more important role as a mentor, even in times of crisis that had nothing to do with work. We worked out my core values together, of which self-respect – something I often struggle with – is number one.

I throw the little stone that travelled with me all the way from Cape Town into the sea. For me the Camino was a rediscovery and confirmation of self-respect.

"I knew I would find you guys!" I recognise the voice immediately. It's my doppelgänger, Robert. We last saw each other briefly outside the cathedral in Santiago de Compostela.

Robert arrived in Finisterre yesterday with Sabine, Sebastian and Alessandro. These three have already gone back to Santiago de Compostela by bus, but Robert wants to stay a few more days along the Costa da Morte. He guessed that we would be at the lighthouse tonight and took a taxi here.

What a privilege to be able to share this special sunset with a few Camino friends. It looks just like the Brierley book cover, only better. Because this is here and now. I sit cross-legged on a rock, with the sun's last rays on my face. Fully present in the moment. And wholly aware of how short and precious life is. This too shall pass . . . These ancient words also apply to this moment.

The sunlight casts a golden path on the sea. From where I'm sitting, it looks like a golden Camino arrow extending from the rocks across the water.

When the sun eventually slips below the horizon, silence falls on Cabo Finisterra.

* * *

One of the pilgrim rituals over the centuries has been to burn something – usually an item of clothing – at Cabo Finisterra. After sunset we make a fire between the rocks. Anna throws a pair of her walking pants on the fire. I follow with a pair of socks.

It's a lovely moment – symbolic of letting something go and of making a new start. But an aggressive French couple almost ruin our ritual. "Why do you make fire here?" the man barks, highly upset. "You Camino tourists! You come here and destroy the environment. This is not the Camino spirit!"

We stand there a bit dumbfounded. The fire itself is tiny, and we made it on a spot where fires have been made many times before. But these two environmental activists are clearly on a mission.

I want to retort with The Dude's words in the cult movie *The Big Lebowski*: "This will not stand, you know. This aggression will not stand, man."

But mindful of the Zen monk's words, I just say calmly: "Is that so?"

* * *

It's after midnight when we walk back from Cabo Finisterra to the albergue, Timna and I right at the back.

She has been a dear friend on the Camino.

I tell her a ghost story from Brierley's guidebook. Here in Galicia people believe in the Santa Compaña – an invisible procession of the dead who wander around the landscape at night. Each one bears a candle. If you see a tiny light that flickers and darts, you know you are in their midst. If one of these doomed souls approaches you and places its candle in your hand, you become one of them.

Timna is a bit superstitious, so the story unsettles her – especially since we're walking around after midnight in dark Galicia.

Then it happens: first, one little light flickers. Then another, and soon ten or more. But happily these are not the Santa Compaña's candles, but fireflies leading us to the albergue.

RETURN

"Doen dit gerus
want dis
'n groot avontuur
alhoewel jy eindig
waar jy begin het."

"Do it anyway
because it's
a great adventure
even though you end
where you began."

– Valiant Swart, "Die Mystic Boer"

Day Thirty-seven, Thursday 11 June
From Finisterre to Muxía
(31 kilometres)

I have only four days left in Spain.

Today I'm walking to the fishing village of Muxía. I said goodbye to Timna and Anna last night. They are going to relax in Finisterre for a few more days and then head home.

Robert also wants to go to Muxía today, but he only wants to set off later. This suits me fine – I want to walk on my own for the last few days. At Muxía I can get a third certificate, a Muxíana. I just need to get a stamp in my Credencial at Lires, which is more or less the halfway point.

I start early. I want to go to Cabo Finisterra again first. But not to the lighthouse – I take a steep footpath to the highest point, Monte Facho. There are two large round boulders here, the Piedras Santas or Holy Stones.

Apparently the pagans used to perform rituals at the Piedras Santas centuries ago. Later, the Catholic Church would rewrite (or hijack) this rich history with a tale that the Virgin Mary appeared at these rocks to help St James in his ministry. I'm standing on top of the Piedras Santas. I'm neither pagan nor Catholic, but I'm interested in these stories and legends, and I do like a nice view. Far below I see Praia do Mar de Fora, a beautiful secluded beach. The Costa da Morte stretches north.

* * *

I'm a walking machine along all the forest paths leading to Muxía today, never too far from the sea. How will it feel, soon, to have to make my way without this rucksack and these trekking poles? The poles feel like a part of my body, a bionic extension of my arms.

I realise I have become much more aware of my thoughts. This has been one of the gifts of the Camino: the silence and separation in nature, and the rhythm of walking, stimulate this greater awareness. The challenge is to not get judgemental about your thoughts. Sometimes it is enough just to acknowledge them.

Eckhart Tolle calls this "watching the thinker": the realisation that you are not your unending stream of thoughts, but the one who is aware of your thoughts. There's liberation in that distinction; making it is how you escape from compulsive and destructive patterns of thought.

* * *

Muxía is a charming Galician fishing village, a bit like Kalk Bay without the tourists. The name refers to the monks who established a monastery here in the twelfth century to convert the pagans.

In contrast to most of the other Camino towns and villages, here I see more locals on the streets than pilgrims. I have encountered only four other walkers today, all on their way to Finisterre.

Robert and I meet at the Bela Muxía albergue, where we each receive a Muxíana. The certificate is written in Galician, with a picture of St James kneeling before the Virgin Mary next to her legendary boat that has turned to stone.

Day Thirty-eight, Friday 12 June
From Muxía to O Logoso
(29 kilometres)

Robert and I quickly want to visit the church in Muxía, the Virxe da Barca, early this morning. It is close to the rock that is claimed to be the petrified sail of the Virgin Mary's boat.

The rock, the Pedra dos Cadrís, does indeed look like a sail. It apparently has healing properties: if you walk beneath it nine times, you will be cured of all sorts of physical ailments. I tease Robert and suggest that he perform the ritual to see if his blisters disappear. But I doubt that even the Pedra dos Cadrís could soothe his wounds. Instead, we take turns to lie on the sail and take photos.

There's something going on at the church. The building has been cordoned off with red-and-white tape, huge vehicles are parked there and I see cameras and other equipment. A man approaches us to tell us that nobody's allowed to access the church today, because Pedro Almodóvar is here shooting a film.

I'm a great fan of the movies of this legendary Spanish filmmaker, such as *Talk To Her*, *Bad Education* and *All About My Mother*. We hang around for a while to see if there's going to be any action, but they don't seem to have started shooting.

As we walk back a middle-aged man in a cap passes us, walking in the direction of the church. I nod, he nods back. I ask Robert to check Google Images to make sure.

Yep, it was Pedro Almodóvar.

* * *

Robert is catching a bus to Santiago de Compostela to rest there for a few days. There's nothing stopping me from doing the same, but I'm addicted to walking. I want to walk back to the cathedral from Muxía.

I still have about eighty kilometres to cover in three days. When I get back to Santiago de Compostela, I will have walked roughly 1 025 kilometres, further than the distance between Cape Town and Bloemfontein. My walking companions are all on their way home, so for the next three days I'm on my own.

Tonight I want to sleep at O Logoso. Fortunately Brierley's Finisterre guidebook has a map of today's route out of Muxía, because I'm now walking "against" the Camino. For the last time, on with the corpse.

* * *

I'm back at O Logoso and sit on my own at a table with a basket full of bread and a glass full of red wine. A few lines from Derek Walcott's beautiful poem "Love After Love" are very much on my mind tonight. I memorised it at the end of last year during a time of great disillusionment.

> Give wine. Give bread. Give back your heart
> to itself, the stranger who has loved you
> all your life, whom you ignored
> for another, who knows you by heart.

I find Walcott's words compelling, and full of consolation and hope, but I realise that, up to now, I haven't been ready to live them. It's a process.

I may be on my own tonight, but I'm anything but lonely. In patient and subtle ways, I'm gradually reconciling with myself, my soul, my spiritual side, my inner life, whatever you want to call it. For all I know, I am closer to "myself" now than ever before. And that's a consequence of something as simple as walking: one foot in front of the other.

I've been a stranger to myself for a very long time. I kept giving, kept trying to rescue and satisfy others. I wanted to achieve the impossible . . . often at my own expense, at the expense of my own life's journey. Maybe this was an unconscious attempt to escape from myself by investing all my energy and dedication and care in other people, relationships and projects.

When you travel so widely, break so radically with everything and everyone you know, with your usual routines and ways of doing things, with social media, when you walk day in and day out with your own thoughts that you alone are responsible for, you realise many things.

I remind myself again: no matter how far you travel, you always travel with yourself. And that's why you may as well learn to live in peace with this ever-present travelling companion.

I'm sitting at a table in a little village in Galicia. I'm eating bread and drinking wine. That's all.

And it's enough. More than that – it's a feast. A feast in the here and now.

Day Thirty-nine, Saturday 13 June
From O Logoso to Negreira
(36 kilometres)

I spot this notice behind the counter at O Logoso: "This establishment has complaint letters for users."

I once complained about my fate to my friend J.P. He suggested I write a letter to the universe in which I explained exactly why I was so angry that things had not worked out how I wanted them to. I could have a proper rant, and could even blame it all on the universe.

All I had to do was post the letter to J.P. in Grahamstown, because he knew where the universe's personal post box was. He would deliver the letter for me personally.

And where is this post box? At the shredding machine in his office, where he's stuck the word "Complaints" on the wall.

* * *

I'm really battling today. Maybe I *should* write that letter to the universe. I was hopelessly over-confident to think it would be easy to walk the same route back to Santiago de Compostela.

I walked this exact route a few days ago, in the opposite direction. Now I keep missing the yellow arrows and scallop shells on the route markers. I'm finding it hard to walk the Camino back-to-front. I've never been good with directions, not even with a map.

I get lost for the third time somewhere near Vilaserío, but only realise this three quarters of an hour later. I have just added four unnecessary kilometres to a day that is already over thirty kilometres long.

And now it's started pouring. I shouldn't complain, I suppose – it's the first time this has happened on my Camino. But it's starting to feel like my most difficult day in Spain.

My emotions are also all over the place. I think I'm already beginning to miss the Camino. I'm not ready to say goodbye to this simple way of life.

Jim White sings in one of his songs: "I've got ten miles to go on a nine mile road".

That's exactly what it feels like today.

Day Forty, Sunday 14 June
From Negreira to Santiago de Compostela
(21 kilometres)

After supper last night, I must have fallen asleep the minute I sat down on my bed in the Albergue San José in Negreira: I'm still wearing yesterday's walking clothes and didn't even get as far as brushing my teeth.

The albergue is almost empty. Most other people have already started walking. My body is protesting and my mood is still low after yesterday, a day of disorientation and doubt. With all the toing and froing I ended up walking almost forty kilometres.

Tomorrow I return to my busy life in Cape Town, without the yellow arrows, the daily walking routine or the "Buen Caminos".

A young man walks out of the bathroom and packs his rucksack on the bed opposite mine. I was so exhausted last night I didn't even see him.

Gustavo is a fireman from Barcelona. He is also a taxi driver and coaches a soccer team at a local school. He applied for a few days' leave and arrived here in Negreira last night. He is walking only as far as Finisterre, then returning to Barcelona.

I envy the Spanish their option of quickly walking a section of the Camino on a long weekend. For me, doing this again will involve a lot of saving – and a great deal of planning. But I can't complain about my hiking options at home. I live barely five minutes' drive (if the traffic lights are green) from Table Mountain.

"So my last day on the Camino is your first day, Gustavo," I say as we go our respective ways.

He smiles. "No. This is not your last day. Remember, the Camino may start somewhere, but it never ends."

* * *

I remember the refrain of Amanda Strydom's "Pelgrimsgebed", a pilgrim's prayer, when I see the cathedral at Santiago de Compostela in the distance:

Alle pelgrims keer	All pilgrims come
weer huis toe	back home again
elke swerwer	every wanderer
kom weer tuis	returns home
ek verdwaal steeds	I'm still lost
op die grootpad	on the highway
soekend na	looking for
U boardinghuis	Your boarding house

* * *

I'm lying on the broad of my back on the Plaza del Obradoiro, buggered and wet with sweat.

I'm back at the cathedral in Santiago de Compostela. I was here a week ago. In seven days I have walked just over 200 kilometres.

The church clock strikes four. The square is full of pilgrims and tourists. I hear music coming from different directions: guitars, a tenor, a string quartet somewhere, maybe.

Robert and I have arranged to meet here this afternoon. We are both sleeping at the Hospedería San Martín Pinario tonight, a monastery dating from the sixteenth century that's right next to the cathedral. Tomorrow morning I fly to Paris, and he to Munich.

Knowing Robert, he'll spot me among all these people any minute now. Which is exactly what happens: "My brother from another mother!"

He can be a handful sometimes, but I am really going to miss my Camino friend and his sense of humour.

* * *

Before we mark our last night in Santiago de Compostela with a gin and tonic, I want to talk to my parents.

I throw a few euro coins into the tickey box and dial the familiar number. I know forty days is not all that long, but in this life one never knows.

My mother answers: "Erns, is that you?!" My father says something in the background. It's wonderful to hear their voices again. We talk until I've used up all my coins.

I'm relieved and grateful that my parents, brother and sister are all okay.

I should probably start making plans to get my laptop and iPhone back. I borrow Robert's phone and contact Martine via Facebook to get Marcelle's email address. Martine responds quickly and within half an hour I've sent Marcelle a message.

She lets me know that my parcel arrived safely and that I'm welcome to pick it up in Paris tomorrow.

* * *

The rooms at the Hospedería San Martín Pinario are in the style of how the monks would have lived here in the sixteenth century. They are sparsely furnished: you have a bed, a bedside table and a small wooden table with a chair.

Before I go to sleep I sit at the table. I think of a paragraph in Will Self's book *Walking to Hollywood*, in which he describes what it's like for him to come home: "Who will I be when I get back? Will I have changed? Will *they* have changed? The world is all used up – only tourists or salesmen set off on journeys; the real explorers strike out for the known."

Monday 15 June
Paris

Marcelle's directions are meticulous and I find her flat easily. And so I get the parcel back that I last saw in Bayonne. Marcelle admits that it was a bit strange when it arrived at the post office out of the blue – especially since she wasn't sure when she would hear from its unknown sender.

It's strange to see my laptop and iPhone and all the Slagtersnek notes again.

I bought some last-minute chocolates for Marcelle at the airport at Santiago de Compostela. You can't arrive empty-handed to meet someone who has done you such a big favour.

The chocolate box has a picture of the cathedral on it. Marcelle tells me that she visited Santiago de Compostela last year and walked the Camino Finisterre. We also realise that she and my friend Sophia were in the same student residence at Stellenbosch.

I'm hardly surprised at this synchronicity – I had so

many similar experiences along the Camino. Coincidence itself is on thin ice.

She asks about my work at *Go* and the types of articles I write. I tell her that Sophia and I both want to write more about mindfulness and try to incorporate a labyrinth somewhere in the magazine as often as possible.

"Wait, I have something for you," Marcelle says and goes to her bookshelf. She takes a book and writes something in the front. "It's a gift for Sophia, but you must also read it," she says. The book is *Mindfulness for Beginners* by Jon Kabat-Zinn.

On the front cover is a photograph of a Zen garden that evokes a labyrinth.

* * *

The Hôtel Au Pacific, where I booked in advance, is a modest two-star establishment. I will have to get used to European prices off the Camino very quickly. At 80 euros per night this hotel is almost ten times more expensive than the average albergue.

But I do have my own room and bathroom. The hotel is also only 1,4 kilometres from the Eiffel Tower, *and* there is free wi-fi.

I was last online forty days ago. Luckily, I remember my PIN now that I have the iPhone in my hands again. My fingers' muscle memory kicks in.

The first WhatsApp message I read is from my father, who sent it on Sunday 7 June, the day I first arrived in Santiago de Compostela:

You definitely won't get this message now – hope it comes through on your cell phone! "I can take it, I can make it!"

Camino, where is Erns? I'm listening to Cohen's "Halle-lujah" and wondering and missing you! At this stage O Cebreiro? Triacastela? Or maybe Sarria on the way to the finishing line? Shoo, this silence is awful, but I believe it's good for you! Pray every day for your safe return and that you find great meaning on this pilgrimage. Love you!

* * *

6:18 p.m. on Monday 15 June 2015, Hôtel Au Pacific, Paris

WhatsApp to Sophia

Wow! Hallooo from Paris! My digital detox is over. I have wi-fi in the hotel. The Camino was an amazing ex-perience, far beyond words or photos. I went rogue a bit, walked a lot more, 1 025 km in 40 days ... I'm now going to check out the Eiffel Tower for the first time, Winand is fetching me on Wednesday morning at the airport in Cape Town. Will be great to see you, maybe sort out the car battery after work and grab a bite? I hope things are going well at the Cape. Jeez, it's surreal to be living in WhatsApp again.

* * *

I buy a little bag of cherries at a shop near the hotel and walk in the direction of the Arc de Triomphe. I've walked with my rucksack for so long that this feels . . . too light. And I miss the tick-tock, tick-tock rhythm of my trekking poles.

I see a little yellow arrow on the ground in front of me. I

stop immediately and look again. Yes, it's not my imagination. On a rubbish bin I see another yellow arrow.

Am I on the Camino once again – or still? If I carried on walking, I'd arrive at Saint-Jean-Pied-de-Port in about 1 000 kilometres.

* * *

I climb the 284 steps to the top of the Arc de Triomphe. It's almost sunset and the view of Paris is unforgettable. The busy Champs-Élysées stretches all the way to the Louvre in front of me. To the right is the Eiffel Tower in all its glory.

There are lots of other tourists up here, but I'm pretty much the only one looking at the Eiffel Tower. All the others have their backs to it and are focused on their phones and selfie sticks. They shuffle around and stare at their screens while trying to get themselves and the Tower into the frame.

I don't want to sound like a prophet who, after forty days in the wilderness eating grasshoppers and wild honey, has now returned to civilisation, but I find this smartphone-and-selfie obsession completely ridiculous.

Can someone just turn round for a second and look at the Eiffel Tower?

Tuesday 16 June
Paris

My last morning in Europe. This afternoon, the long haul back to Cape Town begins. I eat a low-octane breakfast at the hotel: a dry croissant with jam and cheese, and a weak filter coffee.

I miss my morning rituals in Spain, especially the tortilla de patatas.

* * *

The train to Charles de Gaulle airport stops every few minutes. A man with an accordion gets on at one of the stations, a typical busker trying to make a bit of money off the tourists. As Tom Waits said in an interview: "A gentleman is someone who can play the accordion, but doesn't."

The busker plays the well-known hits: Édith Piaf's "La vie en rose" and "Non, je ne regrette rien" and something I recognise from the film *Amélie*.

If there's one instrument I would like to learn to play at some point, it's the accordion, like my mother.

The train stops at a station and the doors glide open. For a moment the man with the accordion looks like he is wondering whether to get off or not. Then he looks up, directly at me. He smiles and begins to play again. It's the "Ay, ay, ay, ay" song.

Sing, don't cry. I don't even try to stop the tears.

* * *

Fight QR 1369 from Doha to Cape Town is not without its challenges. I'm extremely restless because I can't walk. Even last night in Paris, I ended up walking fifteen kilometres easily.

I get up every few minutes and walk up and down the aisle. I wonder what the other passengers think about this frustrated pilgrim who can't sit still.

Later I watch a movie, *The Secret Life of Walter Mitty*, with Ben Stiller. It caught my eye six weeks ago when I flew to Paris, but I was too busy with the Slagtersnek article at the time. It's a feel-good movie about a nerd, Walter Mitty, who daydreams a lot and works in the photo archives at *Life* magazine.

I write a quote that appears on a wall in the movie in my Moleskine diary: "To see the world, things dangerous to come to, to see behind walls, draw closer, to find each other, and to feel. That is the purpose of life."

Walter Mitty goes on a great adventure in search of a specific photo's negatives. He eventually ends up in the Himalayas, where he meets the photographer (played by Sean Penn). The photographer looks through his lens at an extremely rare snow leopard, but does not take a photograph. "If I like a moment, for me, personally, I don't like to have the distraction of the camera. I just want to stay in it," he says.

I identify very strongly with this after forty days without a camera. I think back to many of the photographs I didn't take. But I was there. And that was enough.

The Camino is going to be unleashing emotions in me for a long time still. The tears fall at the end credits as José González sings:

Sometimes there's things a man cannot know
Gears won't turn and the leaves won't grow
There's no place to run and no gasoline
Engines won't turn and the train won't leave

I will stay with you tonight
Hold you close 'til the morning light
In the morning watch a new day rise
We'll do whatever just to stay alive

On the plane, I read the book *Mindfulness for Beginners* that Marcelle sent as a gift for Sophia. The author defines mindfulness: "Paying attention on purpose in the present moment and nonjudgmentally, as if your life depends on it."

Wednesday 17 June
Cape Town

At 1 p.m. I descend the stairs of the plane in Cape Town. My brother is waiting for me at the airport. It's good to see him again and he comments immediately that I have lost a lot of weight.

I feel different in so many ways from when he dropped me off at the airport six weeks ago. I was in such a state that Sunday morning. Bad-tempered, very anxious. I barely spoke to him and his wife over breakfast at Mugg & Bean. Now I'm as calm as a Zen monk sitting cross-legged in a monastery.

We have lunch at Giovanni's in Green Point and he drops me off at my flat. I have a ritual whenever I return to my flat after a long trip, usually for *Go* articles: I drop my bag, sit on the couch and stare at a painting on the wall.

The painting is by Piet Grobler. Years ago I asked him to draw me a melancholy ginger cat. So he drew a ginger cat sitting on a rock, straight from a fairy tale. In its paw it's holding a bird's nest with three eggs in it. The title of the painting is *From: Oscar's travels – Lunar landscape with three small planets*.

Sophia's picking me up at six. There's time for a siesta.

This is going to be one of the hardest things to unlearn, especially when I'm back at the office.

But the siesta lasts much longer than I expected. I only wake up at 18:45; Sophia is waiting in my lounge.

She is surprised enough to hear that I mailed my laptop and iPhone to her friend Marcelle in Paris. But when I hand her the book *Mindfulness for Beginners*, the gift from Marcelle, she nearly falls over backwards.

She looked at that very book on Amazon two days ago, and wondered whether she should order it.

Sunday 21 June
Cape Town

At sunset I'm standing on the top of Table Mountain. For the past four hours I've walked the Pipe Track and Corridor Ravine to the top. I'm still using my trekking poles and wearing my blue Camino shoes, which are completely worn out after 1 000 kilometres.

The reflection of the sun is a golden arrow on the sea. Just like ten days ago, when I sat on a rock at Cabo Finisterra.

I now weigh 79,9 kg. I walked off more than twelve kilograms on the Camino – roughly the weight of my fully packed red rucksack. And I feel lighter in so many ways.

I'm going to need time to internalise all the Camino's lessons and rich experiences. I'm curious about these changes that occur within us, the way they evolve slowly and often subtly.

The Camino was the greatest gift I could have given myself – and the people I love. I needed to go away for a long time and be somewhere else before I could come home to myself. Walking this far does not make you a better or worse person. But it can make you a different person, if you open yourself to it.

Every person's Camino is different. And every Camino is valid, no matter what the reason: fitness, the beauty of nature, vacation, or to process a crisis. Not everyone has to go Forrest Gump like me and walk 1 000 kilometres in one go.

I can speak only for my own Camino. For me, it was about striving to fulfil the potential for change. For the first time, I could care for myself and establish my autonomy. And rediscover the sanctity of life, after a time of cynicism.

I also had a chance to break away completely from all the digital distractions that influence our lives in so many ways. We do not need all these things. I hope I'll be able to do a digital detox more frequently from now on, even if for shorter periods.

And then there were the other pilgrims. People from all over the world, old and young, some of whom have become dear friends. It really says something if you are literally able to walk a long way with somebody. The camaraderie, care and sense of togetherness among modern-day pilgrims are things I will cherish for the rest of my life.

I have learnt that the Camino starts at your front door, but never ends. Every step of the way during those forty days was a confirmation of the Buddha's words: "There is no way to happiness. Happiness is the way."

The challenge will be to reconcile all the Camino's gifts – the discipline, the focus, the greater self-awareness – with the reality of my life and work here in Cape Town.

And to accept that this will not always be easy.

I'm going to miss the yellow arrows, scallop shells and

route markers. But around my neck hangs a pendant with a little yellow arrow pointing to my heart – the symbolic home for an inner compass that's now been calibrated properly.

And now, whether I have a sore knee or a sore heart, my mantra will always be: Walk it off. Going for a walk makes most things better and always helps to put things in perspective.

It is reassuring to know the Camino is there. And that thousands of people are now, at this very moment, somewhere on the road to Santiago de Compostela. And that dozens of pilgrims are now on their way to Cabo Finisterra, to gaze at the sunset in a few hours' time.

But the Camino is everywhere. Even right here with me, on this peninsula where I now stand. Now, I need to keep walking on this journey. On with the corpse. One foot in front of the other. Still on the journey to find meaning in this short life, which the psychoanalyst James Hollis calls "a short interval between two great mysteries".

Mary Oliver wrote a poem, "Sometimes". It includes the following lines:

Instructions for living a life:
Pay attention.
Be astonished.
Tell about it.

I think I'll write about my Camino after all.

Poem written in September 2015

I See a Darkness

"We're all on the brink of despair. All we can do is look each other in the face, keep each other company, joke a little . . . don't you agree?" – *The Great Beauty*

Bonnie Prince Billy you have already said and withheld everything / while you thread words seamlessly into sentences / you sing the light and the darkness with so much rhyme and heart / your voice so pure that each word and chord balance perfectly on the finely tuned cord between pleasure and pain / so that I can only mindlessly concur like a drunken parrot squawking out the words far and wide: I see a darkness.

Yet I won't rejoice but elaborate / God knows I don't know if God is the universe's live-in ADT taking a smoke break a few blocks from here / in a disabled parking bay with a broken two-way radio and disarmed response waiting / for false prayers and the sirens of without doubt struggling mortals like me and you and all of us together here. / It's hard to know about God, the ever-absent presence that flies in the face of all words. / Perhaps in the incalculably long ur-silence before Genesis 1:1 He did not say it but probably thought it: I see a darkness.

Bonnie Prince Billy, despite the firmament and the stars from the distant past that shoot and sparkle it remains a dark business out there / William Stafford writes "the darkness around us is deep" / and even deeper the darkness within me where no "Lumkela Inja" signs grace the picket fences of the psyche / where the Black Dog with foam on its muzzle and a chain round its neck lies skulking / when sleeping wounds awaken and once again the refrain echoes: I see a darkness.

Bonnie Prince Billy, of all the songs that could have come to me / from the unsurpassed and seldom pedantic ether / yours I kept on singing as a repeated mantra on the Camino / mostly out loud with the metronome of my trekking poles that tick-tock tick-tock day in and day out while I lose and find myself / over the Pyrenees through the Meseta's kilometres of wheat fields before the cathedrals in Burgos and León and the other side of Santiago de Compostela / to where the sun sinks into the sea at Finisterre nine hundred kilometres from the starting point your words echoed: I see a darkness.

Thank you for your darkness and your light / two sides of the same coin / we are wounded but undefeated sometimes kings sometimes pawns but may life keep surprising and boring us may we continue to laugh and play / even if we are sometimes headless chickens that cluck-cluck here and cluck-cluck there keep calm and carry on / our lives are a breath long as Breyten wrote another Spanish philosopher whose name has slipped my mind and I cannot Google wrote: "Life is much shorter than death." Remember this, ponder on this. "Life is much shorter than death." Embrace the darkness and the light. May both bless us abundantly – with friends *and* alone.

Muchas gracias

I walked alone, but *Walk it Off* was a huge team effort. It is much more difficult to write 80 000 words than to walk 1 025 kilometres . . . Many thanks to Etienne Bloemhof and Hester Carstens from NB Publishers, who believed in the book from the beginning. Without their encouragement, expert input and patience (especially when I got up to my writer's tricks), *Walk it Off* would simply never have seen the light of day. Many thanks to François Haasbroek for the map, Dian Wessels for the cover design, Edwin Hees for the translation, Angela Voges for her careful editing and Susan Bloemhof for the typesetting. Sean Fraser's proofreading eye was very reassuring. As the first reader of the book-in-progress, Yvonne Beyers made an enormous contribution towards keeping me on course when I wrote the Afrikaans version. Le Roux Schoeman also read large sections of the original manuscript and encouraged me throughout. Thanks to Toast Coetzer for the Departure photo. I also want to thank Pierre Steyn, my editor at *Go*. Pierre approved my leave of absence for a full six weeks to walk the Camino and later allowed me the space between *Go* trips and deadlines to work on the book. And thank you to my dearest Catharien Robbertze, whom I met only after the Camino. It could not have been easy to run a home with a sometimes neurotic debut writer. Her love and support have been of inestimable value, especially when it came to injury time in producing the book. She also gave the English version a final proofread.

Finally, a very big thank you to all my fellow pilgrims on the way to Santiago de Compostela. You enriched my trek through Spain infinitely. And thank you to Bill, Rubí, Robert and Timna, who sent me photographs, some of which appear in the book. Buen Camino!